Love At First Sight

Stepping Out on a Maybe

REBECCA MERZ

WESTBOW
PRESS
A DIVISION OF THOMAS NELSON

WestBow Press books may be ordered through booksellers or by contacting:

WestBow Press
A Division of Thomas Nelson
1663 Liberty Drive
Bloomington, IN 47403
www.westbowpress.com
1 (866) 928-1240

ISBN: 978-1-4908-0047-9 (sc)
ISBN: 978-1-4497-7643-5 (hc)
ISBN: 978-1-4908-0048-6 (e)

Library of Congress Control Number: 2013915936

Printed in the United States of America.

WestBow Press rev. date: 4/18/2014

To God:

Thank you for the gift of your Holy Spirit that is with me to guide me not just when I work but even when I play. You inspire me to want to share my love for Jesus.

To Adam:

Thank you not only for looking into my eyes and allowing me to look into yours, but also for encouraging me to write by showing me your desire to read my work and expressing that you find every word good.

Table of Contents

Preface

This story would never have been told had it not been for the faith and prayers of my husband. I was married to George for almost thirty-one years. In 1995, he was diagnosed with stage four-colon cancer. After George learned of his eleven-month prognosis, he told me that he wanted me to remarry one day and that he prayed for God to provide a good husband for me. My response was, "You aren't going to die, so stop talking about me marrying someone else. I only want you."

George and I both experienced pain whenever we thought about our marriage ending. I couldn't imagine my life without him. For that reason alone, I never dreamed I could want another man. During the last few years of his life, George often told me he was still asking God to provide another husband to take his place. We actually had arguments over that prayer. George would remind me that God had answered his prayers when we'd met each other. I believed that, and I suppose I believed God would answer George's prayer about finding me another husband too. I think that's why whenever George would tell me he was still asking God to bring me another husband I would reply, "Who knows—I may die before you. Besides, I don't want to get married again." George explained why he wanted me to remarry. His love for me prompted not only those conversations but also his prayers. George believed in marriage and wanted me to have a special someone. He knew the happiness being a wife in a loving relationship brought to me, and he didn't want his death to rob me of ever experiencing that again. He said, "You are still young and have a long life ahead of you. I don't want you to be alone." He shared that he worried about that most of all.

Amazingly, George lived thirteen more years after his diagnosis despite his prognosis. After my husband died, some people asked me if I'd ever remarry. With tongue in cheek I used to say, "If God has someone for me, He will present him."

I met Adam on July 17, 2009. The moment we looked into each other's eyes and he smiled something happened to me. I sensed that God was in that moment. After meeting Adam, I went home and asked God this question: "Is this the man you are presenting to me?" I said it with more than a tinge of sarcasm because at that time I didn't believe I would ever be involved with or care about another man. However, in time I began to hope that Adam was the answer to my late husband's prayer. I even jokingly said, "God, I guess the reason I'm so attracted to Adam is that you and George picked him out for me."

In some ways, George knew me better than I knew myself. He knew I would want another man again if the right one came along. George was a loving husband, and he was very special. Even while battling cancer, he was concerned about me. As I reflect back on the words George said to me, I'm reminded of the reason God created Eve. "And the Lord God said, 'It is not good for the man to be alone. I will make a companion who will help him'" (Genesis 2:18 NLT). I see this verse is meant for me too.

Sometimes, I felt certain that Adam was the one God had presented to me; at other times, I wrestled with that idea. I questioned God about whether the desire I felt was really from Him or merely my own. I even questioned the discernment God gave me when it came to things regarding my connection with Adam. I started doubting that this was a "God connection" and began to think it was purely born out of my imagination.

While I found it easy to believe that God was involved in my love life, I had a harder time coming to terms with the task God was calling me to do to move forward in this area of my life. This book is the product of that call. Trusting that God wanted me to write this book and give it to Adam was difficult. What if I was wrong? I realized I was counting on the outcome of the story to determine if I was meant to give this book to Adam. That was when God stepped in and showed me this was about trusting God "for Adam." Maybe it was "for Adam" meaning Adam and I would be together and God would use this book to help arrange it. Maybe it was "for Adam" meaning Adam needed to read this book as much as I needed to write it but for an entirely different purpose. Either way, it was all about trusting God. Adam has known for some time that I pray for him. I was pretty sure Adam sensed our relationship was not ordinary. Maybe he was confused too, and this story would shed some light. Maybe he just thought this whole thing between us was crazy or that I was crazy. I had no idea what Adam thought about any of this; that was part of the problem. I knew only what I sensed in my spirit. Maybe, in some ways, I was reaching out to Adam for confirmation.

At times during the writing process, I wondered if all the thoughts and dreams I had about Adam were just part of an addiction to love. I didn't know if I was writing about a woman obsessed or a lady in waiting. Because of this experience, I developed a bit more understanding about how God is obsessed with us. He wants us to be in relationship with Him, and He thinks about each one of us. In the end, He wants nothing but good things for us. "If you sinful people know how to give good gifts to your children, how much more will your heavenly Father give good gifts to those that ask him" (Matthew 7:11 NLT). I believe God has more good gifts waiting for me when the time is right.

I do know I am a friend of Jesus, and that is the role that defines me. "You are my friends if you obey me. I no longer call you servants, because a master doesn't confide in his servants. Now you are my friends, since I have told you everything the Father told me. You didn't choose me. I chose you. I appointed you to go and produce fruit that will last so that the Father will give you whatever you ask for, using my name. I command you to love each other" (John 15:14—17 NLT). I trust that God is moving me forward to live a fruitful life. I pray this book will produce some fruit too.

During the times I struggle and am tempted to rely on myself, I am thankful for this serenity prayer to get me through. This is a powerful prayer when put into practice.

> God, grant me the serenity to accept the things I cannot change; Courage to change the things I can; and wisdom to know the difference. Living one day at a time; Enjoying one moment at a time; Accepting hardships as the pathway to peace; Taking, as Jesus did, this sinful world as it is, not as I would have it; Trusting that you will make all things right if I surrender to Your Will; That I may be reasonably happy in this life and supremely happy with You forever in the next. Amen (Reinhold Niebuhr)

I'll admit there were times I was anything but serene when it came to writing this book. In those moments, I had to trust God's promises. "Even youth will become exhausted, and young men will give up. But those who wait on the Lord will find new strength. They will fly high on wings like eagles. They will run and not grow weary. They will walk and not faint" (Isaiah 40:30–31 NLT). This verse is the word I stand on when praying the serenity prayer, especially when I am wrestling with making a decision. I need courage to change the things I can, and releasing this book is going to be a change for me. I have no idea what, if anything, it will do for Adam. I need serenity to accept whatever the outcome is after Adam reads this. While I have no control over his reaction to this book, I don't want this story to harm him in any way. God knows that is my desire. No matter what happens, I trust in the end it will all be good. Trying to pretend my feelings away wasn't working; I'd hoped writing about my feelings and sharing them would bring me some peace. This was a big step for me because I'm used to striving to keep the peace. I am not saying I want to start a fight; however, God showed me that in order to have peace of mind and be an effective writer I needed to honestly bare all without worrying about what others, including Adam, thought of me. Always a people pleaser, this was hard for me to do. I learned I needed to be concerned with only what God thought of me.

Even though I struggled, God found a way to let me know He had heard my prayers and was directly involved in this situation. When some of my thoughts were confirmed to be true, I giggled. I still don't know if this thought that Adam and I will be together one day is a foretelling, but I know the idea is good material to base this book on because it is the dream God gave me. Perhaps one day I will understand it all. One thing I know for sure, God let me know He has His eye on me. Through this situation, God taught me not to run ahead of Him and to trust Him for discernment and confirmation. I am waiting on God, and perhaps Adam, to see where this relationship will go.

Dreaming of a life with Adam gave me a new focus, and it broadened my relationship with God too. When I've talked to God about Adam, we've laughed together and I've felt my spirit soar. During these times, I not only had peace, I had true joy. The feeling is a foretaste of what it will be like when I am with God in heaven one day. Even though, at times, I get frustrated with wanting to have all the answers, I am thankful for the situation. I've learned that when I think about Adam, I do not have to hide it from God. Many times these thoughts help me be aware of God's presence. It's so refreshing having God involved in my love life. I say "my love life" because dreaming about a life with Adam is one thing I love about my life right now.

I don't really allow myself to think about details of what a future with Adam might be like other than to dream that Adam is a man who loves God. I know God loves him. I try to concentrate on the idea of what an amazing story this could turn out to be, and I don't just mean for the book. I hope Adam wants to share this amazing story about what God has done to bring us together. In my dream, Adam not only desires to be with me, he also wants to be involved in promoting my work. Adam delights in telling everyone what a good God we have who brought us together. He wants to be in a ministry that gives hope to people who have had their lives affected not only by cancer but also by depression, addiction, divorce, or unhealed hurts. He understands firsthand how these things can stand in the way of living the life God has planned for all of us.

In this dream, Adam loves to tell everyone about my first book, not only because he believes in its message and that it was God inspired, but because of his joy in knowing God destined him to be involved in its creation too. In my dream of dreams, this book, *Love at First Sight, Stepping Out on a Maybe*, changes the direction of both our lives, putting us on the same path walking hand in hand.

When I dream along with God, I know I dream big. It is not because I think I am able to accomplish anything by my strength, rather it is because I know there is no limit to what God can do. I know He can do the impossible. I know God is pleased that I believe in my dreams, but He wants to see me act too. Believing in dreams is one thing; acting on those dreams is where faith comes into play. Big dreams call for bold action. God can make big dreams come true, especially if He is the one who initiated them, but He also wants me to trust Him in the small things. Giving this book to Adam is a small thing by some standards, but God knows just what a big and scary deal it is to me.

At times I get carried away with my dreams, such as when I think my books will become best sellers. I dream about starting a nonprofit called "Love One Another" and using the proceeds from my book sales to help others who are struggling financially. I know these are my dreams, but I will have to wait to see if they are God's too.

I don't know if having a life with Adam or starting that nonprofit are what God has planned for me. Regardless of whether those dreams come true or not, I believe I was meant to write this story. The writing process helped me acknowledge the Holy Spirit. I am now in an intimate relationship with Him. I trusted Him, especially when my mind thought this whole experience was just plain crazy. Sometimes I thought, *This really cannot be happening or I am just reading way too much into things.* Then I realized if I have faith in what I wrote, I have to show it by acting on it. I am delighted to say God found ways to help end my doubts. God kept arranging so many coincidences that involved Adam. I deduced that God was not going to stop prompting me until I gave Adam this manuscript. God used visible signs to keep me encouraged and help me believe He was involved in this. Many of these signs were in black and white, or shall I say in print—and not just what I printed, either. God you are so amazing. That's all I can say at this point. I truly believe I was meant to experience those things and write about some of them too. Trusting that writing was what God called me to do is enough of a dream come true for now.

I do believe the bigger picture is what is most important. This book is not just meant for my Adam, the name I call my crush, but for all Adams, meaning all humankind. God wants all of us to learn to trust Him. God wants us to know we can learn to discern the voice of the Holy Spirit among all the other voices. He wants us to know praying is not a one-way conversation; He speaks back to us in many ways. His Word, the Bible, is the measure of all things spoken. Because I believe that, I have confidence and obey what God asks me to do.

God is with me, and He leads me. He knows my every thought. I want to have this ministry through my books that reaches others and brings hope, encouragement, and healing into their lives. I want to have someone beside me to share in my dream to reach others for Christ. Most of all, I want each one of my readers to believe God loved you at first sight. He has plans for you too. "For we are God's masterpiece. He has created us anew in Christ Jesus, so that we can do the good things he planned for us long ago" (Ephesians 2:10 NLT).

If Adam and I end up together and share this ministry, it would truly be an awesome bonus. Even though I am writing the words to the story, God is really the only one who has the power to bring it from a fairy tale to a reality. No matter how this love story ends, one day all God's children will experience the greatest love story of all. We will know what it feels like to be swept away by the King of Kings and have the experience of being loved for eternity. We will each be one of the characters in the most magnificent love story of all time. We will be in that romantic state of love with Jesus and will live happily ever after with Him.

I am willing to give this book to Adam and risk looking foolish, because I am willing to love Adam in the way God wants us to love each other. We are to reflect God's love and love unconditionally. I believe God wants to use this story to let Adam know he has been chosen by God to be a friend of Jesus. He may already know this, but just in case he doesn't or he has doubts, I don't want to risk missing this opportunity to tell him. I am willing to look foolish so Adam will know for sure that God loved him at first sight too. I am also willing to take this risk because I don't want to live a life of regrets, either.

I trust God with my life, including my love life. I am counting on God to guide me. Next to accepting Jesus as Lord and Savior, becoming one with another person is the most important decision I will ever make. Whether or not Adam is the one, or if I ever remarry, I need to trust God for discernment to reveal the plans He has for me. In the meantime, I am doing what He has called me to do. I want to obey God not only by keeping his commandments, but also by living the life He has called me to live. I believe God has called me to write about my life experiences and share how He has been there for me in good times and in bad. By doing this I hope to encourage others not only to trust God, but also to dream along with Him. Dreaming is a way to discover what He has planned for you. It is one of the steps to fulfilling your destiny. Then be willing to step out in faith and act, knowing that even if it isn't the right call it will bring you one step closer to finding what is.

Knowing that this eternal life I dream about will all come true and that I will spend eternity with my bridegroom Jesus helps me to dream and act. I know God is pleased that I have faith and trust in Him and am willing to take risks for Him. Right now I am here on earth, and I am writing about what I am experiencing. I am a woman who thinks she has met the man God is presenting to her—but for some reason, there is a pause in the story. What I thought was moving right along came to a screeching halt. And that is where this story really begins.

Adam and God

When I first saw Adam—I would call it a chance meeting—I was surprised. He was the first man to catch my eye since I'd met my late husband, George, thirty-three years before.

I met Adam at his workplace. My sister Nora came with me that day. She was there to listen because two heads are better than one, but I was the client. Although I was there for a professional reason, Adam and I began to strike up a conversation that had nothing to do with my reason for being there. As the conversation took on a more personal slant, we both began exchanging lots of information with each other. My sister sat in the corner as she listened and watched Adam and I interact. While Adam and I were conversing, he removed a fallen strand of hair from my shoulder and held it up for both of us to see. It was such a natural gesture that I normally wouldn't have given it a second thought. But as we looked at that strand of hair, our eyes met. At that moment Adam smiled, and the look on his face mirrored that of George's whenever he would look into my eyes. Adam's face just lit up, and I was shocked. That's when I heard this voice say, "Adam is 100 percent German". For a brief second, I actually thought Adam was attracted to me. Then I concluded it was just his reaction to the joke I'd made about the hair. "I know it has to be mine," I had teased because his head was shaved.

During this initial conversation, we learned we both had houses in Indiana and South Carolina. Adam told me of his plans to spend his winters in South Carolina after he retired. He went on to say, "Did you see the older married couple that just left my office? They have a house here and in South Carolina too." It was as if he was lost in thought as I heard him say, "This is so strange … and now you're here." Initially, I thought he was referring to the coincidence that all three of us would have the same dual residency. Later, I wondered if he was thinking something more.

As Adam continued to talk about the house he was having built, he said, almost as if he were thinking aloud, "I don't know why I'm building such a big house for just myself."

Inside my head, I heard a soft voice speak, "Maybe he isn't going to be there by himself. You'll be there with him." That was quite a shocking idea considering I didn't even know this man. I started to wonder about Adam's marital status, and instantly he gave me an answer to my unspoken question.

Adam blurted out, "I'm single." He went on to say, "I am going to be retiring in a few years." That was when I made the mistaken assumption that we were the same age. Later in the conversation, he mentioned we were around the same age, so he falsely assumed that too.

I could hardly believe the turn in the conversation. Everything was happening so fast. My mind raced to absorb all that had transpired, but part of my brain felt like it was trying to clear out cobwebs. I pushed all thoughts of Adam being in my future away. I thought I had put the prospect out of my head altogether, but it merely snuck into the recesses of my mind. We continued to talk. We had so much in common. When he spoke about how he had been to every beach in Florida, it was as if I was speaking. I had said that very same thing many times. For that reason alone, I didn't find Adam attractive; he seemed too much like me—and not in a good way. I thought he talked too much.

As Adam and I compared beaches that day, I found out that Siesta Key was Adam's number two favorite. The beach he rated number one is found on Florida's panhandle in Destin. (Is that short for destiny, I wonder?) He said he favored it not only because of the pure white sand but also because of the direction the wind blew across the sand. He mesmerized me with his description. Later, when I reflected back on the conversation, I could imagine being at that beach with the gentle ocean breeze blowing each grain of white sand softly across my toes as we walked hand in hand.

My first impression was Adam seemed nice enough, was quite a talker, but was self-absorbed and not a good listener. Later, he proved me wrong.

Adam was detailed in his conversations, which included information about his personal life. I would love to share all the particulars, but I cannot because his stories are not mine. Someday Adam and I might openly share these stories, but for now it would be premature. What I can say, however, is that from the moment we met I felt so safe and comfortable when I was with him, I didn't want to leave his presence.

At first, I didn't understand why I felt that way, but I sensed he felt the same. We had long since finished up the business at hand, and yet we continued to talk. Eventually he opened the door for me to leave. When he immediately shut it, I knew he didn't want me to go. I perceived he felt comfortable and safe with me too. Adam's words and actions matched what I sensed.

"No, don't go," he said when it was time for me to depart. "Stay and talk some more."

Sometimes when I reflect back on this exchange, I wonder if I am dreaming it differently than it happened; however, my sister remembers it happening this way too. This moment is the one thing that I cling to when I feel like this romance is all a figment of my imagination. I pray for the day when everything between us is clear and simple again.

I'll admit that by the end of that first meeting, I was beginning to enjoy hearing Adam talk and wanted to learn more about him. I was pleasantly surprised at how open this man was and that he shared some private things with me—a stranger. Even though he had been the one to close the door and ask me to stay, I'd thought I'd better leave because I had taken up so much of his time. I finally said something to that effect.

When my sister and I finally did leave, she said, "He is so nice and cute and single! I could see you two together."

I heard myself say, "I would date him." That was what shocked me the most. I almost looked around to see where that voice came from, because I couldn't believe my ears. I wasn't interested in dating anyone, especially not this guy that, except for his smile and his shaved head, I didn't really find attractive.

My sister said, "He is so much like you. When he took that hair off your shirt—that was something you would do. He's detailed like you and notices those little things." She commented that she thought he was doting over me and was interested in me.

I was amazed to hear her say that; it confirmed that maybe I had read Adam correctly when I thought he might be interested in me. I'd been thinking that very same thing about the two of us being alike, but for different reasons. After my sister's comment, my mind took off on a tangent, and I thought, I guess I do notice little details that others miss. All this prompted a memory from my past.

I recalled a remark my friend Lynn made when we were in seventh grade. She had just bought her first pair of contact lenses. One lens had the tiniest red dot on it to distinguish it from the other. When I asked Lynn why she had a red dot on her eye, she replied, "Rebecca, I knew if anyone would notice the red dot, it would be you." I guess others might see me as detailed, different, and perhaps outspoken. Some things that come in my mind pop right out of my mouth. I later discovered that Adam had trouble filtering things sometimes too.

After Adam had held up that hair and our eyes had met, we held that gaze. We could not stop looking into each other's eyes. It was as if we knew all the while that something beyond our understanding was happening.

On that first encounter, we talked and talked—at the same time, I might add. Later, I realized we were able to do that and still listen to each other. I found that fact rather remarkable because sometimes when I talk I know I'm difficult to follow, since I jump from subject to subject. Sometimes I even mumble to myself. Yet Adam proved over and over again that he heard every word I said. Once he astonished me by repeating word for word something I had sort of mumbled almost three months earlier. I was surprised he picked up on it, let alone still remembered it verbatim.

Each time I met with Adam, we continued to share more about our personal lives. After Adam told me about building his winter home at Red Rock Lake and that it was thirty-five miles from my home, I looked up the area. The next time I saw him, I smiled and said, "I looked up your lake. It's seventy-five miles from me, not thirty-five."

He replied, "Either way, it isn't that far away. It's only about an hour's drive." He had the biggest grin on his face. I'd hoped he recognized that I was sending him a signal that I was interested in him. The week before, he'd mentioned he was single and didn't know why he was building such a big house for himself. A week later, he seemed to be reemphasizing his status by saying, "I don't know why I am building such a big house. I am single and all alone." I interpreted the fact that he added the words "all alone" as his way to let me know he was available and interested in me.

Keep in mind the fact that this is coming from a woman who had been married for almost thirty-one years up until nine months before this exchange. I was at a loss for words, but in my head I recalled the little voice whispering that Adam and I would be together one day. Remembering it, I felt fearful. I wondered where that voice had come from. Soon that fear was replaced with a sense of a peace that I interpreted as a spirit-filled moment. That moment quickly vanished too.

I reminded myself that I had just met this man and wasn't interested in another man, because I was still grieving the loss of my husband. I decided I must just have a vivid imagination. I denied that this was coming from the Holy Spirit, even though I had learned to recognize Him as the still, small voice inside of me. I wondered to myself, *Who is this person who is flirting with Adam, and what in the world is she thinking?* I still didn't find Adam all that attractive, which added to my confusion. But I felt very comfortable and safe with him, and that was the feeling I never wanted to end.

After we established that our homes in South Carolina were only about an hour apart, Adam mentioned that his house was around

2,600 square feet. I commented that my house was that same square footage. He proceeded to tell me about the very large rooms in his house. I thought we were in a "gotcha beat" match for a moment.

Then, with this beaming smile on his face, he announced, "The guest bedroom is sixteen feet by sixteen."

I sensed he was inviting me to stay over if I drove to his house to see him. The fact that he gave me directions to his place added to the allure. I thought he was such a gentleman because he didn't mention the size of his master bedroom, which I believe he would have had he been trying to send a sexual invite to me. I began to imagine the main room inside his house, but I fought against letting my mind run away with this fantasy. The mental picture was replaced with the thought, *I don't know if I could stay with you there. God surely would have to help me stay in my own room.* In that instant I realized I was beginning to feel an attraction toward Adam. I felt safe and comfortable with him because he was so nice and sweet ... but there was more to it. I realized I really wanted to get to know this man. I just had a sense that he was a good guy and I could trust him—maybe more than I could trust myself. I wondered why I had all these thoughts running through my head. Though at the time I didn't find him sexually attractive, it was as if I was seeing this off in the future. I realize this all sounds very weird. In retrospect, I believe that the Holy Spirit was indeed giving me insight. I was very confused and conflicted, but my feelings were starting to come through a little more clearly each time I was with Adam.

I saw Adam several more times over that summer. He talked about how he looked forward to spending his winters in South Carolina. He was so excited about the house he'd just built, and he wanted to show me pictures of it. But we would get so engrossed in our conversations that he'd forget all about his house, so I never did see those pictures. It was funny because sometimes when he'd mentioned showing the pictures to me I would think, *I am able to wait to see the actual house.* I didn't want him to ruin the surprise.

As I reflect back on the day I met Adam, the fact that the couple from South Carolina had been in his office right before I entered made me think that was a God sighting for Adam. Was he waiting for a woman who would be happy to live half the year in each state? Perhaps he thought that arrangement would somehow make it possible to share a life with someone else. I could sense the coincidence certainly did get Adam's attention. I don't know what personal significance it may have had for him, because I don't know what things he had been talking to God about. Maybe he hadn't been talking to God at all, and God was using it as a little nudge. Only Adam can say if that coincidence had any personal meaning for him. For me, it meant God was there in that very moment. He wanted Adam and me to have that assurance too.

Later that summer, I mentioned to Adam that I would soon be heading back to South Carolina. Adam used my announcement as an opportunity to offer to provide his personal cell phone number to me.

He said, "Think about it. If you want my personal cell phone number, let me know when I see you again."

I wondered if I'd heard him correctly.

Then, as he reached into his jacket pocket, he repeated the offer. "If you'd like my personal cell phone number, not the one here at the office, you can let me know the next time you come back."

I just smiled and thought, *Hum, I like a man that takes his time and doesn't pressure me.* Then he began to ramble on about the reasons I might want to call him regarding our professional business together. I began to become confused about what his intentions were toward me. I doubted myself and wondered if I really understood what Adam was trying to tell me. It was in this moment that I realized I truly was finding him attractive in every way. Any confusion I was having about my feelings toward him left. I wanted to ask for his phone number right there and then, but something stopped me. I found him to be so cute while he was nervously babbling on; it made me realize he wasn't very good at lying. Instead of asking for his number, I said nothing. Maybe my smile said it all.

Adam and I did what I like to call a little dance with each other. It was fascinating to me because I'd never experienced anything quite like it before. George and I met shortly after I was divorced from my first husband. We coined our attraction "love at second sight" because the second time we saw each other we both knew our relationship was special. We believed that God brought us together, and we were up front about it. This was different. Adam and I were in a professional relationship. I knew we shouldn't be getting personal with each other, but for some reason I couldn't help myself. It wasn't all the interests we seemed to have in common that had me behaving like a schoolgirl; it was the expression on his face that he couldn't hide that let me know how he felt about me. It was more than physical attraction. I could tell he found me captivating. Once he commented that I was like a little child, and he smiled as if he found that part of my personality really appealing.

During another visit, Adam was walking behind me on the way down the hall and he was clicking his pen. As soon as we were in the office, he asked, while he continued to click the pen, "Does that noise bother you?"

I replied, "What noise?"

As he clicked his pen he said, "This noise. It drives one of the girls here crazy, but I don't even notice that I do it." He laughed and then said, "I was clicking my pen as I walked behind you, and I wondered if it bothered you."

I said, "No, I didn't even hear it. My husband was a pen clicker too. The only time it bothered me was when George would click his pen while he was talking to someone on the phone. Then I would scold him and motion to him that he was clicking in someone's ear." As I said this, I waved my hand in the air the way I used to do to get George's attention while he was deep in conversation.

Adam found this whole scenario really funny for some reason. I thought, *Is he testing me to see if I would find his habit annoying?* If my memory serves me right, this exchange took place the same day he made the cell phone number offer.

About a week after he'd made that offer, I decided to be brave and give him my cell phone number. I had written mine on a piece of paper and put it in my pocket for safekeeping. I knew I'd be too nervous to write it in front of him. I had rehearsed what I wanted to say to him. It went something like this, "I thought about the offer of your personal cell phone number. Here's my cell phone number, so when I call you'll recognize it." That was the day I put on an extra spray of perfume for courage and to attract a honeybee.

As soon as I entered the room, Adam said, "I really like your perfume."

Maybe he saw the look of panic on my face as I silently scolded myself, *Why did you put so much perfume on and make yourself so obvious?*

In the next breath, Adam said, in this ever so reassuring voice, "I meant to tell you that last week."

I was shocked to discover he had been thinking about me since last week. Then I wondered, *Is this man a mind reader, or is he just that in tune with me?* If this had been the first time I'd felt like he could read my mind, it might not have had such an impact—but it wasn't. There were so many other times I'd thought we had a connection. I recalled the moment when it first happened: the time I'd wondered about his marital status, and he immediately blurted out that he was single. The thought that we had this connection helped give me the confidence I needed to make the next move.

The meeting had started out all well and good with the compliment about the perfume. Knowing this guy had been thinking about my perfume since last week reassured me that he did, indeed, want to give me his personal cell phone number. I wasn't going to make him squirm, either; I was going to bring up the subject. I sensed he was a little nervous and seemed to have rehearsed what he would say too. I knew how he was feeling. So I was going to, let's say, assist him. My plan of action was business first, and then I'll ask for his phone number.

It was apparent that Adam and I had something going on between us. I was excited to ask him to coffee, although I wasn't even sure he liked it. I wanted to sit and talk outside the office and get to know him better. There was a part of me that was afraid too. I started to think things were moving too fast for me, and then I felt panicked. I clearly remember thinking, *What if I don't like him?*

Even though I had finally admitted to myself that I found him attractive, I was concerned that once I got to know him better I might not like him. It wasn't, "What if he doesn't like me," that had me worried. I just didn't want to hurt him. After my thirty-one year marriage to George, I wondered if I would ever really be able to give my heart to another man. I also wondered who would ever be able to meet my expectations, because I'd had such a good and loving husband. It wasn't that I didn't think Adam was capable, I just knew I was very picky. I was also concerned to let him into my life and have him see what a mess my family was in at the time. Since my husband's death, everything seemed to be falling apart. Frankly, all my children were having marital problems. I had relapsed into a codependent relationship based on what was going on with them. In addition to the marital problems, my children were also not getting along with each other. It seemed as if my entire life was crumbling around me. I wasn't sure I should bring a man into the mess. I felt so embarrassed, too, as if it were somehow a reflection on me. All these thoughts were going on in my mind. But I wanted to move past those fears and offer Adam my number, even though I was nervous and even a little afraid. The thought that it would be totally inappropriate for us to even see each other socially never entered my mind.

While all of these thoughts battled it out in my head, we were chatting away as usual. The feelings of safety and being so comfortable with him began to return. I was moving beyond that panicked feeling, and I started to relax. He mentioned playing 500 Rummy with his daughter when she was younger. He talked about his theory of how good it was for her because it gave her the opportunity to learn many things as they played. There it was again; he was just like me. I used to say that exact same thing. My daughter, Ann, still teases me saying, "Mom, you were so clever making me count the cards at face value so I'd have to use my math skills." I mentioned to Adam that I was going to be teaching my granddaughter Marie how to play 500 Rummy now that she was almost seven.

I noticed Adam looked a little shocked after hearing my remark. He quickly asked, "How old are your children?" That was immediately followed by "I presume you have children, since you have grandchildren." As soon as I heard his question, I feared what might follow. I had done some investigating, so I knew he was fifty-one years old. I'd recently turned sixty-one.

When I'd learned of his age after looking him up on the Internet the first thought I'd had was, *It's a mistake.* He looked older, which was rather ironic. When I came out of denial, the next thought I'd had was, *He isn't really interested in me in the way I think he is.* As things unfolded more each time I saw him, I figured my age didn't bother him. It didn't bother me that he was younger. I thought he looked and acted my age, and that was all that mattered to me. I'd assumed he'd seen my birth date on some of the important papers he handled for me and had done the math. He was so detail oriented; how could he have missed my age?

So when Adam asked about my children's ages, I immediately thought, *Oh no, he* doesn't *know my age!* I answered that my daughter was thirty-nine. I said my son was thirty-five, though that wasn't even right. I was so rattled. I couldn't even remember my own son's age. My mind was racing ahead to what was sure to follow. I remembered the feeling of disappointment I'd felt when I had learned Adam was younger than me. But I'd had time to adjust to the idea and consider that he might not care that I was older. Now I was anticipating his reaction, because he looked so startled and shocked.

I was right. Adam asked the question no man should ever ask a woman: "Well, how *old* are you?" He said it almost as if I had lied to him and got caught.

When I answered him with "Oh, I'm ancient," he ran over and looked up my birth date in his computer.

I wanted to say, *That's not fair, I can't even lie to you about it.* It was so ironic because, just for fun, I used to lie about my age all the time. It took years for my kids and my family to figure out how old I really was. At my sister-in-law's fiftieth birthday surprise party, I was still fibbing about my age. I was forty-eight at the time, but that day I told everyone I was forty-five. I loved to make myself younger, and I constantly changed my age too. I thought others would catch on or at least be confused because I would say different ages, but usually no one but George caught on. He knew I was just having fun, so he kept quiet. However, that day my sister-in-law actually thought I was going to be turning fifty as well, and that lead to my son and niece sneaking into my purse to look at my driver's license. That was the day my son figured out the secret to remembering my age was to add twenty-five years to his age. After that day, I couldn't get away with fibbing anymore. Now, when my grandchildren ask my age, I make up all different ages. My granddaughter knows how old her dad is, so I usually make myself about five years older than my son. Marie doesn't catch on; she isn't a math person. Neither is Adam, I can tell you that much. Or maybe he just didn't want to say that I was almost ten years older than he was.

For whatever reason he said, "You are ah … I am ah … I am eight years younger than you."

I was thinking, *No, it is really almost ten years,* but I didn't want to have to explain how I knew his age. I didn't want to go there. It was too embarrassing to tell this man that I looked him up on the Internet. I honestly don't know how I managed to keep my mouth shut or hold back my laughter, because some part of me was already finding this too funny. I also thought, *He has some codependent issues.* I sensed he was wording this ever so carefully so he wouldn't hurt or insult me. Maybe he was feeling a bit embarrassed for the way he overreacted to my age. He didn't know that I understood how shocking it could be when you are so off about someone's age, since I had just gone through this very same thing when learning how "young" he was. He was wrong about upsetting me. When he looked at me that certain way, I still felt like a teenager.

Whenever I think about what happened that day, it still brings tears to my eyes because I laugh so hard. I hope when Adam reads about this, it will bring him to tears as well—happy tears from laughing too. I pray no matter how this turns out between us, he loves this story. I want him to say every word is good. I want him to get something out of this story as well. One thing I am pretty certain about is Adam will be able to say he had the experience of getting into a strange woman's head and knowing exactly what she was honestly thinking. Most men have to get married first in order to do that. Even then, some men have wives who aren't open and honest about what they think or how they feel. Other men aren't all that interested in what a woman thinks. I just know Adam isn't like that. How many men can say that they knew exactly what a woman was thinking the first time they met? It reminds me of the movie with Mel Gibson titled *What Women Want*. I found that movie to be a laugh-out-loud funny one. I loved it!

What you have to understand is every time I saw Adam, other than the day I told him I looked up "his lake," I never intentionally showed my hand. Why bother? He could see it on my face, and he could read my mind—at least, it felt like he could. I would never have teased Adam about his lake if I had known it would make him feel so conflicted. Adam told me how much he paid for his house, the interest rate on his mortgage, and gave me the exact direction on how to get to the house. He started to open up about other things in his life too. At first, I thought that was not unusual, because I am open when I feel comfortable with certain people. Later, I wondered if he just felt so comfortable with me that he just naturally started to tell me all the things he wanted to share with someone special. Sometimes, I think I surprised him by walking into his life when he wasn't expecting me, either. Maybe my age scared him, or maybe it was an excuse to not get involved with someone who could read him so well or, perhaps, could make him feel so out of control.

I know that sometimes Adam speaks his mind like I do. When he said, "I thought you were my age. Did you have work done?" it didn't come from a man who sensors what he thinks. Maybe he doesn't know that is the other question you should never ask a woman.

Although I took it as a compliment, I think he was feeling like he'd been tricked. I snapped back and said, "No, I just have good genes."

He replied, "You *sure* do!"

The way Adam said it told me in that very moment just how attracted he was to me. Maybe hearing himself say it out loud scared him too; the moment the last words left his lips, I sensed a total change in him, as if he panicked. I still find it hard to believe that I was so tempting to him that he couldn't help himself.

That is when this crazy story took a sudden turn ... or maybe it was just a detour. I will tell you as simply as I can what happened after what I refer to as "the incident." That is how I'll get around not mentioning every detail of what transpired the day Adam closed the door. All I will say is after Adam told me in his wooing tone that I sure did have good genes he did a complete turn around.

I sensed the walls slowly being erected, but not before Adam said, "I know you're going to be mad ..." Then he went into what I call "his babble" about why he thought I would be mad. It had nothing to do with what had happened, but I got his message. It was his way of saying I changed my mind. I'm sorry. You have every right to be mad. He painted this picture of his fiancé and her child and his commitment to help raise the child. He kept calling it a child even though it was awkwardly worded. I thought his commitment was to his inner child and he wasn't going to get involved with someone again that could make him fear another loss. I sensed that he didn't want to get involved with me because I was older and what if I died. I sensed I had him very rattled. Maybe I was just projecting, but I don't think so. I wasn't feeling afraid to get involved with him for fear he might die although even though he is younger than I am there are no guarantees. I thought that if he was just playing with me my age would not have affected him like this. He couldn't look at me. I did not believe him when he told me this new information. Maybe he was going through a midlife crisis and the fact that he was attracted to an "old lady" messed with his head. I have no idea, but in all seriousness I think he was very shaken.

I understood how he was trying to make the connection with what he had just told me. I have learned to read between his lines. It is one of my gifts; however, many times, I later doubt my abilities. While Adam tried to explain his way out, I stood there the entire time with my arms crossed, tapping my left fingers on my right bicep. I kept looking at him, and I thought, *Just keep digging a deeper hole.* He couldn't even look me in the eye. I wasn't sure if it was because he was lying, had lied, or just felt ashamed, embarrassed, or guilty. Maybe it was a little of all those emotions going on inside of him. I didn't feel mad at him during this conversation he was now having by himself. I never said a word; I just watched him panic. I was starting to feel sad and helpless. What I was feeling more than anything was disappointed. Yet, another part of me found this to be amusing. It's hard to say why. Maybe it had something to do with the thought that Adam couldn't talk his way out of this one. I could see right through him. Perhaps it was because I had a sense or foretelling that God was going to use this to create a story that would speak to us in a lighthearted way but still get across the seriousness of this message.

There might have been some truth to what Adam was saying as he stood there looking down at his shoes, but he was lying about what had been transpiring between us. I remember the shoes he was wearing that day too. They were what I call "old man shoes." I think those shoes were what I used as a basis for determining his age that first day I met him. All this was going through my mind as I stood there with a smirk on my face. I don't think he saw it, because he wasn't able to look at me. As he continued to talk and I started to absorb more of what he was saying, I felt my expression turn to stone. I felt almost like a mother when a child is making up an excuse for why he got caught with his hands in the cookie jar. I guess I was starting to feel more than a little shocked too.

That day is etched in my mind because I've gone over it hundreds of times trying to see if I could figure out the truth. I know he admitted to not being honest, in a round about way, when he said, "I am honest. I don't lie but I have to tell you I am engaged." I believed he was lying about being engaged because he no longer wanted me to ask him for his phone number because I was too old for him. Then again, I wondered if he was telling the truth that even though he was engaged he was still considered a single person. More than that I thought if you are engaged you aren't committed. I couldn't help but wonder if he was the most dishonest to himself. There may have been a great deal of truth being spoken that day, but facts are one thing—true honestly with oneself is another. I often wonder if he too had already written his phone number on a piece of paper, had it in his pocket, and was hoping I would ask for it. More than that, I wonder if on the first day he met me a tiny voice told him we would be together one day. I guess that is what drives me and keeps me believing that dreams do come true. It's what makes me feel crazy, confused, but at times, oh so hopeful.

I left there that day very disappointed when Adam had found a way to renege on his offer of his personal cell phone number. I was shocked, confused, and left thinking, *What just happened?*

My friend Gabrielle knew what had happened the day Adam found out my age and closed the door on a relationship. She knew how disappointed I was. In an attempt to help me work through this, she said, "Let's go out to dinner."

Over dinner, I talked about all that had transpired with Adam from the first day I'd looked into his eyes. Gabrielle and I laughed so hard we had tears in our eyes.

In fact, our waiter asked, "What's making you laugh so hard? I want some so I can bottle it to give to my other customers. I'm enjoying waiting on you two."

I replied, "You can read about it in my book one day."

Gabrielle and I had so much fun thinking about all that had happened that had led up to this day. I don't think either one of us believed what Adam said after he learned my age. We both saw it as his way to get out of the situation because I was too old for him.

I told Gabrielle, "Now, I do have to write that book I'm always talking about."

I never thought for a minute that I would actually be writing this entire book about Adam. At the time I made that offhanded remark, I was just thinking about how unpredictable my life was. I thought maybe I would write about my life and devote a chapter to this incident. I had never dreamed I would have one book published, let alone be writing a second one and dedicating the entire book to Adam.

When I got home from dinner that evening, I sat to watch TV. Gabrielle called and, through her laughter, I heard her ask if I was watching TV. I knew immediately that she too had seen the introduction to the new show *Cougar Town*. The day Adam found out my age was the exact day *Cougar Town* premiered. It was so timely because I was feeling the same as the main character, Jules, as she looked at herself in the mirror. She examined her sagging skin under her arms and scrutinized her body to see all the changes taking place. I had done that very same thing as I was dressing to go to dinner with Gabrielle. It was like seeing my life debuted on TV. Well, not exactly—I wasn't dating anyone yet or having sex with younger guys—but the similarity of having a younger man interested in me was, nonetheless, very amusing. The theme of that first show was older women dating and sleeping with younger men. The women were referred to as "cougars." In the strictest sense of the word, I'm told a cougar is at the very least fifteen years older than her male counterpart; so my pursuit of Adam would not make me a full-fledged cougar. Anyway, Gabrielle and I didn't stay on the phone very long that evening. We were laughing so much we couldn't really talk, let alone understand each other.

Before Gabrielle hung up, between those giggles, I was able to understand when she said, "I hope he is watching this too."

There is a map of Florida that appears at the beginning of each episode of the TV show showing Cougar Town located just the tiniest bit south of Sarasota. This is in the exact spot where George and I lived for five years before moving to South Carolina. It is also the exact spot I was planning to take my seven-week respite at and where Adam's second favorite beach, Siesta Key Beach, is located. That is the very same beach I referred to in a letter I'd written and had planned to give to Adam. Yes, Siesta Key Beach is where I told Adam we could meet, take a walk, and start a friendship, if he was willing and available.

When the map showing Cougar Town's location appeared on the TV screen, I couldn't stop laughing. I said to God, "This is too funny. Sarasota, Florida, of all places. You've got to be kidding."

I was planning on returning to Sarasota for a final walk down memory lane. After meeting Adam, the purpose of that trip started to have a different meaning. All I could do was dream I would see Adam and we would walk on Siesta Key Beach hand in hand.

While I watched the TV show, I talked to God, saying, "I couldn't have planned this any better. I could never make this whole thing up. Oh God, you do have such a sense of humor."

That moment brought me so close to God that I broke out in holy laughter. That's what I call it when I am with God and giggling. It goes beyond any sense of happiness that I think could humanly be possible under any other circumstances.

The next time I saw Adam, I had the letter with me. I had rewritten it several times, and I was proud of the finished product. It was clever, accusing, thought provoking, and stupid—and it was what I later termed my "incident" or mistake. But at the time I didn't see it that way. I couldn't just let go of things, let go and let God. No, I had to take things into my own hands instead of trusting God.

The day I was prepared to give Adam the letter, he started out our conversation by asking me this question: "Aren't you the one who lives on a golf course?"

I answered him with a question: "Are you talking about here in Indiana or in South Carolina?" I went into some babble about living in a golf community in Indiana and actually having my home on the fifth fairway in South Carolina, although I am not a golfer. I may have told him that my late husband and I had dreamed of living on a lake one day but ended up on a golf course.

Then he proceeded to ask, "Didn't you say you had a friend that likes to fish and came to see you and wanted to go fishing on Red Rock Lake?"

When Adam repeated word for word what I had said to him earlier, I thought, *What kind of man would remember word for word what a client had said almost two and a half months earlier?* I knew what he was getting around to. He really wasn't interested in the golf course or fishing, for that matter.

I answered him by saying, "Oh, that was Jim, my friend Patty's husband. They came down to visit us once. That was the first time I'd heard the name of your lake."

Adam started laughing, and it made me think he had mistakenly believed I had a boyfriend. He seemed to be beginning to see the irony of the situation too. I wondered if he thought I was the kind of woman who would cheat on a boyfriend or have a boyfriend come and stay over with me. I sensed there was something behind all this, but I didn't know what it was. I began to wonder if, perhaps, he knew my friend Jim. I thought maybe the two guys had actually fished together or knew each other some other way.

This conversation made me wonder if there were other women that Adam was flirting with while at work. He started out by saying, "Aren't you the one who lives on a golf course?" I clearly remember thinking, *How many other women do you flirt with? I thought I was the only one.* I could see how the comments he made after discovering my true age had affected my relationship with him. I started to pick up on the littlest things he said, and I wondered if he was playing with me. I didn't want to believe that about him, but he was the one painting that picture. I felt confused. I didn't sense he was that kind of person, and that is what bothered me the most. Maybe I was looking at him with rose-colored glasses or was in denial. Or was I looking at him through eyes of love, seeing him the way God sees him. Over time, I thought about this quite a few times too. Either way, I see him forgiven.

In my heart, despite everything that had happened between us, I believed that Adam was doing what I was doing. He was going over our time together and reliving it. That is why he remembered every word I'd said. I felt certain there was more going on between us than meets the eye. I couldn't believe he was doing this with a handful of women. If he was, he would have had to keep very detailed notes or have an excellent memory. This is part of what I think keeps me obsessed. I want to know the truth, because his attempt to get honest left me very confused. I don't like when things don't match up and aren't logical. I sensed one thing about Adam, but I heard something else. Usually when that happens, I go by the person's actions, body language, expressions and the tone of their voice instead of their words. When the words conflict it is a red flag to me that something isn't quite right. I wondered if Adam was confused and that was why he didn't know what to say. I question whether his confusion was what has me feeling that way too.

When I first saw Adam that day—I now call it D-day (D for door closed)—I gave him a picture of my perfume that had been in an advertisement that, coincidently, had arrived just the day before. After he had complimented my perfume the last time I'd seen him, he'd asked the name of it. I couldn't remember the name at the time. I still have trouble remembering it when others ask me what perfume I wear, which always leads me to think about Adam. (After he reads this book, I may have to find another brand of perfume.) Anyway, I thought it was rather timely that I now had this advertisement to give him. I told him the story about how I had returned my bottle to the store because I thought it was broken when I couldn't get the rest of the perfume to come out. I hadn't realized there were two bottles, one for day and one for evening wear joined together to form one bottle and I needed to take them apart. The advertisement actually pictured the bottle both ways, which was perfect. This prop helped to keep me appearing calm as I talked to him, because I was so nervous inside.

When he went to return the ad to me, I said, "No, you can keep it."

He replied, "Sweet."

I couldn't believe he used that word. When I described my opinion of him in the letter I was about to give him, I had alternated between using the word "sweet" or "nice" at least a dozen times before deciding on the word "sweet." When he chose that word, I was thinking, *Another coincidence? What is going on?* It wasn't so shocking this time, but I just found it all so amusing.

Although I was feeling uneasy about what had happened between us the last time we were together, I wasn't able to brooch the subject. All in all, we had a nice visit and talked as usual, but I was already feeling very sad. Those feelings of being safe and comfortable with Adam were gone. I asked God to help me get through that visit and keep it together. As I was about to leave, I gave Adam the letter I'd written. Of course, I'd sprayed it with my perfume. In the letter, I teased him about not seeing my age and about the offer of his personal cell phone number for business purposes. When I went to hand him the letter, he didn't even wait. He reached over and grabbed it from me. He had the biggest smile on his face as he began to rip open the envelope. I panicked and was too embarrassed to have him read it in front of me.

I said, "No, don't open it now. Read it later, and pray about it."

In a way, I think I was afraid to know his answer or maybe I wasn't ready to move forward. I often wonder what would have happened if I had only been brave. I would have loved to see his expressions as he read the letter. I know now that wasn't meant to be. I wasn't meant to know his answer that day, either. Looking back at all that has happened since then, I wouldn't change a thing. God was there in that moment too.

I watched him put the letter into the breast pocket of his jacket. In the letter, I asked him, "What were you thinking?" I sarcastically mentioned the possibility that my age had something to do with his memory. I mentioned that maybe age didn't matter and suggested that was why he'd never noticed it. I even gave him my cell phone number and told him that if he changed his mind to call me. I implied we could walk on the beach when he was going to be in Sarasota, Florida, coincidently, at the same time as me. He had let that fact be known when I'd told him I was going to Florida with my dogs and couldn't wait to walk with them on the beach. My letter was confrontational, and, maybe, it was confusing to him as well. I think it may have embarrassed him. I didn't mean for it to do that. I wasn't straightforward, and I used humor and sarcasm to hide my true feelings. I wanted the letter to be used to prompt Adam to think about how he was presenting himself and how he was living. It was meant as an encouragement for him to do some self-reflecting.

That day, I tried to shake Adam's hand good-bye. I wanted to thank him for taking good care of me, and I truly thought it was really going to be good-bye. I didn't know if I would ever come back. I wondered what having our hands touch would do for us. I didn't get the opportunity to find out, because that offer didn't go over well. I was left with my hand held out in midair. Perhaps Adam couldn't bring himself to touch me, say good-bye, or pass the peace. I guess God didn't want that to take place that day, either. I reminded Adam that I was heading to South Carolina and then to Florida.

I told Adam, "It is getting so cold out. My hands are freezing. Feel them." I extended my hands toward his, but he resisted that invite too. Maybe in some small way I was testing him. I said, "It's time to go South." I was thinking, *This relationship had already gone there.*

He said, "I hear you there." Was he responding to my words or my thoughts?

Looking back on it, I see how insecure I was about the possibility that he could truly be interested in me, especially after what he had told me the previous week. That is why I wrote the letter and wasn't able to talk to him about all that had happened between us. I wasn't able to be straightforward. The fact that we were meeting at his work didn't help make this conversation any easier for me. So I took the coward's way out and gave him the letter. I think it made him uncomfortable, and it certainly didn't show me in a good light, either. While I don't regret any thing that happened, at the time I wished I'd had the courage to just talk to Adam. But now I see it in an entirely different way.

I had turned this situation over to God the very day I met Adam and asked the question: "Is this the man you are presenting to me?" Now I see this is all part of the journey. I think God is giving Adam and me choices, just like He gave them to Adam and Eve in the garden.

As I was leaving, Adam said, "If you need me, call me." Then he turned to the secretary and said, "You'll get me if she calls, won't you?"

There was no offer of the personal cell phone number and, after asking his secretary to get him if I ever called, he limited that offer to the business at hand. I felt he was trying to rewrite history and take back everything he'd said to me. Maybe he added the business part because he noticed how uncomfortable I was. I think I was even blushing. Either way, I was feeling so hurt, confused, and embarrassed that I just wanted to run away. On a previous occasion, he'd mentioned if I needed to ask him any questions regarding our business together I was to call him at the office. His exact words were, "If you need anything, anything at all, just call me here. I'll tell the girls that if Rebecca ever calls they are to come and get me right away so I can talk to you." He had said this before he found the way to offer me his personal cell phone number. I think every time I heard these things, I was slow to get his point, confused, or in denial.

Adam came highly recommended by several people. In fact, before I met Adam, three people all said the exact same thing to me on the exact same day: "You are really going to like Adam. He's so nice." It kind of grabbed my attention at the time, but then I forgot all about it. So when he would say such nice things to me, I remembered what others had said about him. I thought he was just a really nice guy. When he took extra time to talk to me, I merely thought that perhaps he just likes to spend time with the clients. But when the "I like your perfume, I am single and all alone, if you want my personal cell phone number, and if you need anything, anything at all, call the office" comments were accompanied by his body language and his smile, I thought, *I must be pretty thick not to get his message.* I would go home and replay in my mind what he said and think, *He is interested in me!*

As I stood there remembering how he'd closed the door the past week on any future between us, I heard him say, "You're coming back again in January, aren't you?"

I said, "No, you know I'll be in Florida."

Then he said, "Well, you'll be back here in the spring, won't you?"

I said, "I don't know if I am ever coming back." That is how we left it that day. I went home and cried.

Looking back on it, I realize I was sending him some mixed messages too. Part of me wanted him to know that if he called me and we saw each other socially and things worked out, I could go somewhere else for my business dealings if it would be a conflict of interests. The other part thought if I don't hear from you, I don't know if I can face you again. In a way, I started this mess by flirting with him at his workplace. I never thought of the consequences. I only wanted him to know I was interested in him if he was interested in me. I just didn't think it through. I didn't know if our professional relationship was one of the reasons why we couldn't be together or if I was just making up another excuse to keep myself in denial. Maybe Adam had come to his senses, and I was still living in this fairy tale.

The very next day, October 1, 2009, I started to write my first book, which was about George. I wrote about how we met and married, and then I was stuck and couldn't write anymore. I had written about Adam in that first chapter too. Eventually, I would write more about my life beyond that wonderful year of courtship with George. I would write about our entire life together. I wrote about discovering George's diagnosis of terminal colon cancer, about experiencing God's many blessings those last thirteen years, and about evolving from a wife, into a widow, into a single woman. Adam was the reason I really started to write, because he made me feel alive again and attractive. In the first letter I wrote to Adam, I told him how he made me feel. I didn't know at the time that writing down those feelings for Adam would enable me to face the memories about George that were too painful to recall before meeting Adam, allowing me to begin writing that first chapter.

October 26, 2009, I left Indiana and headed to my winter home on the golf course in South Carolina. I wasn't able to stop thinking and praying about Adam. He not only awakened a playful spirit in me, which reminded me about George's love, but Adam also brought me to the place where I wanted to be loved and love again. Thoughts of him distracted me from writing, and I couldn't work on my book.

Even though I was over six hundred miles away from Adam, I couldn't stop thinking about him. A few weeks before Christmas, I wrote to Adam and told him that very same thing, I couldn't stop thinking about him. The day after I mailed the letter, I took him up on his offer and called him at his office. I left a message with someone to have him call me. I was having second thoughts about sending that letter, and I wanted to warn Adam that I had sent letter number two to him at his workplace. I didn't want him to be caught off guard. It was getting close to Christmas, and I was still waiting for him to return the call. In the letter, I told him I was confused and wanted to know the truth. I told him I didn't want what had happened to come between us and implied that I forgave him for what transpired. I remember writing something about the New Year that was ahead of us, and that I was reflecting back on the old one and wanted to resolve any old issues.

In that letter I asked him for answers to my questions. I made it real simple for him to just send me a response of either ABCDE or F. The key was: A...you were attracted to me; B... I was attracted to you; C... we were attracted to each other; D... it was moving way to fast; and E... you really are engaged; F... I should have talked to you instead of all my girl friends. I wished I had written G... for all of the above. Regardless, he never did answer me. All he needed to do was send me a "letter!"

After waiting for what seemed like an eternity for him to either write or return the phone call, I ended up writing another letter to him. In that letter, I shared some of my dreams about writing my first book and maybe helping others with cancer. I held back sharing some of my dreams—especially the one I was dreaming about where Adam and I ended up together. I was stuck not only on him, but I was stuck on moving forward with the book too. After writing that letter, I was able to envision that manuscript becoming a book. I worked day and night on it, whenever I felt inspired by the Holy Spirit. During that time, I wrote a great many poems too, including some about Adam.

This is part of that third letter that I wrote to Adam around Christmas 2009. As you will read, I told him I would call him Adam instead of his real name. At that time, I had no idea I would be writing this second book and calling him Adam. I just knew God wanted me to have Adam in my life for a season. I still don't know where or how that season will end. Only God knows that for sure. It now seems very appropriate that an excerpt from this letter be included in this book I am titling *Love at First Sight, Stepping Out on a Maybe*. I started the letter by telling Adam that he had an opportunity to share with me about his dream of building his house and retiring to South Carolina. Now I wanted to share my dream with him, too. I deleted some parts of the letter that were just what I call "small talk" so please trust me when I say the heart of the letter hasn't changed.

> I have tired numerous times to give this, whatever
> it is we had between us, back to God, but He

will not take it away. You were the inspiration I needed to start to write my book. So maybe that is why He keeps bringing this desire to talk to you back to me. I hope you are smiling, and I am not scaring you—but somehow I get the feeling you are a brave soul too.

I have always wanted to write about the unbeliev-able story of how and possibly why my husband survived an eleven-month prognosis of stage-four colon cancer. But I couldn't write it until he died, because how can you write a story that hasn't ended, and that took thirteen years. We had gone to hospitals in Indiana, where we first lived. After he went into remission—following liver surgery to remove the right lobe of his liver, chemo, and radiation—we moved to Florida. I wanted him to live his dream. We really had no idea how long he would live, but I was brave. I still am, because I am writing this to you. If I were doing this on my own, I would never do it. But I've learned to listen to God, gut feeling, compass or heart, whatever name you give it. You see, not only did my husband survive thirteen years, he had so many complications it would take so long to tell you them all. He survived, and we were able to enjoy life and even experience some extensive travel. We didn't let cancer rob us of a great life.

That is what I think you saw. You saw the amaz-ing person I have become. If you'd only known me when I was twenty or thirty or even forty, for that matter, you would know I am not the same person I used to be. I believe God doesn't waste any hurts or mistakes. I also know He has given me full permission to write to you. He even demanded it. I am following my heart. I didn't give up my life and follow God to turn my back on Him and any dreams He gives me. Right now He gave me you, and the only person that can put a stop to this is you. If you don't want me to write to you anymore, all you have to do is say STOP. Somehow, I just don't think you will. Time will tell.

I feel so playful when I think of you and my heart sort of has a little pitter-patter. I have no clue what it means. I just know that when I met George— you know, the other pen clicker—I knew he was good for me. I had no fear of him. And if you knew the messy marriage I'd had the first time, it is remarkable that I could trust George or myself again. I feel I can trust you because I see myself in you. Think about it. How many people have you met in your life and felt an instant connection with them? I know that was the way I felt about all my close friends when I first met them. When I think of all the people that have crossed my path, it is rare.

So I have this all figured out in my mind. Do you watch *Castle*? Well, it will be reversed. If you haven't, you ought to at least watch one episode. I am teasing and serious too. I do want to write this story to give hope and inspiration to people with cancer, maybe to hospice workers or to those whose spouse died or even to people that are struggling in bad marriages. I don't know where or how this is going to be used, but I know I am called to write this story.

Whenever George and I would go to a new doctor, and we had plenty because besides living in Indiana we lived in Florida and South Carolina and in every state George's doctors were amazed that he was still living and beating this cancer. When the cancer finally went to George's brain and he decided to do some more radiation to give me a little more time with him, it turned out just right. My husband always trusted me to guide him, and, somehow, great things always came of it. I think that is what happens when you do things for others. I am sure you know that, because I see how caring a person you are. I think it was my faith that really kept George alive. Sometimes, I think God did it just for me because he loves me so much. He has done amazing things in my life. Unless you've had that experience, it is hard to explain.

I hope it is okay to send this to you. It is a heartfelt story, and I can only write it if I feel safe to express my thoughts and feelings. It is a wonderful love story, and you should feel honored that you were my inspiration. That is why I chose you to hear some of it.

I love to tell my stories. I guess someday I want someone who understands what my husband and I have been through and would not be threatened if I made telling this story, to whatever audience, a purpose in my life. I need someone who wouldn't be jealous or think I am not over my husband. I am over grieving for him because I just let the tears flow but, of course, I will always miss him. I don't want to disrespect my husband and never get on with my life. He would hate that. I was not going to have his life be wasted through his death. My husband is more alive now than ever, and I am happy for him.

I don't want my story to be sad and hopeless. I want the world to see that George and I were able to live not knowing how much time he had. We were able to move to Florida in the midst of what would normally be crippling to most people. We were a team. We gave each other a reason to hope. I want to give hope to others, but if I have none for myself I don't know if I can do this. I am trying to do this for others and for God.

So right now I am going to use you. I'll just call you Adam in my mind. You sort of represent someone I am holding out for one day. Maybe together we can do something good. All I ask is that, if it's okay, I can write to you if I need a little daydream. It is hard to write when I have no one to give it to just yet. I don't want to bring any more pain to those people who loved George and aren't ready for this. Seriously, if this is making you uncomfortable, I understand, just tell me to STOP.

I wish you all the best. I don't know if I'll write to you again or not. I just take it day by day. I may have to yell at God first and ask Him why

He made me look like such a fool. Honestly, I am
not nuts, just a little fun crazy. Are you clicking
your pen?

I went to Florida on January 20, 2010. I was hoping Adam would
call me while I was there. He had my cell phone number, and I
knew he was coming to the area sometime during my seven-week
stay. Though I highly doubted I would hear from him, part of me
remained hopeful. I told myself, "If I don't hear from him after
this, I won't think about him anymore. I'll give up any hope that
he is the one. I'll face the truth that there's really nothing between
us." I was really restless, and I was having such a hard time getting
over this. I wrote two more letters to him, but I never mailed
either one. I titled one "pathetic" because that was what I was
thinking about myself. Those letters were just a purging of my
thoughts. I continued to talk to God about Adam, and I kept
praying that if God hadn't put that desire for a relationship with
Adam in my heart that God would take it away. I knew He could.

I thought if I talked to some of the women I met in Florida about
Adam I would get a different perspective, so I told several of them
about the story. It was interesting to hear their takes on it. I started
to notice a pattern too. Women who were happily married had a
different take away then some of the ones who were either single
or divorced. I think that shows how we project what we think
and believe into our dreams or onto others, for that matter. Some
of them shared their stories about how they met their husbands.
Many encouraged me to write to Adam again. One woman said,
"It's Valentine's Day. Why don't you call him?" I really wanted
to, but I just didn't believe in my heart it was the right thing to
do. I wasn't feeling prompted by that inner voice. In fact, I think
that voice was the one who warned me not to write anymore.
One thing I learned from talking to these women was, no matter
their age, most women love romance. Although these women

were strangers I'd never see again, everyone I spoke to said they couldn't wait to hear the ending. Some said they would pray for me. I knew because I probably wouldn't ever see these women again that they would never know how this story ends until they got to heaven. I hoped it didn't take that long for me.

I was free to talk openly with the women I met because no one knew Adam or me. I did talk to a friend of mine who still lived in the neighborhood where George and I had our home before moving to South Carolina. She and I went to lunch, and it was great to see her again and catch up. I talked about Adam, and she commented about how my face lit up when I spoke about him. She said she was glad to see me looking so good. She knew George, and she understood what a good husband I'd lost. She commented that it was a good thing that I could still have my heart open to the possibility of love.

My daughter was back in South Carolina going through her own marital crisis. It was hard for me to be in Florida, but I knew it was best for me to stay there. Talking about Adam did my heart good. It kept me hopeful and focused on my life rather than obsessing on all the struggles my daughter was experiencing. I believe God gave me Adam for that purpose too. Thoughts of Adam not only helped me feel hopeful, they also kept me lighthearted. They reminded me that no matter what struggles we are going through at any given time our lives can change for the better overnight. We never know what good things God may have waiting around the corner for us.

The weather in Florida those seven weeks was unseasonably cold and damp. I didn't get to walk on the beach as much as I'd hoped. My son and his family came to visit, so I did get to spend a few days with my grandchildren. I went back to my former church, went on a planning retreat with some of the leaders from the singles group, and started some new friendships. I even considered the possibility of moving back to Florida. I went house hunting just to see if I would find a house or a neighborhood that called my name, but that never happened. Two of my girlfriends from Pittsburgh, where I had lived before marrying George, came to spend the week with me. We had a great time. It wasn't the vacation I expected because the weather was so disappointing, but it was a stepping-stone to living life as a single person. Although I didn't like being alone, I learned I was capable of driving to Florida and staying there all by myself. I was pleased because I felt victorious.

When I arrived back in South Carolina after that seven-week trip, among the pile of mail that accumulated I found a letter Adam had sent me. It simply said, "Please stop writing. Hope you're well. Thanks," followed by his signature. The first thing I noticed was the letter wasn't on his work stationary, but it did have his company's name hand stamped across the top three times. He had written his note very close to the top by those stampings. I wondered if he was saying, *I am at work, stupid! What are you doing? Are you trying to get me fired?* That thought quickly vanished. After rereading his words, my second thought was, *He's so polite.* Finally, I thought, *Thank goodness I didn't send him any more of those letters! I wouldn't have wanted him to think I disrespected him or that I was some kind of stalker. It was bad enough that I wrote to him to begin with.*

Then I looked at the postmark; the letter was sent January 25, 2010. He would have received my letter long before that, since I mailed it before Christmas. I couldn't help but wonder if he was thinking about his response for a while before answering me. By now, it was the middle of March. I knew I would be returning to Indiana soon and would have to make some decisions about whether to see Adam again or not, professionally speaking that is. I thought this was the closure I was seeking. I shredded his letter along with the copy of the handwritten letter number two. Then I talked to God and asked him to take away this desire for Adam and heal me of my obsession.

After shredding the letter from Adam and talking to God, I still wasn't cured of my obsession. I attempted to make other arrangements to take my business elsewhere, but things weren't working out. I've learned that if the door closes, God doesn't want me to try and go through it. I took this as God's way of saying I needed to face this and stop running away. I figured out a way I could go to Adam's workplace without seeing him. I thought maybe after that I would have a better handle on what to do.

Reading Between the Lines

When I arrived back in Indiana, I had no idea what changes, if any, the coming summer would bring. But I knew I wanted something to change. I wanted this obsession with Adam to end. I wasn't sure if facing him and the situation would be the key to finding the peace I longed for. I felt as if I'd lost my serenity, and I wasn't willing to exchange it for happiness that I know doesn't always last. If I'm honest, I wanted it all. I wanted to have peace, serenity, and the happiness I know is possible to have in a marital relationship. I wondered if this obsession with Adam would ever go away. I prayed for God to take away the desire for Adam or bring a change in our relationship. Pleading with God, I said, "Please don't leave me stuck in limbo." I wanted to surrender all to God and have Him transform me into a woman who was at peace waiting or, better yet, have Him provide a revelation about where this relationship was heading.

I arrived back in Indiana in early May. A few days later, I ended up at Adam's workplace. I wasn't even sure if Adam would be in the office that day. As I stood in the reception area talking to the secretary, I was extremely nervous. Then she commented on my cross necklace I was wearing. I told her I'd bought it at a holiday shopper's sale when I was in Greensboro, North Carolina, for the Women of Faith Conference. After that, I felt a peace come over me because the cross was a reminder about everything that Jesus means to me. It gave me prospective, you could say. I remember telling the secretary about my favorite jade cross, which had been my grandma's. I told her it is my most valued possession because it represented my family and the faith that was handed down to me. She said, "Bring it in the next time you come. I'd love to see it." I never saw her after that. But as I was talking to her that day and signing some papers, I noticed something out of the corner of my eye. I looked up and saw Adam standing in the hallway, waving his arms back and forth high in the air to get my attention. He was smiling. I just gave him this meek little wave in return, but I really wanted to wave back to him the exact same way he was waving to me. I was so happy to see him. I wasn't sure how to act, and I felt awkward. I sensed he was happy to see me too. Then I started to read more into it. I thought that he was possibly trying to send me the message that it was okay for me to be there, or perhaps he was overreacting because he was so uncomfortable with even the sight of me. Maybe I was a reminder of all he wanted to forget. I was thinking, I am still stuck not only on you, but stuck not understanding what really happened between the two of us. I knew how hard I was fighting these feelings for him, which I now labeled as inappropriate. When he came out into the waiting area to see another one of his clients, he made this "whoa" sound. I thought he was telling himself to hold his horses. I know it sounds so silly.

A little over a month later, around the middle of June 2010, I had a meeting with Adam. It was the first time we were alone together after I'd written him those three letters. I was feeling tense and confused. There was some mix up when I tried to schedule that appointment with him. Someone had written a note saying not to schedule me with Adam anymore. I asked the woman at the other end of the phone why that note was there. She assumed it was at my request. I told her I didn't initiate that request, so she went ahead and booked my appointment with him. I thought I heard her giggle. Then I wondered if I was imagining that too. This just added to my confusion. I wanted to see Adam at least one more time, because I had planned to bring everything out in the open to clear the air. I started to doubt if I should be seeing him for my business transactions at this point in time. I wanted to talk to him about that as well. What if he was being insincere when he waved and he was the one who requested not to work with me anymore? I didn't want to believe that was the truth. After seeing how tense he appeared and knowing I was feeling the same, I started to think this meeting wasn't good for either of us. Maybe there was no reconciliation and no moving forward.

As I stood there in the office, I could feel the tension. Adam seemed so different. Remembering the meek little wave I'd given him last time I saw him, I wondered if it had made him think I wasn't happy to see him. I didn't mean to send that message. I had planned on having a point-blank conversation with him in hopes that it would clear up all the confusion that had taken place since the day we'd met. I had prayed for God to give me the right words to say that day. For some reason, I remained silent. Later, I looked at it as God's answer to my prayer. The way Adam's eyes looked grabbed my attention; I didn't remember his eyes being such a dark color. I stared into them as if they would give me the answers I was looking for.

After some small talk and an odd compliment about my purse, Adam told me that he wasn't going to be able to work with me anymore. I immediately assumed it had to do with what had happened between us, and I could feel my heart sink. In the next breath, he told me his father had died of cancer three years ago. He told me he had taken care of his dad before he died, and now his mom had cancer. He talked very little about it, but I knew it wasn't good.

He said, "Today is my last day at work, because I am going to be taking care of my mom."

I just said, "I am so sorry about your mom."

He said, "Thank you for saying that." That is when he said, "I don't know when I'll see you. I don't know if I'll ever see you again."

I was shocked to learn this about his mom, but I felt God was once again involved in this timing, and I was meant to be there for Adam. I normally would have seen him much sooner and we would have finished up the business for that quarter before that day even came. I'd been praying about Adam and for him; now I really had some specific things to pray about. I realized that the letter I wrote to Adam about wanting to write my first book for people who have cancer and their loved ones was directly addressing Adam's situation. I wondered how much that letter affected him. I had no idea when I wrote to him that cancer hit so close to home. I only had discerned from God that for some reason Adam might be the one who would want to help promote the cause because we had the same passion. Hearing about his parents confirmed that my discernment was somewhat correct.

Since Adam would be taking a family leave from work, I didn't know if or when I would ever see him again. I wondered if that meant good-bye. Maybe God was closing the door on this relationship. Other people at the office would be able to take care of my business transactions. I thought, perhaps, Adam wanted it this way. I could sense how uncomfortable he was, but I wasn't sure if it was because of what had happened between us or because his mom was dying. I felt guilty for even thinking about the situation between him and me at a time like this. I was just thankful that I hadn't said anything to him about what had transpired between us and that God helped me to be a good listener that day. When I reflected back on that day, I realized what I saw in Adam's eyes was his pain.

When I saw Adam that day in June, we managed to talk a little about my first book. Adam acknowledged its existence and asked if I had found someone to help me with it. In the last letter I'd written to him, I had suggested sending him my manuscript and having him help me with it. His question about finding someone to help me was the only time we broached the subject of the letters I had written to him. I felt bringing up the letters was taboo. After sensing how tense he was and seeing how his eyes looked so different, I wasn't able to clear the air like I had hoped. I began looking to him to take the lead in directing our conversations regarding those letters. I knew those letters had made him uncomfortable, because he'd written to me and asked me to stop sending them. So I didn't want to cross the line.

In a way, I was trying to figure out why God had brought us together. I thought Adam might have some insight about this. I was searching for answers and asking God why this was happening. This was the first time I spoke to Adam about a God sighting. I told him about the coincidence that happened when I was trying to find a publisher for first my book. I told Adam I was riding in my car and talking to God like I usually do. I had just asked God's help in getting the book published, when I heard a man's voice on the car radio as I was using the seek button to help program the stations. The voice on the radio said that if you feel that God inspired you to write a book go to this certain website. The timing of this announcement was perfect. It was as if God used that moment to assure me He was there coaching me as I took my next step when writing that first book. Adam called this déjà vu. That's when I explained that I call those coincidences a God sighting. It meant that God was there in the moment, letting me know he hears my prayers. Sometimes these sightings are just little coincidences, and other times they are bold clues that lead to direct answers to a prayer. I told Adam that these coincidences happen to me quite often.

I didn't end up using the publisher that I first heard about on the radio. That God sighting was just God's way to confirm that He'd heard my request. For some reason, I didn't rush into using that publisher. I believe God was trying to teach me not to rush into things. It was important for me to be confident that I was working with a publisher that I believed God was finding for me. Other coincidences that happened after that helped me feel assured that I was to wait and would be confident when the right publisher came along. As a result of waiting, one day I was having a conversation with someone from another publishing firm about my writing and the person suggested that I might want to write a story about Ruth and Boaz. I started to giggle because I had already written a poem to God asking if Adam was my Boaz, the man God chose for me. That statement grabbed my attention and I talked to God about the possibility of writing this book. Even though I had tremendous doubts, I kept enough of an open mind to bring it to God and consider that He might be trying to tell me something.

Then I thought about the poem I had written in December 2009, right before I sent Adam letter number three. I went back and reread the poem. When I wrote it, I thought of it as purely another God sighting. I thought, perhaps, God was letting me know there might be something to this idea about Adam being my Boaz. I had no idea when I wrote the line about writing my love song that one day I would see how that refers to writing this book. I believe I am supposed to share the poem with you now.

Sometimes I read between the lines of my own poems, and I'm
surprised at how they are a foretelling of what eventually happens.

Here with You God

My heart is a flutter, I don't know why.
With all that's going on, you'd think I'd cry.
When I leave this, my safest of places,
I wish I would feel his warm embraces.
So here with you, God, is where I belong.
I will stay here while I write my love song.
If I am truly honest, God, with you,
I sense there's something you want me to do.
I trust you with all of my secrets inside,
I do not want it mistaken for pride.
I feel safe, and you always make me smile.
With you, please, I just want to stay awhile.
Will I ever be the same as before?
Was it my wounded heart he tried to lure?
I feel such a fear building up in me.
God I know you do not want that to be.
Someday soon with you to heaven I'll fly.
That will happen on the day that I die.
Until then, am I to stay here alone?
What if he has a heart purely of stone?
God, when will you send me my helper mate?
When can we go on that very first date?
Let me know if there is something amiss.
Do you think he's ready to handle this?
I listened and trusted you from the first day.
Now, God, please take the confusion away.
Do you have me acting a silly fool?
I am not going to break any rule.

I'm really growing stronger day by day.
When can my waiting child come out to play?
I have such heaviness inside of me.
I want to do all these things meant for Thee.
I think I have learned all I really can.
Is it time now for him to show his hand?
I'm getting impatient for the first date.
Do I have longer that I have to wait?
Now I know I need to have faith, I see.
Did I do everything you've asked of me?
You have proved you hear every single thought.
Some I certainly wish you could hear not.
I sometimes blush like an innocent bride.
If he has feelings for me, will he hide?
I'd like a husband with me in the flesh.
Though, Jesus, you still are the very best.
I want to be in heaven now with you.
I know while I have a life, there's work to do.
I have a silly question for you, Lord.
Do you really think that Adam's on board?
You know I thought I'd like him for my mate.
How ridiculous, we never did date.
He has a soothing gentle healing hand.
I believe he's a very special man.
If these things are not all honestly true,
What then do you want me to do for you?
Is he truly down, praying on his knee,
Requesting he be purified by thee?
I feel conflicted. The truth cannot wait.
Was our meeting merely an act of fate?
If he a righteous man does not appear,
Do not let him toward me take one step near.
It's a hard thing for me to know it's true,
But I've truly spent so much time with you.

How will I control all I feel inside?
Am I ready, my face, from him to hide?
When I am sure this test from you is done,
Will he and I together see the sun?
I needed a rest and desire one too,
I know my only true rest is in you.
Will it ever be safe to show my heart?
Am I acting foolish, not very smart?
God, I have a serious question for you.
Is he understanding of all you do?
Or is he just a goofy little man,
Not meant for me, then I will understand.
I will have my answer to this riddle,
I'll no longer be stuck in the middle.
For if he is not meant for me I see,
It doesn't matter; it's more time with Thee.
I made a fool of myself it is true.
I should have known first to confide in you.
I've had this problem since I have been young.
When will I ever learn to hold my tongue?

When I thought about the story of Ruth and how she sowed into her situation, I knew one thing for certain: if I was going to sow into my situation, that meant I better pray for Adam and his family.

I was hard at work finishing my first book. My goal was to send it to the publisher on July 6, George's birthday. I used that date not only as a motivator to put the final touches on the book but, also, as a way to remember my husband on the anniversary of his birthday. I thought that would be very fitting.

Thoughts of Adam continued to come into my mind. I knew I needed to pray for him. Having gone through being with my husband during his last days helped me relate in a way to what Adam must be going through. The memories were still fresh in my mind. I knew what walking through the valley of death with a loved one was like. I remembered what it felt like to lose my mom, too, and what it is like not to have either parent alive anymore. I had some idea about what Adam might be dealing with and felt such heaviness in my heart for what he was going through. I was concerned for him. I wished there was something I could do. That was when I realized I was doing the most important thing of all: I was holding Adam up in prayer. I believed with all my heart that I was there that day—his last day at work before venturing on that journey—because God had so perfectly arranged it. I now see that God wanted me to be a strong and courageous woman who would push through my insecurities and overcome obstacles, like the scheduling mix up, to follow my heart so that I could be with the man my heart was longing to see. I believed this is the type of behavior God will bless.

I searched through the obituaries daily because I wanted to know when Adam's mom died. During this time period, I found the prayer card we'd used at my mom's viewing. It had the date of her death on it. I often had so much trouble remembering the date my mom died. Maybe it was because George and I were vacationing in California at the time or my mind just didn't want to remember. When I came across the obituary for Adam's mom, it didn't have her date of death on it. The obituary was printed on July 17, 2010. That was exactly one year from the day I had met Adam. Coincidently, July 15, 2010 was the ten-year anniversary of my own mother's death. I never did ask Adam the exact date of his mom's death. The fact that it might be somewhere in the middle of those dates is enough of a God sighting to let me know that I was Adam's angel now, meaning God was using me to pray for Adam and ask for protection for him.

When I read the obituary, it included his parents' love story and the fact that they were both born in Germany and had come to the United States after they married. Now I knew for certain that Adam was 100 percent German. It was just like God to reveal that to me in that most special way. I believed the Holy Spirit had indeed been gifting me with that discernment. When Adam reads this, I hope he will see it that way too. I hope this story not only brings Adam comfort, but also grows his faith in a God who has His eye on Adam and loves him more than he could have ever thought possible. No matter how this story ends for Adam and me, it is a beautiful love story indeed. It shows the love of God for His children and how He can open our hearts to love one another.

So much has happened between Adam and me to bring this story about. From the day we looked into each other's eyes, the connection we made that opened me up to write my first book, and now this connection with the death of his mom—it is no wonder why I can't just let this man out of my heart. I don't know if God is creating a love story that will lead to romantic love in the earthly sense, but I know it is a love story in the heavenly sense. I know what I want. I pray that after Adam reads this book he won't have a doubt about how much I care for him. He will know it is enough to motivate me to write an entire book and dedicate it to him. He will know that, while I still love George, I am capable of loving another man.

Sometimes I wonder if Adam's mom is in heaven talking with my husband. I like to think they agree Adam and I would be good for each other. That picture brings me peace when I think I am about to go crazy because of all these coincidences. I do believe God brought Adam and me together to help us get through this rough time in both of our lives and to help us each grow stronger too. I honestly admit to God that I want it to be more. God knew that all along; he just wanted me to stop pretending I didn't want a romantic relationship with Adam. I keep praying, "God, if Adam and I would be good for each other, let it be. If not, help me let it go." So far, there is no letting go.

I pray this book will give me the peace and serenity I want. I pray it will bring me happiness too. I believe, with God's help, I can have it all. I have faith that God can do the impossible. When it seems Adam and my signals are so crossed, I wonder if this mess will ever get straightened out. I guess that is part of what this book is about. It is my attempt at being that "open book" my first husband, John, used to call me. At the time I thought it wasn't a good thing to be so open, because I saw it as a way of not protecting my heart. Now I see it as the way into my heart. I never thought in a million years when John said those words about me it would be a foretelling to what I believe is my chosen calling. I believe my willingness to open my heart to all of you reading this book is part of God's plan for me.

I was able to write my first book about George because, in a way, Adam brought me out of my grief and brought hope back into my life. I had originally written about Adam in the first chapter of that book. The woman who edited it asked if I had remarried. After I read her comment, I quickly wrote Adam out of that chapter altogether. I only mentioned him briefly toward the end of that book as "the stranger" and "my angel." I said when I met him I'd thought it was love at first sight, but later I concluded it was a fantasy. Either way, I didn't think the story about Adam belonged in that first book. That book was my dedication to George.

I know George wanted me to remarry, but now I see this part of my life without George is not a new chapter—it is an entirely new book. It is beginning with this story, which I will dedicate to Adam. I hope I can write his real name on the dedication page, but if he isn't comfortable with that he'll still know it is meant for him. That is all that really matters. I know when George prayed I would have someone again, he knew I wouldn't settle for just anyone or for living a boring life. George knew I would only consider being with someone I truly love and that would be the only reason I would ever remarry. Although at times this part of the journey has been a rough ride, I believe God has me on a romantic adventure. Women love romance. And this woman loves adventure too.

This leads me right into the time I experienced another adventure, which I can label as a very silly one. I actually had one of these God sightings in the form of a printed book. I had been carrying this little book in my purse for quite some time. I know it was there that day in June when I saw Adam. It was in the purse I had bought in February 2010 when I was in Sarasota, the day my girlfriends and I went shopping at St. Armand's Circle. We were shopping at our favorite jewelry store when I saw this white purse I liked. It cost much more than I'd usually spend on a purse.

Liz talked me into buying the purse when she jokingly said, "You'll look dazzling with your new bling and purse when you see Adam again this summer."

Deb, Liz, and I giggled.

Now imagine my amazement and amusement when the first thing Adam says as he moves my purse so I could sit down is "Nice bag."

I couldn't even talk. I was dumbfounded. As he was speaking, he held it up high so we both could see it. Unlike the hair that he had held up using a similar gesture, this object was large enough to hide my face from his. I was thankful for that because I couldn't hide the expression on my face; it was similar to the Cheshire cat, when he catches the mouse. I immediately changed it to my poker face and just thought this is *unbelievable.* Adam was the first man who has ever complimented a purse of mine. I thought about God and how He was with me now—and that day in St. Armand's too.

I knew God was trying to have me lighten up because I was so anxious about seeing Adam that first day after having written all those letters to him. God was reassuring me that I was being obedient when I felt His calling to write to Adam. Somehow, I felt my purse was a little gift from God, and Adam gave his stamp of approval. Maybe I have it reversed. If it wasn't for Adam, I would never have splurged like that on myself. I thought what I spent on the purse was extravagant, considering it was around two hundred dollars, though maybe in comparison to what some people spend that isn't that much money. I still think it was expensive, but now that it has such a wonderful story to go with it I am glad I bought it. It is a good leather purse I will have for a long time. I just hope it always brings me good memories of the day God was there and was pleased that Adam and I loved one another in the way God intended, despite what was a rocky start. I know one thing for sure: we were holding each other up during rough times.

A few days later, I noticed something in that white purse. It appeared to be a book of some kind, still in its wrapper. Then I remembered it was the prize that came with my grandson Robert's lunch that day we went out to eat at Chick-fil-A. As I took the book out of its wrapper, I noticed the title: *Cliff Hanger, the Lap Dog, and the Riddle.* The words and the picture on the cover grabbed my attention and reminded me of my riddle, my poem to God. Intrigued, I opened the book and began to read. It started out with a little girl (me) and her father (Father God) sitting on a bench at the edge of the cliff. The father says he wants to get his daughter a lap dog (husband). She seems more interested in telling her father a riddle (poem). The father then says, "You can tell me your riddle after I get you that lap dog. That is why we are here." In the meantime, Cliff (Adam) hears their conversation and thinks this is his opportunity to finally be rescued from this cliff he is hanging over. He gets out his survival manual and decodes the situation. He is instructed to put on the dog costume and dog collar. The dad throws a leash over the cliff and, naturally, Cliff hooks it onto his dog collar. The dad pulls Cliff up, and Cliff lands right in the little girl's lap. I could hardly turn the pages because I was laughing so hard. At the same time, I felt like I had just interpreted a dream or a vision from God.

I said to God, "I don't have a doubt that you've heard my prayers and read my poem about Adam."

I had actually written the word "riddle" in the poem. I knew God was answering me in a similar fashion. The book was a riddle from God to me. A few other words that can be used to mean riddle are charade, conundrum, dilemma, mystery, enigma, or teaser. *Webster's* definitions of riddle are a puzzling question requiring some ingenuity to answer or any puzzling person or thing. That is so powerful, to think it requires ingenuity to answer a riddle. Who do I turn to in those times when I need answers? The answer to that riddle is simple: my Father God. I am not saying I am the genius, but all the persons of the Trinity are.

As I turned the page of this little book, I knew once the little girl asked the dad the riddle, "What do you lose when you stand up?" what would happen to Cliff. I knew the answer to her riddle was "your lap." I knew Cliff would be propelled off her lap and fall back down over the edge of the cliff. This Cliff Hanger story ended with a caption that read, "Can't hold on much longer." I sure could relate to Cliff's hanging on, waiting to be rescued.

Immediately, I felt without a doubt that God had arranged for me to have this book. God had heard my cries and pleas to him, and God was acknowledging that He knew I stood up for what was good when I confronted Adam with my first letter. Even though I used humor and sarcasm, I stood firm and resisted temptation. God also knew I was still trying to lure Adam. He also knew why. I thought Adam was available and meant for me. I thought he had landed right in my lap the day I met him. Through this book, God arranged an intimate, unbelievably humorous but miraculous way to speak to me. This definitely was a time I experienced the presence of God.

After reading that book, guess where I went for lunch that day? I ordered a children's meal for myself. I asked the woman who waited on me if there were any more books in the Cliff Hanger, Reading Between the Lions series. (Reading Between the Lines!) She said there was a total of four books in the series. The book that came with my meal that day was titled *Cliff Hanger and the Giant Snail.* The title gave me a little inkling that this situation with Adam was going to take a while to figure out.

The story was about a snail on its way to get help to rescue Cliff as he hung there waiting. Each picture page represented a season, with only the corresponding word at the bottom. As I turned each page and read "autumn, winter, spring, and summer," I giggled out loud. The order of the seasons was exactly the same as the progression from the last time I saw Adam at the end of September when I confronted him with my first letter to the time I saw him again just a few weeks ago in the middle of June. I thought, I have been waiting through all these seasons, and I still don't know any more than I did the day this confusion started.

In the story about the snail, Cliff was angry because the snail had gone only seven feet on the journey to rescue him. I worried that Adam was indeed angry that I was still there. Maybe he had written that note stating not to schedule me with him anymore. Maybe I bothered him. I know I could relate to the snail (me) disappointing Cliff (Adam). Like the snail, I wanted to help Cliff, but it didn't seem that I could since I wasn't even in a relationship with him. Adam did seem to be dangling. I could sense how emotional he was that last day we'd met. I still felt confused about the truth. I didn't know how either one of us could hold out. At this point, I wanted some help too. I wanted to know how this would end. And now, besides this situation between us not getting resolved, his mom was dying. I felt helpless. I concluded that I didn't know any of the answers, but God was telling me these things take time. I could relate to the snail's pace. I still wasn't certain what this all meant other than God knew my thoughts. It was more for my affirmation that God was indeed involved in every aspect of both Adam's and my life.

The realization that almost an entire year has passed since I'd met Adam made me laugh. God knew I was still thinking about Adam and I couldn't run away. I had only gone seven feet, just like the snail. I loved that the number of feet was seven. That number has significance to creation, completeness, and rest. I kept asking God to take Adam out of my heart, but God's answer was "No, not yet." This isn't finished.

I know this little book was meant as a way to let me know it was going to take a while to complete this story, but when it is done I will get to rest. Jesus is my rest, because He has given me salvation. But I want to rest knowing I am doing what God has planned for me too. I was already trusting God for that. This was just confirmation. Just like the snail, I did want to help Adam get off the cliff, meaning make up his mind or get over his confusion. I didn't want to leave Adam behind. I know I cannot rescue him—only God can.

After reading this book, I was really curious about the other two remaining books in the series. I approached the woman behind the counter and asked, "Do you have the other two books available?"

She said, "Yes. If you'd like, you could buy them today."

We figured out which two books I still needed, and I got a free refill of ice tea too. I sat down to read the remaining books. I couldn't believe my eyes. The book I called book number three, because of the order I read it, was titled *Cliff Hanger, the Mole, and the Rope*. In this book, a mole comes up out of the ground and throws one end of a rope to Cliff in an attempt to rescue him. As Cliff begins climbing up the rope on his way to safety, he is so happy. The mole says something along the lines of, "Since you like this rope so much, here—I'll give you the whole rope." I was sitting there laughing out loud reading these books. I thought about how I had told God to take this Adam business away from me. I was tired of the whole situation and was throwing in the rope, giving the situation over to God. It reminded me that it took my frustration, me being at the end of my rope, to motivate me to give in to God. I must confess that, at times, I trust God is handling this; at other times, I want to take back that rope and stay frustrated. I let fear and other emotions rule instead of my trust in God, and I stay paralyzed.

The last book was the clincher. It was titled Cliff Hanger and the Sneezing Zebu, a bull of sorts. I am a Taurus. I don't believe in astrology or waste my time reading my horoscope, but I know that I am a bull. Because I was laughing so hard sitting at this restaurant, I was thankful it was off-peak time and there was only one other customer there. I could hear the Christian music playing in the background. It was the perfect setting for this amazing God sighting. In the story, the bull pulls Cliff up from where he is hanging over the cliff by its horns. Then the bull sneezes and Cliff says *gesundheit,* which is German for "God bless you." I sat there shaking my head thinking of that coincidence, although the day I read this I hadn't yet had confirmation that Adam was German. Then the clincher comes. After the bull sneezes, Cliff gets out his red hankie to give to the bull. I just thought, *Yeah, red flag—the same thing Adam waved in front of me the day he closed the door.* You probably guessed the rest. The bull gets mad and charges at Cliff. I couldn't help but think of how mad I eventually realized I was when Adam waved that red flag, closed the door, and left me stuck.

I wanted to give Adam those books. I had planned on giving them to him the next time I saw him. I really didn't know if or when that would ever happen since I was no longer seeing him professionally because he was taking that personal leave from work. I had written my little Cliffs Notes on the pages of the books to interpret the story for Adam.

One day I was so angry with Adam for leaving me hanging, I shredded all those books. I remember the exact date; it was September 8, 2010. I was so frustrated with not knowing what was happening between Adam and me. I just wanted to get Adam out of my heart since I wasn't getting my way. I thought that shredding those books would be a way to rid myself of all thoughts of him once and for all. That never happened. God had a different plan for those Reading Between the Lions books anyway. And who knows, I may come across them again somewhere in my travels. In a way, I regret shredding the books, because I believe God gave them to me. However, I will have this book as the true gift from God.

In my first book, I wrote that I thought God was going to give me some interesting and fun work to do. I never believed it was a foretelling for writing this story. After I had these books fall in my lap, I knew God was providing not just the work, but also the material to get the job done. I thought, *God wants me to lighten up and not take life so seriously at this stage in my journey. He doesn't want me to work so hard, and He wants me to know He has it all under His control—from my writing, to my love life.* When I wrote my first book and wrote God has joyful work for me to do, I had no idea I would be writing this second book and laughing my butt off. (lmbo not lmao for all you texting lol) Oh, don't I wish my butt would go away so easily.

Discovering these Cliff Hanger books was the first time I really, in all seriousness, felt that God used something so tangible, so personal, and so humorous all at the same time to help me sense His presence. God is amazing. The books provided me with a very intimate moment with God. I don't mean this in an egotistical way, but I truly believe God arranged for those books to be at Chick-fil-A just for me. He wanted me to know how much He loves me, and He wanted me to know He'd received my poetry and these books were my present from Him. God found a way to let me know He is watching, and through the books He said, "I hear you. I received your poetry, your prayers, and I am with you during this time of confusion." It was God's way of telling me He knew I loved Him too. I felt God was answering me back in a humorous way that would make me feel so loved I'd be unable to doubt that He is with me always. It touched my heart. In that moment, I knew God not only exists, He is in a personal relationship with me. I knew He was going to use whatever it was I needed to grab my attention so I would believe, beyond a shadow of a doubt, that He is involved with the relationship between Adam and me too. I don't think it could get more personal than this. So, Adam, I pray you will take it as a personal message for you, too. I can tell you I heard God say, "Never doubt my love." That message is from Him to both of us.

Since George's death, there have been times I've felt as if Jesus is my husband. He is the one that I go to now for all my wants and needs. When God showed up with all His magnificent sense of humor, He knew how much I love a sense of humor and desire a husband that has a great one too. I think God is using all this humor to reach out to me and let me know I am not alone. He is right here with me. I wondered how I could ever put this into words so that other people could know this wasn't just meant for me, either. That is why I believe He put this desire to write into my heart. God is using this amazing story so you, too, will understand that He comes to each of us in different ways. We need to open up our minds to the idea that God doesn't just appear in tongues of fire, burning bushes, or awesome sunsets. He will find countless ways to let us know He is our God. He will do whatever it takes to bless us, increase our faith, and gift us for His purpose. I still don't know what will happen between Adam and me. I do believe God is sending a message, loud and clear, that He holds the moon and the stars up in the sky, He knows all, and He hears me. That is why I am not waiting. I am stepping out in faith. I hope Adam finds this story as laugh out loud funny and ironic as I do. I also hope he understands why I am writing this story. This really isn't just all about me. I never thought that the day I agreed to send Adam that third letter, God would reward me with His presence to show He is pleased with my faith in Him.

After much prayer, the Holy Spirit used all these silly coincidences to convince me that I was the woman who was meant to write the story about Ruth and Boaz. I still don't know if Adam is indeed the man God has destined for me—my Boaz. Maybe, after Adam reads this book, I will know that answer. While that is partly what this book is meant to accomplish, from God's spiritual prospective it is much more. I think God wants this book to be used as a way for others to see that God will use whatever means He decides to get our attention. When we are seeking Him and know His Word, we will be able to make that connection. We will be able to know His voice, so to speak. Even though I still didn't have all the answers I wanted, I was able to see God was helping me to be honest with Him and not hide anything. I think that is a good place to start, if I am willing to have God transform me into the woman He intended for me to become.

My Heart's Cry

J am at a stage in my life where I can see God's amazing workings in all areas of my existence, yet there are still things that I question. Meeting Adam has been a wonderful experience, but it has also led to some confusion. Maybe it is because I'm one of those people who can't just appreciate things for what they are. I get caught up in wanting to know the future. I thought I had learned to live in the present, but it seems after George died and I met Adam, I have relapsed into that old way of thinking.

In the beginning, it was so shocking that I would feel such an attraction to Adam when I was so opposed to the idea. How did I go from not even giving romance a foothold in my mind to being so obsessed with thoughts of Adam?

I don't know how this could have happened to me. I wonder if I am in an obsessive-compulsive nightmare. I question if this is from God. If it's not, I don't understand why He doesn't take this away when I plead to Him to take away these thoughts and desires. I beg God to release me from this hold that Adam seems to have on my mind and my feelings.

Thoughts of Adam bring me joy. Sometimes joy comes in the form of laughter; other times joy comes in the form of tears, especially when I allow myself to believe this dream will come true. When I trust that feeling that comes from somewhere deep inside of me, I think this is meant to be. But then my emotions come into play, and I start to have doubts, fears, and even sadness, thinking this isn't real. Sometimes I doubt myself all together. I begin to think this is all just my vivid imagination. It gets so tiring. That is when I cry out to God and something miraculous happens to let me know He hears my prayers. That is what keeps me hoping this dream will come true. I believe God wants me to trust that the time will come when I will have my answers.

So I pour my heart out to God and ask Him all these questions: How could I have such a strong feeling for someone I hardly know? Why do I think Adam has feelings for me? What is the attraction? Is he safe? Is it that I can't face the fact that I am alone, and no one wants or loves me anymore? Will I die alone, never experiencing love again? Is that what keeps this going, or is it that I felt a true connection to Adam and know he felt it too? Or is it that I am not willing to let go of what seemed to be such a strong connection? Is it that I don't want to face that it wasn't real, or that it is broken because, for whatever reason, Adam doesn't want to go there? What keeps me hoping against all odds that this will ever come to fruition? God, why do I feel you are telling me to trust you and not give up on this relationship just yet?

It is crazy because no matter what I feel, it has nothing to do with what will happen. I have no control over Adam, and I certainly have no control over God. I am totally dependent upon God to give and take away. There is nothing I can do or think to make this come true. So why, when my head knows all of this, does my heart keep wanting and hoping this will really be a dream come true? What is it about Adam that grabbed my heart to begin with, and why do I still want him to be an important part of my life? Is it the rejection that has trapped me? What made me feel such a strong attraction to him? This is what I need to figure out.

I know I loved to see the way he looked at me and see his face light up when he looked into my eyes. Did I imagine that too? I don't believe so. Was it the fact that I felt so safe and comfortable with him that I didn't want to leave his presence? Or was it how I found him so attractive and couldn't believe I could be so drawn to him in every way? Or was it his laugh and playful ways that made me want to be with him? Or perhaps it was the fact that he listened to me and remembered every word I spoke to him. Was it because he admitted that he found me attractive when he expressed that I had "good genes" when he mistakenly thought I was almost ten years younger than my real age? Or was it his boyish ways when he seemed so nervous when he mentioned giving me his phone number? I cannot say it was any one of these things, but it certainly was my reaction to him that seemed to get my attention. And then there was the feeling that he was reading between the lines and both of us were thinking and feeling the same way. There seemed to be this connection and then, in one moment, there was a complete turn around and the door closed. I felt his panic, and I couldn't do anything to stop it. And now I just feel sad. I feel this sense of loss, as if someone else important in my life has left me. Only it is much worse because he is still out there, leaving me tethered to the feeling that there is the slightest possibility that I could recapture the happiness I was beginning to feel. The hope that maybe he is my next wonderful love keeps me trapped. What will be the key that will release me from this prison I have allowed myself to be locked in? God, do you really have a bigger purpose in mind for why Adam and I have this connection?

Grandma's Dream or a Silly Fairy Tale

$\mathcal{I}$ have three grandchildren; they are the loves of my life. Because I have two in Indiana and one in South Carolina, I divide my time pretty equally between those two states. I want to spend as much time as possible with them while they are young and still interested in Grandma. We have play dates, dinner dates, shopping trips, movie nights, card marathons, Monopoly tournaments, and sleepovers. I usually alternate my visits with my Indiana grandkids, Marie and Robert, so they don't have to share me. Catherine is an only child, so she doesn't have that problem. It works out great. Once in a while the two grandchildren from Indiana will both stay overnight; when they do, we get in my king-size bed, eat popcorn, watch movies, and cuddle with the dogs. It is great fun—although somehow I always end up with the tiniest part of the bed. One night in May 2010, Robert and Marie came for one of those sleepovers.

For whatever reason, when we were snuggled together in the crowded bed, Robert asked, "Grandma, are you going to get married again?"

"Why are you asking?" I questioned.

He replied, "Grandma, I don't want you to get married. Marriage is yucky."

I said, "Well, what if I just have a boyfriend?"

"That's okay," he said. "That would be fun."

My heart was sad that at the age of not-quite four Robert had already formed this opinion about marriage. I hope he will soon witness how wonderful a marriage can be and that will change his mind.

The next time Marie was staying over, we were having one of our "girl talks." The conversation turned to boys. I think Marie had mentioned a boy liked her, and I confided in her that I might be interested in having a boyfriend someday too.

Marie said, "Grandma, you're too old to have a boyfriend."

"No, I'm not!" I quickly responded.

That's when I heard her ask, "What about Poppy?"

I said, "Poppy isn't coming back, and I know he doesn't want me to be alone."

"Grandma, I understand. It's okay," she said.

I was thinking, *Marie, are you sure you are only seven?*

Then she started to tease me, chanting, "Grandma wants a boyfriend. Grandma wants a boyfriend."

I told her, "I do like a boy." I guess when you're almost seven liking a boy and having a boyfriend are pretty much the same thing because she changed the chant.

"Grandma has a boyfriend. Grandma has a boyfriend."

She just kept it up until finally I started to tickle her. Then she could only giggle. It works every time.

In early June, Marie came to spend a week with me while her parents were away in Florida. I was fixing my hair and doing my makeup as Marie watched.

She began to chant, "Grandma has a boyfriend. Grandma has a boyfriend."

I asked her, "What makes you say that?"

Marie replied, "I can tell by the way you're smiling and making yourself look beautiful—you like a boy."

I said, "I always fix my hair and put makeup on."

In a very serious tone, Marie said, "Grandma, you just look different."

It was very strange because I was going to be seeing Adam that very day. I never said anything to her, but somehow she just knew I was getting ready to see "the boyfriend." I guess it was the look on my face that gave me away.

On Labor Day of that same year, I went to visit Marie and Robert for the afternoon. I had my agenda, as usual. I wanted to spend a little quality time with Marie and hear all about her first few days at school. As soon as I arrived, the new puppy, Sabrina, came running over to me. I was looking past her into the family room, so I didn't see her. Not once, but twice I stepped on her paw and she yelped. I'm thinking, *Good start to my visit.* Marie came running into the kitchen to see what was going on with her puppy.

My son followed directly behind Marie and said, "Mom, what's going on? What did you do to the puppy?"

I don't blame them for responding in this manner; this was their new baby, a darling black-and-white Shih-Poo, and both of them are very protective of her. They have inherited that protective trait from me, I must say. So I had to explain how the puppy put her paw under my foot.

My son said, "Twice?"

I said, "Well, yes she did. I can't help it, and that's why I stepped on her paw."

I felt defensive, and this was my playful way of saying clumsy grandma wasn't looking and stepped on the puppy. I picked up Sabrina and told her I was sorry. Luckily, she hasn't had a lifetime of hurts to deal with like some of us humans, so she easily forgave me. She spent over an hour of my visit just sitting on my lap. Dogs have that ability to show unconditional love. Holding the puppy on my lap reminded me a little of what it is like to spend time with Jesus and just have that feeling of being forgiven and accepted. As I sat with Sabrina, I felt such happiness.

Even though I had a vision of what I wanted my visit with the kids to consist of, Marie had other ideas. She was excited to share the movie she was watching with me, so I sat on the couch petting Sabrina and watching *Ella Enchanted.* As Marie explained the story line, I began watching.

When I got up to speed about the story, I heard myself say, "Oh my." I felt as if it was my life I was watching.

I started watching right at the moment Ella gets sprayed with perfume. I laughed because it reminded me about Adam and our perfume connection. Then, when Ella has to be obedient and truthfully answer everyone's questions or do what she was told, it reminded me of writing that third letter to Adam. When I wrote that letter, I did it believing I was being obedient to God. There was a part of me that didn't want to send it; I even wrote that to Adam in that letter. I could relate to Ella having no control over being obedient. This fairy-tale story seemed to be revealing things to me, and I wondered why I felt so strange as I watched it. I never dreamed I would be writing about this day, let alone sharing this story with Adam. At that time, I just knew it totally reminded me of Adam. The words he'd said to me about my perfume came back into my mind along with the feeling that he and I had a strong connection. As I sat there watching this movie, I sensed God was in the midst—and I don't mean the mist of the perfume.

Marie started teasing me again about how I liked a boy. Marie is a quick study, and even though I didn't say anything but "oh my," Marie saw it in my face. Little girls who watch fairy tales learn to recognize that look.

She began to chant again, saying, "Grandma has a boyfriend. Grandma has a boyfriend. Grandma wants to kiss a boy. Grandma wants to kiss a boy."

At first I was really laughing, but as Marie kept repeating her chant, I got angry and said, "Okay, Marie, stop it. That's enough."

I think her seeing that desire in me upset me because it was true—I wanted to kiss a boy. I knew exactly which boy, but I didn't think it would ever happen. I still struggle with that, and sometimes it brings such frustrations to me. When I think Adam and I will be together, the thought brings happy tears to my eyes. Through it all, I still have faith that God has something good planned for me.

As I sat with Marie and watched the movie, there were so many words that popped out as if they were exactly referencing my situation with Adam; part of me couldn't help but believe that God was using this to get my attention. He was telling me it's okay to have my dreams. At times I get carried away, and I can't leave it at that. This is usually about the time I begin to talk to God about Adam, and I ask, "God, do you just want me to have fun with this daydream? Are you using it to open me up to all the possibilities that you have for my life? Is this really just about Adam being the inspiration for me to write? Is Adam really going to be my boyfriend? How much longer do I have to wait?"

I think the fact that I am still thinking and dreaming of Adam these many years later is what makes me want to finish this story. Maybe once the book is finished, Adam will have served his purpose in my life and I'll be free of what I, sometimes, think is an obsession.

I wrestled with the idea of giving out so much detailed information about Adam, because this is a true story and some people know Adam—"the one I want to kiss," as Marie puts it. My family and close friends know of him. I'm sure many of them think I have gone off the deep end or over the cliff. Some of my friends see this as my way of having fun. Others will not entertain the idea and are just plain sick of hearing Adam's name roll off my lips. I try my hardest not to mention his name, but, at times, my conversations just ends up being about the latest "Adam" story God has brought my way.

My daughter is so sick of hearing about Adam that she once suggested therapy, and she is a licensed therapist herself. She admitted to me that she talked to a girlfriend about me.

Her girlfriend said, "Ann, you know how us women are when we meet that guy we think is the one. We have a hard time letting go, and it doesn't matter if we are thirteen, thirty, or any age really. Your mother is just going through that too."

I guess Ann was thinking like my granddaughter. She thought I was too old to fall head over heels for someone or have a crush on a guy. She even had me list what it was that I thought I saw in Adam that I could learn from to help me in the process of finding my next husband. I tried to appease her, but it really didn't work. She's too smart, and she saw right through me.

One day when Ann and I were shopping, I promised not to talk about Adam anymore. I explained that I was honestly trying to forget him, but God just kept bringing things up that reminded me of him. Well, about an hour or so later, a woman from my church called me on my cell phone. Ann and I had signed up for a woman's retreat, and the woman needed me to send her the payment for the retreat. I told her she could text me her address. She did and, of course, wouldn't you know it—she lives on a street that bears his name. When I opened the text and read it, I just couldn't stop laughing; I saw it as a God thing. Now Ann was able to see with her own eyes an example of what I had tried to explain to her. Unfortunately, I don't think Ann found it quite as funny as I did, but that's okay.

These coincidences keep happening to me so much that now I'm used to it. I just go with the flow. Sometimes I even anticipate them. I can't help it. I didn't wish for this. In fact, I am constantly asking God to stop teasing me and either make my dreams come true or take this desire for Adam out of my heart. He usually answers by producing more evidence that Adam is still supposed to be in my thoughts and prayers. So for now, I am just writing this silly "love at first sight" story about a grown woman falling head over heels for a guy she hardly knows.

Adam and Eve

When I met Adam it reminded me of what I think it might have been like for the original Adam in Paradise after he awoke from his sleep and saw Eve. I had been grieving the loss of my husband, and it was like I was asleep. I was oblivious to the world around me. That all changed when I saw Adam. When I was with him, we were in our own little world. I felt so comfortable, cared for, and safe. There was an innocence about the two of us getting to know each other a little more each time we were together. It was a playful time, and I longed to be with him between those visits. I missed him when I wasn't with him. I started to allow myself to dream about us being together, and I had hope that I would be loved and love someone again too. It seemed almost magical that in an instant my whole life could change, and I wondered if God really was presenting another man for me to have as my husband. I was falling for Adam, that much is true.

Just as fast as the dream appeared, it was gone; everything changed, and reality was replaced by denial. It left me wishing and dreaming I could go back and erase everything or that I could just keep dreaming of it over and over again. I realized I had fallen in love with the dream of Adam and with Adam's dream—and, well yes, with Adam.

I imagined the first Adam and Eve were like that too. I pictured them in the garden just being together, talking and enjoying the world God had created just for them. Frequently, they would spend time with God. It was Paradise, and everything was perfect—the way God intended it to be.

Adam might have fallen in love at first sight when he awoke from his sleep only to find his rib missing and a woman called Eve now occupying some of his space in the garden. She seemed so much like him, yet, different. He wanted her to stay with him, but he didn't even know why.

When Adam and Eve were in the garden, it was a perfect time. Their life together, like the garden, was beautiful. But with one action everything changed for them. Was Eve the blame? The serpent twisted the truth just enough that Eve ended up eating of the forbidden fruit, and then she convinced Adam to try some too. Adam and Eve were each responsible for their own decisions, but Adam blamed Eve, and Eve blamed the serpent. They both made excuses instead of accepting the blame for their own choices. It was the beginning of sin, deceit, lies, confusion, doubt, denial, and fear.

"But the Lord God called to the man, 'Where are you?' He answered, 'I heard you in the garden, and I was afraid because I was naked: so I hid'" (Genesis 3:9–10). God knew exactly what had happened. When Adam and Eve sinned their eyes were opened to their nakedness and they felt shame. They knew the difference between good and evil because they ate from the fruit of the tree of knowledge. Since they had disobeyed God, they knew they would surely die. God had clearly told them that would be the result. Instead, God graciously killed an animal in order to clothe Adam and Eve. That was the first animal sacrifice to cover human shame, and it was the beginning of grace too. However, Paradise was created to be the home to innocence, so they were banned from the Garden of Eden. Sin led to denial and more sin, and neither Adam nor Eve took responsibility for their own sin. It only took one act of disobedience to bring sin into the world.

There were consequences to sin; God said Adam would have to do labor in order to eat and Eve would know the pain of childbirth. But in the midst of judgment, God gave grace to man and He allowed the human race to continue. But for Adam and Eve, death would be the final consequence of their sin.

Why would God allow all of this to happen? He knew once He created man that we would fall from grace and sin. He and Jesus knew the entire plan, and yet they still said, "Let's do it. Let's make man in our own image." Jesus knew He would eventually have to give up His heavenly home and come to earth. He knew He would have to suffer and die. God knew He would have to watch His Son be that pure and perfect sacrifice. They had the plan all along. God didn't make Adam and Eve to be like robots; He made them in His own image, knowing full well what it would mean. He did this because He saw each and every one of us in His mind's eye— and He loved us all at first sight. God knew without the freedom of choice, none of us would be able to truly love Him back. He knew the love of Jesus would be the remedy for sin and one day change the world back to the way it was meant to be. He knew the beginning of the end and the beginning of the beginning too. God sees the big picture. He knows it all. And He is motivated by His desire to be in relationship with all of us. He is waiting for us to freely love Him, for He knows if love isn't freely given it really isn't love at all. God also placed the tree of life in the garden, next to the tree of knowledge of good and evil. Man's desire to be equal or above God spurred him to rebel, and he ate of the wrong tree.

Since Adam and Eve ate from the tree of the knowledge of good and evil, they had to be banned from the garden.

Playful Adam and Eve is what I like to call Adam and Eve before they disobeyed God and committed the first sin. They ruled over all the earth and were able to spend time with God too. God placed them in charge of the garden, and they were able to roam freely among the animals. They had all they needed to eat in the garden, and they did not have to work hard to be fed. Everything in the world was perfect. There was no disease, no pollution, no crime, no politics, and no death. It truly was Paradise. But it did not last.

Now, Adam and Eve are Fallen Adam and Fallen Eve. They have sinned. They were free to have choices, but because they wanted to be like God and know all God knew, they ate of the tree of the knowledge of good and evil. They went against God's instructions and tried to hide from the consequences.

Adam and Eve's behavior was not much different from ours when we choose to sin. Sin leads to separation from God. It isn't because God leaves us; it is because of our own guilt that we feel separated. No matter how much Adam and Eve regretted what had happened the day they chose to disobey God, they couldn't go back and change what had happened. They didn't understand that God wanted them to come to Him and be honest. Instead they hid because they didn't know Jesus yet. They didn't know He was the answer to their problem with sin.

If we live under the power of the tree of the knowledge of good and evil, we will judge ourselves and be found guilty. We can find ourselves in a trap of sin and guilt. Or we may pretend we don't sin, deny our sin is a big deal, or rationalize it by blaming circumstances or others. But God gave us a choice to eat of the tree of life, and because of Jesus we now understand there is an option. When we get honest about our sinful nature, we can see the need for a savior—and accept one in Jesus. He is the way to eternal life. We have a second chance. When we look back and revisit our sinful choices, we can confess them to God. We can have full confidence that, even though we cannot change the past, we can move forward knowing we are forgiven because of Jesus.

God sees us as sinless. He sees Jesus standing in our place. That is why God can look at us and not see our sin. Jesus paid that price for our forgiveness; we were bought with His shed blood. Now we are free and have the power to change. The Holy Spirit is with us, and through His gifts we can accomplish things that would be impossible without Him. He gives us courage to reach out to others and share the gospel. We are required to forgive others and ask for forgiveness. It is this reconciliation that was bought and brought through Jesus. As Christ's followers, we are expected to live this way. It isn't optional. Sometimes it is expressed in nonverbal ways. I like to think when a husband and wife are one it goes without saying. To quote a line from the movie *Love Story,* "Love means never having to say you're sorry." There are times when it most definitely needs to be communicated both verbally and nonverbally. We need to speak it and act it. By that I mean we need to say we are sorry, ask for forgiveness, forgive others, treat others like they are forgiven, and act as if we are forgiven too. When we do this, it is good.

Because of the Holy Spirit, we are able to understand that not one of us is without sin. God sees all sin the same; He does not grade on a curve. How would we ever know we passed, since that grading system exists only after all the tests are finished? We would go through life full of anxiety, wondering if we were truly good enough and if we were really going to heaven. God is fair and would never make a curve grade that could include me but exclude you or vice versa. God would not be just if He allowed a set number of sins to be the make it or break it point that would decide where you or I would spend eternity. Sin is sin, and death is the punishment for it. There are no exceptions! So all you Adams and Eves do not fool yourself by thinking you are not that bad. Don't compare yourself to others. God doesn't. He only compares us to the perfection He requires, and when we are compared to that we all fail. We are all Fallen Adam and Fallen Eve. Remember, your sinless state is nonexistent; playful, sinless Adam is gone forever.

Then there is Play and Work Adam. I like to call him that because he sins and then works hard to try and earn forgiveness. This Adam is confused. He's striving to earn a passing grade to get to heaven. I think many of us that grew up with religious teaching received this false idea about salvation. We have all the elements in our head. We know Jesus as Savior, but we are still somewhat confused. We understand both Jesus on the cross and risen Jesus and our need to become like Him, but we try to become like Him by working hard. We have the "works" mixed up, and we think we have to work to earn. But we can never work away our sin.

Thankfully, death has lost its sting. Jesus conquered sin and death. The price for sin has already been paid. We do not have to prove to God or anyone else that we are forgiven. Working to earn forgiveness is dangerous because we can be deceived into thinking we don't need a savior. Trying to add to what Jesus has done actually takes away from what Jesus did. He has done it all for us. There is nothing that we can do to earn God's forgiveness. We need only to accept that Jesus took our place. He took on the punishment we deserve. When we are in this state of mind and know Jesus as our personal Savior in our heart, we will move into the state of playfully working.

When we accept Jesus, we become the New Adam. We will be so awestruck by what God has done for us that we will want to have

God use us for His purpose. The Holy Spirit will help us discover all the gifts God has given us. When we use them to serve God, it won't seem like hard work. We will have a passion to do what we believe God has destined us to do. That is why we will be able to playfully work, because we will know God's presence. Even though we are in this world, we can still go to be in the garden with God to be renewed and strengthened. We have the power through the Holy Spirit to live out the dream God has for us.

God always knew we would fall short, and He had a plan to combat the sin that would enter into the world when we did. He knew one day He would sacrifice His only Son in order to pay the price of sin. God does not change, and He does not go back on His word. Jesus willingly agreed to give up His throne for a time and become fully human and live a life of obedience, the way we were meant to live. In this sinless state, He was able to take our sin upon Himself so He could be the sacrifice for all of us. He was the perfect lamb without a blemish. Jews no longer needed to reenact the sacrifice. When the scales from their eyes were lifted, they would fully understand and see that Jesus is the Messiah—the One who was promised. Once they understood that, they would also know Jesus is the second Adam because He began life anew for all who accept Him. He was the beginning of the new man, just as we are when we proclaim that we are one with Jesus. God can now look at us as sinless, too, because the blood of Jesus covers our sin. Jesus was the sacrifice once and for all, for Jews and non-Jews alike. It is because Jesus willingly obeyed His Father that God placed Him in the highest place of authority and honor. Jesus is worthy of all praise! And one day every knee shall bow and confess Jesus is Lord.

Through the Holy Spirit working in and through men, New Adam is now able to become more like Jesus. However, the more New Adam learns about God, the more he sees he will never attain the state of perfection until the day he, too, is risen from the dead to reside in heaven, perfect and one with God. But in this world, New Adam does not have to spend his days focused on his sins or other's sins, but rather expresses his passion for God through serving others. As New Adam becomes more like Jesus, he develops a heart for the lost, the sick, the confused, and the lonely. New Adam has a desire to find his passion and purpose so when he walks through those pearly gates on the last day, he'll have the pleasure of seeing what he was able to do with the gifts he was given. Upon seeing this, New Adam will know Jesus found these acts to be more precious than gold, incense, and myrrh. As we live our life, discover our passion, and share the Good New about Jesus, we will know how sweet that is to God. Only with the aid of the Holy Spirit coming to teach, preach, convict, convert, comfort, and most of all bring understanding, could this life be possible.

Ask yourself, which Adam or Eve am I? I don't want you stuck in the state of confusion. It's a terrible place to be, and it can lead to death. I pray that the Holy Spirit comes to you, and—no matter where you were before reading this book—you now see things a little clearer. I pray that this is the day that you sense in your spirit that God loves you so much that He destined me to write this story so you would read it and have a true understanding of God. God does not want to give up on you, Adam and Eve. You see God loves all of us. He wants no one to perish but all to have eternal life.

I mistakenly tried to get into the head of the man I affectionately call Adam, because I thought I could find answers hidden in there. I thought I saw his heart for me when we were playful in the garden together. Then I realized I might not be able to trust what I saw. I am not Jesus, and I cannot see into other people's hearts. When I desire to know the future and know all God knows I am no different than Adam and Eve when they sinned in the garden. Because I have confessed this and brought this to God in prayer, He found a way to use everything for His purpose. I believe out of this situation a story developed that will help Adam, you, and me look into our own hearts. That self-examination is critical for each and every one of us, not only for this silly love story but also for the real love—tested love story between God and us. I pray one day Adam and I might have an open and honest conversation based on this self-examination, but it may never happen.

Part of the reason I believe I met Adam was so I would have a passion for him. But Adam seemed confused. I don't know if it was because of me tempting him that he lied, but, either way, he did admit he lied. If he hadn't told me, I never would have known or been confused, for that matter. When he said, "I'm honest. I don't lie but I have to tell you I'm engaged," I believe he was lying because he was trying to backtrack. I'll admit it did rattle me and confused me. I still think he panicked. Maybe he realized he wasn't acting professional either and we should not be involved with each other at his workplace. Maybe it was his way of getting honest, but it left me more confused than ever. He might have been trying to say he lied all along or that he was about to tell a lie. Either way, I know he knows I forgave him. I sense we are reconciled, but the truth is still important because I need to know how to act with him. I know how I want to act, but that behavior might not be appropriate. I am so tempted to flirt with him, but if he is truly involved with someone, even if he didn't get married, I don't feel comfortable flirting. If he did get married, I don't know if I can be around him anymore. It is too hard. Like it or not, I have strong feelings for him; I don't want to be tempted or tempt him. Maybe once we talk, I will understand why things happened as they did and everything will be resolved. I am counting on God for this resolution.

I believe the passion I have for him is real. I don't know why God allowed this to happen. Maybe, just maybe, I was meant to share this story, so others can imagine what the result would be when a New Eve knows just what it is like to receive the power of forgiveness and extends it to others. For whatever reason, Adam and my paths did cross. Maybe that spark Adam and I had when we first met was a glimpse of what it will be like when we go through those pearly gates and are with Jesus in paradise. Maybe in heaven Adam will be my neighbor, just like all of us are to each other, right now, here on earth.

I want all of you who read this to know Adam is real. His name has been changed because the last thing I ever want to do is have him feel embarrassed or ashamed. This book was fueled by my desire to go back to a moment in time with him when I felt a refuge from the storm. I felt safe, comfortable, awakened, hopeful, and accepted. I needed to be seen, to be visible to someone, and he gave that to me. He led me to believe he held me in his thoughts even when we weren't together, and I wondered if he had been praying for me. Maybe he didn't even realize he was. But something in his spirit knew what I needed, and something in mine, maybe, knew what he needed too. I trust this moment in time to the Holy Spirit who knows all things, sees all things, hopes all things, and desires all things to be done to give glory to God and point to the risen Jesus. I believe the Holy Spirit has gone before us to prepare for this day. No matter what was meant to harm Adam and me, God used it for good. I just have a gut feeling that Adam is never going to be the same after reading this story. He may want to tell everyone that he is a New Adam all because of a girl named New Eve.

The Little Bride

Confusion is a terrible state to be in—especially when it comes to love. I know the effect wondering if love is true or not has on me. I suppose it is not a peaceful state for anyone. But not everyone deals with uncertainties the same way as I do. When I was young, I felt this same type of confusion when it came to the love God had for me. I thought of it almost as a "He loves me, He loves me not" relationship that was dependent on my behavior. It took years to sort this all out and finally come to a true understanding about God's love—not just for me, but for all His children.

The title of this chapter was inspired by memories of my first confession and Holy Communion. Funny, I would have thought that would have been the last place this story would take me. Maybe the confusion I felt about Adam and his feelings toward me prompted a memory from the past, and that is what led me to write this chapter. I really had no idea about the story within the story that would evolve when I began to write what I originally titled *Love At First Sight, Really.* I believe God has stirred these memories up in me for a reason. I think they are part of the story He wants me to tell.

My first Holy Communion was confusing to me as a child, but I understand the meaning behind the bride's dress worn during the ceremony now that I am older. Back then, I felt like anything but a beautiful bride in the plain, dotted Swiss dress that I wore. All the other girls had on the most beautiful wedding-type dresses, which I wished I had. It was not so much about being envious of having one of those dresses; it was more that I was concerned about not wanting to stand out by being different. I was disappointed that I didn't even get to have a say about choosing that dress. I remember that much, for sure. I wanted to fit in and be exactly like everyone else. If I am honest, looking back on it, I wanted to feel like a beautiful bride too. But on my first Holy Communion day, I forgot all about my dress and focused on Jesus. I remember keeping my hands in that most reverent, prayerful position as I walked down the aisle. In my heart, I felt beautiful and wanted. Today, I have a glimpse of what Jesus saw. He saw my heart and my love for Him in the way only a child of eight can love. I had a knowledge given by the Holy Spirit that I was to trust Jesus as a man who was also God and lived, died, and lived again in heaven and who loved me. I was going to marry Him when I took the first taste of Communion, and I would have Him in my heart. That I understood. I had prepared myself in the best way I knew how. I was pure and ready to accept Him and have Him accept me. This story conjures up what I want it to be like if I ever have another wedding day. I still have a dream of feeling beautiful and loved by my groom and being pure and ready to accept him. If that day happens, it is not going to be about the dress for me that day, either.

We were taught that our first Holy Communion day was going to be the happiest day of our life if we really loved Jesus. We were even told to go home and ask our parents what the happiest days of their lives were. I took everything so literal, so I went home and talked with my dad.

I asked him the very question that the nun had posed. I said, "Daddy, what was the happiest day of your life?"

There was not one second of hesitation before my dad answered, and I will never forget his response. He said, "The happiest day of my life was the day I married your mother."

I told him what the nun had said. He agreed his first Holy Communion day was a happy day too, but that wasn't the day that came to his mind. He said he had Communion at his wedding, so he had both my mom and Jesus.

Then I told my dad about my dress and that it seemed different from what all the other girls were wearing. My dad said that the day was not to be about the dress, and my dress was plain for a reason. My mom had bought it because it was simple, and that was good because I was to be focusing on the Communion not the dress. I think I had some pretty smart parents who understood the separation of tradition and the true meaning of Communion. It still made me sad that I couldn't pick a dress that would make me feel special. When I married, I didn't buy a beautiful wedding gown either. By then, it wasn't because of those pure reasons. I just didn't think I deserved to spend much money on myself. If I am honest, I felt that way as a child sometimes too. I believed that my parents didn't think I was worth spending too much money on either. Back in the day, I didn't understand that they were living from paycheck to paycheck.

I did not have a big first Holy Communion party, but having one never even entered my mind. We just didn't do those types of things. We spent the day with our extended family but did not have all the festive party time that some have after the first Holy Communion. It was more somber and low key. I did love spending time with my extended family though, and I have fond memories of them.

To me, Holy Communion was a special time when I could bring my prayer request to Jesus. I always prayed that my grandfather, who had suffered from a severe stoke, would be healed. I believed Jesus could heal him. There was a time I would go to Communion every day. I went to a Catholic grade school, and we had mass every morning. That daily observance provided me with an opportunity to be in an intimate relationship with God. I remember myself as a little child who believed that God could do the impossible. I believed that I was closest to Him when I received Communion and that He would hear me at that very instant. For that moment, I felt pure and worthy to be with Him and receive Him in my heart.

As much as I believed that Jesus loved me when I first took Communion, my conviction in that belief was not immune to faltering. The more I would go to confession and feel I could never measure up, the more confused I became. After I would enter that box of shame, the place where the sins of the world find their voice, I would leave feeling anything but forgiven. I felt ashamed and guilty, knowing I would be repeating the same sins again. I went in there desiring to be honest and came out feeling condemned. It was like being trapped, not knowing how I could ever free myself of the sins I had just confessed to, knowing all the while I would repeat them again and again. That is what kept me trapped in a circle of sin and guilt. The connection to Jesus dying on the cross for the forgiveness of my sin got lost in translation. I was stuck in a trap of confusing thoughts and conflicting ideas. When I was in that dark box, I wondered when God or Jesus would appear to set me free. I wanted to believe God could really bear to hear my sins and still love me. But when I went to confession, I didn't hear about sins being forgiven because Jesus died for me and took all my sins with Him to the cross; instead, it was more about what penance I needed to do to be forgiven and make a good act of contrition. I was stuck in this place, somewhere between sorrow and guilt. I didn't feel free of sin's hold on me. No one told me that my sins were as far as the east is from the west, meaning God remembered them no more. I didn't know God. "Who is a God like you, who pardons sin and forgives the transgression of the remnant of his inheritance? You do not stay angry forever but delight to show mercy. You will again have compassion on us; you will tread our sins underfoot and hurl all our iniquities into the depth of the sea" (Micah 7:18–19). I'd never heard that the blood of Jesus covers me, symbolically speaking, and God sees me as He sees Jesus—sinless.

Thoughts of Jesus surrounded by little children brought images of being safe, cared about, and loved by Him, so that is where I longed to be. "Jesus said, 'Let the little children come to me, and do not hinder them, for the kingdom of heaven belongs to such as these'" (Matthew 19:14). I pictured myself with the group of children who came to Jesus. I saw Him loving me equally as much as He loved all the children who were gathered around Him, no matter what I had done, because He just wanted to be with me. This was such a contrast to how uncomfortable I felt before, during, and after making my confession. I didn't feel forgiven. I didn't learn anything about the meaning of the word "repent" either. And after I continued to find myself falling back into that sinful state, I eventually stopped making an honest confession. That added to the viscous circle of guilt that became my relationship with God. I did not understand what the fear of God meant, but I sure was afraid of both Him and the priest. I also worried I might go to hell, so avoidance seemed the easiest way out for me.

God does, however, supply. Over the years, I came to an understanding of what it meant for Jesus to have died for my sins. I was able to talk to God and confess to Him. Today, the whole idea of keeping track of all my sins until I can go to confession and tell the priest how many times I did exactly what I did is foreign to my way of thinking about God. I don't even know if the practice of confession is handled the same way today. I am not making a judgment here on the Roman Catholic Church. I am merely telling you my experience. Hopefully, the act of confession is now seen as an opportunity for a priest to be encouraging and counseling; most importantly, I think it should provide a chance to once again give the Good News to a person who may be feeling and believing they are separated from God because of their sin. I believe it should be a time of remembrance and reassurance that Jesus has done it all. The whole idea of having to make a perfect confession in order to be forgiven is so far from my way of thinking and believing. Looking back, I can see why I was confused about God and His salvation plan for me. I thank God that He has revealed to me that Christ died once for all. I know in the moment Christ died, by that very act, my sins from yesterday, today, and tomorrow are forgiven and cast into the sea. Because of this belief, I don't take sinning lightly. It is not because I fear God, but because I love Him. I want to become that person He sees when He looks at me. That is why I am open to hearing from the Holy Spirit and being convicted of my sin so I can repent. It is a process—and sometimes, it moves at a snail's pace.

But back when I was a child and had to keep confessing and keeping track of my sins, I started to picture God as having a big gun. I thought if I wasn't good enough He'd shoot me, you know, send me to hell. There would be no stop in purgatory if I died in the state of a mortal sin. Now, if I passed go and made a pretty honest and good confession, I could earn myself a free pass; no, not free—I needed the tokens of the prayers like Hail Mary or Our Father. If my list was long, I might end up getting the Rosary. Every time I went to confession, I looked around to see who had the beads. I hoped and prayed it would never be me. In all seriousness, this is where the confusion about Jesus and Father God came from. It was a lot like a juggling act.

As I thought about my past need to confess, God reminded me about some of the lies I'd told Adam. I had forgotten all about them. They weren't intentional, but they were lies never the less. I think God brought them back to my mind because He wanted me to share one of them with you. The day I met Adam, we were going over something that was pertaining to the reason I was there. He explained something in great detail. Then he asked me if I understood him.

I admitted I didn't. I remember him going over it again. Maybe he added more to the explanation; that part of the conversation I cannot honestly remember. Even after the second explanation, I still had no idea on earth what he was talking about. But I didn't want to look foolish or stupid, so I remained quiet.

When Adam asked me the second time if I understood him now, I clearly remember lying and saying yes. God and I sure had a laugh over this when He brought it back to my mind. It was God's way to remind me that I lie for different reasons, and sometimes I don't even know I do it. In the end, it is important that I realize if I say I have no sin, the truth is not in me and I deceive myself. I like to think of myself as an honest person. I say I don't lie, but God just reminded me that's a lie too!

Over the years I've learned going to God with my sins is for my healing, not something I need to do to earn forgiveness. It is not about good record keeping and keeping the letter of the law. Rather, it is about the spirit of the law. This means it is about my heart and my relationship with God. It is not about playing by the rules just for the sake of saying I don't sin. It is about desiring not to sin and asking God to help me be obedient. I can never attain perfection. I sin, and I need a savior. I cannot free myself by my own effort, but that freedom was freely given at the cross. When I say freely given, I mean free for me, but at a great cost for Jesus. He truly did suffer a terrible death. It was not free for God, either; He knew the pain and suffering Jesus would have to endure for the cost of my sin. It makes me feel ashamed, but at the same time, it makes me feel so loved. God wants me to believe with all my heart that even though I did not do anything to deserve forgiveness, He forgave me all my sins before I even committed them. He knew them before I was born—He is all-knowing. I now believe that God had me in mind when He planned out salvation, because He is capable of intimately knowing each and every one of His children. The only way I can explain this concept is that God knew exactly what I would do and when I would do it but gave me the freedom to commit every sin, knowing He already had His redemption plan in place for me. Even more powerful is the belief that He knew everything about me and, yet, still gave me life—in every sense of the word. You see, God fell in love with me at first sight! He created me, and He saw His creation as good.

I am happy to know how much Jesus loves me. In many ways, I feel like He is my husband. He protects, provides, and cares for me. I understand about the relationship of Jesus being the bridegroom and the love He has for His bride, the church. I am part of that church—not because I go to a church; I am part of the church of believers because I have accepted Jesus as my Lord and Savior. He is the bridegroom, and I am His bride. I understand the depth of God's love for me and for you. God fell in love with you at first sight too. If, like me, you were once confused about God's love but now understand, you know how wonderful it is to believe and receive His perfect love.

The Bride and Groom

I believe God placed a desire in me to have a soul mate, someone I was destined to be with during a particular season in my life for a special purpose. I had this in George. After he died, God showed me he brought us together for a purpose that was beyond just the two of us. When George lived so much longer with his cancer than was expected, I saw that as part of God's plan for our life together as well. It provided an opportunity to tell others just how much God blessed us and showed us favor. I believe God loved me so much that He spared George from dying just for me. God answered my prayers and allowed George to live longer than any doctor could comprehend was possible.

I was blessed to see the big picture too. When I wrote my first book about why George lived so long, I sensed its purpose was to let other people know God does hear us and answers our prayers. I was able to give God the glory for all the miraculous things He had done.

Looking back on our relationship, I don't have a doubt that God arranged for George and I to be together. We felt that almost from the onset. At the end of my marriage, I was more certain than ever that what we sensed from the beginning of our relationship was indeed true. God arranged for us to be together, and He gave us the insight and confidence to recognize it.

Eve was created out of Adam's rib; she was a missing part of him. I believe that is why when we find the person we believe is the one God arranged for us to be with, it may feel like we found that missing piece that fits just perfectly with us. From the beginning of time, God has ordained marital relationships and arranged them too. There are many stories in the Bible that speak of situations where God made arrangements for His children to be blessed through relationships. Since I am writing about the blessing of finding our intended mate, I will compare not just the story of Ruth and Boaz but also the story of Rebekah and Isaac to relate to what I believe applied to my circumstances. These two stories represent what I like to call "arranged marriages," meaning God destined or planned it.

Sometimes I wonder how I could have such strong feelings for a man I really don't know. I still remember the feeling of panic I had when I sensed that Adam was interested in me. I wasn't sure I could ever be with another man. At that time, I know I was still grieving the loss of my husband. The story of Rebekah and Isaac gives me confidence that when God arranges the relationship, it will work. I am not unrealistic about the possibility of problems; they will occur in every relationship. But when there is a strong attraction that doesn't wan with time and prayer, it is most definitely worth pursuing the idea that this relationship might work. Both Isaac and Rebekah and Ruth and Boaz had what we would consider today to be unusual romances. What I think is timeless about their stories is that they each trusted that God was involved in their relationship.

For Rebekah and Isaac, it was most certainly about families trusting God to unite the two. It was because of their trust in God that

Rebekah's family was able to let her go to a foreign land to marry a man she'd never even met. Even though I don't know that much about Adam—and he knows a great deal more about me through my first book—I already know things about Adam that I find appealing. I can sense he is compassionate and intelligent. I think he is someone who is reliable, and his coworkers think very highly of him. I see Adam as a playful person, and I find that quality very attractive. I believe he is interested in me and he takes my work seriously. I see he wants to help me, and I know he remembers the things I tell him. I believe we have a special connection and relate well to each other. I can still recall the look he gets on his face when he allows himself to be relaxed with me; it tells me he finds me attractive. I have to trust myself enough to know I am able to recognize when a man is interested in me. I am confident that I am someone that a man would find interesting, so that helps me be open to this possibility. If Adam confirms that he is interested in me, I will trust that God is leading us and believe Adam and I should see where this might go. I have often prayed concerning this and have fasted too. I know God honors that, and He will guide both of us toward the path we should be on. If Adam and I end up together, it will be because of his faith too. I have to trust God and believe He has searched Adam's heart to see if He is a righteous man, meaning made righteous through his faith in Christ. If this relationship with Adam ever develops, I will truly have confidence that it came from God. I believe if Adam sees this relationship is a God thing, it will give him the confidence he needs to move forward. I know I still see that look on his face, and he has made a few comments that confirm he finds me attractive. His alluring tone also gets my attention. I take it as his way of opening the door just a crack. I know he sees I am still standing there, and now it is up to him to act. When Rebekah and Isaac finally met, he brought her into his mother's tent and Rebekah comforted him. I hope, one day, Adam will bring me into his life, and we will see if we were meant to be a blessing from God for each other too.

The Book of Ruth is one of my favorite books in the Old Testament of the Bible. It used to be because I loved the relationship between Naomi and Ruth. For those of you who are not familiar with this story, it is about three widowed women. Naomi was the mother-in-law to Orpah and Ruth. After Naomi's two sons died, she told her daughters-in-law that she was going back to her hometown of Bethlehem. She explained why they needed to return home to their mothers, but Ruth refused to leave Naomi. Rather than be separated, Ruth left her country of Moab and accompanied Naomi back to her homeland, Bethlehem in Judah. Because Naomi had lost not only her husband but also her two sons, she was resentful. She focused on her loss. When Ruth and Naomi arrived in Bethlehem, people were excited to see Naomi. She told everyone not to call her Naomi anymore. She said, "Call me Mara, because the Almighty has made my life very bitter" (Ruth 1:20). She was blaming God. Despite the beautiful declaration of love from Ruth, Naomi felt empty. Others in the town saw Ruth's great love for her mother-in-law and her willingness to take care of Naomi.

I was a young woman and happily married to George when I first read the story about Ruth. Even though I didn't have a mother-in-law because George's mother had died before I met him, I thought of it as a beautiful love story. Maybe the fact that I didn't have a mother-in-law made it easier to love it. (Women can make mother-in-law jokes, too.) On a serious note, I've been on both ends of the spectrum.

Today, thinking of myself in the role of mother-in-law makes me feel sad because it reminds me of my loss. It is not the loss of my husband, but rather of my two daughters-in-law and my son-in-law through divorce that comes to my mind. It has been an extremely painful time, especially with this all occurring so soon after George's death. In some ways, when I think of how my family has been torn apart through death and divorce I can totally relate to Naomi. I am thankful every time God helps me recognize my state of self-pity and move past it. I find comfort in believing if my God is their God, even though we are separated by divorce, we will all be united again in heaven.

At this stage in my life, Adam has brought an entirely new meaning to the story of Ruth. The attraction I have for Adam has brought me to an entirely different place. I now relate more to Ruth, and I feel hopeful. I believe in the possibility that God will have another husband for me one day too.

This sets the stage for me to further explain what took place next for Ruth. Being a widow and under the Jewish custom of her time, Ruth went to a field to gather the barley that had fallen to the ground when the workers were picking the harvest. This barley was purposely not picked up, and widows were allowed to collect it as a way to help feed them. One day Ruth was out in the field taking care of her business, and Boaz noticed her. He inquired about her identity. He learned she was Ruth, the woman who had left her own country because she refused to leave Naomi. He also heard about how long and hard she worked in the field. Normally, because Ruth was not Jewish but was instead a Moabite, she would have been judged by the town's people and considered not a godly woman; but her loyal acts of love earned her a good reputation.

To make a long story short, when Naomi found out Ruth had gone to work in the field owned by Boaz and that he gave her extra food, Naomi became very excited. She knew Boaz was a distant relative, so if he were to marry Ruth the property rights would remain in Naomi's family. Naomi saw the fact that Ruth ended up in Boaz's field as no mere coincidence. She saw it as a God thing. Naomi interpreted Boaz showing Ruth extra attention as a hopeful sign too. Naomi still trusted God, so she was able to look at the situation this way.

I saw Adam and me meeting and having this attraction as no accident either. Naomi believed God is good, and she was feeling hopeful that God was going to change her circumstances. I relate to that way of thinking too. Naomi figured out that Boaz must have taken a liking to Ruth. This increased Naomi's faith in God. Because she had hope, she decided to mentor Ruth on how to get a man. I see God as my mentor, especially when he answered some of my prayers and revealed or provided things for me regarding Adam.

Naomi told Ruth to get all perfumed up and lay down at Boaz feet while he was sleeping. Yes, you heard right. Was Naomi telling Ruth to go sleep with Boaz, meaning go have sex with him? No, not exactly. It was the custom of the day for a woman to lie down at the feet of a man as a symbolic gesture to let him know she would be willing to marry him if he asked. She was really proposing to him—or as we would say today, she was making a move on him. Since Boaz was older, this was designed to boost his confidence that this younger woman had an interest in him. Bottom line, Boaz took care of his business and did what he needed to do to marry Ruth. He didn't waste any time once he knew how she felt about him.

I certainly had a perfume connection with Adam, and I took that as a sign from God too. I also prayed that God would put the desire I thought Adam first had for me back into his heart. I talked to God and sought His advice concerning this relationship with Adam. I believe giving this book to Adam is my equivalent to Ruth going to lie at Boaz' feet. I had actually asked God to symbolically lay me at Adam's feet that first Christmas I wrote to him. The fact that God has supplied all the material for this book helped me know that He wanted me to use this book to inform Adam that I'm most assuredly interested in getting to know him and exploring a romantic connection. God let me know that praying is good and He will bless my prayers, but sometimes I need to do more than just pray. Ruth had to take a risk and get all perfumed up and follow her mother-in-law's advice. God showed me I needed to get all perfumed up and follow His promptings too. He certainly has given me the most unique way to let Adam know I am interested in him. And believe me, I have not written this book all on my own. God has indeed supplied. I know Adam will believe that much is true.

Ruth invested into the situation. She not only got extra barley, wheat, and food, she got the whole field. Ruth ended up a happily married lady. God blessed Naomi with a grandson, and he would eventually inherit the land. Obed was the son of Boaz, and Jesse was the son of Obed. Jesse was the father of David, and Jesus was from the house of David. Yes, Jesus is a direct descendent of Ruth's. He has some Moabite blood, but it was from good stock. It came from a woman who proved she knew the true meaning of love by taking care of her loved ones. When Boaz discovered all Ruth had done for her mother-in-law, he told Ruth, "May the Lord repay you for what you have done. May you be richly rewarded by the Lord, the God of Israel, under whose wings you have come to take refuge" (Ruth 2:12). Ruth was richly rewarded.

I want to believe that God does truly have someone for me for this second half of my life and that He does indeed plan on blessing me. Whether this book becomes popular or I only give it to Adam and others in my sphere of influence, ending up with a loving and caring husband would truly be a dream come true. Although I have big dreams that go beyond marriage, I know having a good marriage again would be so wonderful. If this is what God has planned, it will be just one more way others will see God is a loving and giving Father that takes care of me. No matter how the story ends, I want to praise God all the time. I want to worship and praise Him because He is God and deserving of all my love. On my own I can't even do this, but the Holy Spirit enables me. I am open to all the possibilities, trusting in the knowledge that God is my God. He has me in the palm of His hands.

Although I was prompted to write this book because of a suggestion someone made, my familiarity and love for the Book of Ruth is what helped me be open to the idea and pray about it. I see the journey God has me on is deeply rooted in my heritage as a Christian woman. God knew all the signs that would get my attention, and He used them to encourage me. I must say none of this would have ever happened had it not been for that look on Adam's face when he first saw me. When his face lit up it grabbed my attention and made me think I was the woman he had been waiting for and praying would come into his life. However, I think God gives us choices. He doesn't force us to love someone or marry him based on a spiritual connection or a purely physical one either. God knows we need to be connected on a physical, emotional, and spiritual level—what I call body, soul, and spirit—in order to be married, because we are all those things too. When Adam's face lit up, it grabbed my attention. After God healed my hurts, I allowed myself to take a risk and act on this. I considered Adam to be the man God presented to me. I wanted to get to know him and pursue the possibility of a relationship. I wanted him to be attracted to me, not only in the physical and emotional sense, but also spiritually. I believe in order to be married in every sense of the word it is vitally important for both my husband and me to know Jesus as Lord, meaning the head of the household. I wanted Adam to see that I was a woman with a good reputation. I wanted him to know I was a loving woman who not only stood by her husband for better or worse, for richer or poorer, in sickness and in health, but also fought for him to live. I wanted Adam to see my good character and fall in love with me. I also wanted to be able to use all the lessons I'd learned from my previous marriages to be a wife Adam would feel blessed to be given by God. I wanted Adam to know, through me, how loved he is by God. Most of all, no matter how this ends between Adam and me, I want my God to be his God. Maybe to some that sounds silly, but these desires are what I believe God had put in my heart.

I trusted God enough to take a risk, because I sensed God wanted me in this relationship with Adam for some reason. He wanted me to consider the possibility that Adam is the "one" and that is why Adam and I have this connection. It is hard to explain, but through all the coincidences and the time I spent praying and talking to God, I knew that maybe, just maybe, God was arranging for Adam and me to be with each other. I trust God, and I believed if Adam understood that God has brought us together things would work out for us. Only Adam can say if this is what he believes has happened too. If he has been thinking, feeling, and sensing the same things, then that would be confirmation that this is meant to be.

It has been hard to be in this situation and trust. I felt compelled to continue on hoping and praying that God would reveal His plan and either bring Adam into my life or show me the reason God wanted Adam to be in my heart for a season. I know God showed me I was capable of loving Adam in a Christ like way, especially when we had such a long separation. From the beginning, I felt I was not to let go, but rather to write to Adam and be reconciled with him. That was the strangest part, because it would have been so easy to just dismiss what had happened and forget all about him. For reasons only God knows, I was not able to do that. I could not stop thinking about Adam and wanting to go back in time so that our relationship could continue in the direction it seemed it was first headed. I believe it is because of the love of Christ that I was able to not only confront Adam, but also forgive him. For some reason, that was very important to me. I think it had to do with the fact that Adam had already found his way into my heart. All I know is this kind of love is the kind that can make a relationship work.

What scares me is that maybe I am wrong. Maybe someone else is the person that is meant to be with Adam. If that is true, I will look at this as a time in my life when I risked all and had a selfless kind of love. I will also look at this as a test for me, because I needed to be a good Christian woman and do the right thing. I needed to listen to what I believed God put on my heart and follow that still small voice even though I had times of doubt. I will trust that all of this is written for Adam too. We both need to work through this so there won't be any more confusion about what our relationship is and is not. I just don't want to be seen as forbidden fruit or see him that way either. That will be the true test. If he isn't forbidden, I will enjoy smiling and flirting with him again. It's been several years since we had that door closed. I don't know where he is in his personal life today. I'm just waiting for his answer. I hope this book leads to that clarity.

Some marriages conjure up anything but this kind of selfless love. While it may be the kind of love we think we have when we meet "the one," too often it is short-lived. Jesus loved the church in a sacrificial way, meaning He died not only to self but He also physically allowed Himself to be a living sacrifice for us. While He lived, He was the perfect model of a servant for us. I think that kind of love is reflected in the verses that are often recited at weddings. "Love is patient, love is kind. It does not envy, it does not boast, it is not proud. It is not rude, it is not self-seeking, it is not easily angered, it keeps no record of wrongs. Love does not delight in evil but rejoices with the truth. It always protects, always trusts, always hopes, always perseveres" (1Corinthians 13:4–7). I was once told to substitute Jesus for love when reading those verses. It certainly does fit. Even though we may not humanly be able to achieve this state of being a perfect lover, I do believe there are many times, with God's help, we can be in that type of loving relationship with our spouse. I have not given up that belief. That is why I can live in hope that because I desire to be a loving wife, God will match me up with my Boaz—a man desiring to be a loving husband. God will help spouses become more and more the way He intended them to be, if they only ask. I trust that God won't leave me stuck and I won't be embarrassed, humiliated, or ridiculed because of this story. If I am, I will count it as an honor to have suffered for Christ.

I began to wonder if marriage was something I should even think about at my age, and I started to become concerned that this desire was not coming from God. Then I read 1 Corinthians chapter 7, and it gave me comfort. "But since there is so much immorality, each man should have his own wife, and each woman her own husband" (1 Corinthians 7:2). "But if they cannot control themselves, they should marry, for it is better to marry than to burn with passion" (1 Corinthians 7:9). I am not saying I cannot control myself, but my desire to be with Adam has made me realize that if things worked out between us I would want to marry again and share my life with him. Even though I don't need a man to survive, I still want Adam to be by my side. Having experienced that type of partnership before, I miss that lifestyle. I want a man that has a passion for God too. It was wonderful to serve God together with my spouse. When I was able to do that, it was the best of both worlds.

I believe my desire to be married is the same now as it was when I was six, sixteen, or sixty, and I think it comes from God. I know God created me. He put the desire to be a wife back into my heart around the time my grieving for George was coming to an end. If I think about it honestly, that desire never ended. When

I was grieving the loss of George, I still had that desire for my husband. I knew that George would no longer be my husband in this life or the next. When Jesus was questioned about a widow who remarried and was asked whose wife she would be at the resurrection, this was the answer Jesus gave: "When the dead rise, they will neither marry nor be given in marriage; they will be like the angels in heaven" (Mark 12:25). I do believe I will be with George again but not as his wife. When we are in heaven, we will have God; earthly things will pass away.

I have always wanted to be a wife. I remember playing house when I was little. I fondly recall an incident when I was six years old and my dad saw me kiss my pretend husband. My dad asked me what I was doing kissing a boy. I told him Sammy was my pretend husband, and Sammy had just come home from work so I kissed him hello. I hated that because I didn't like this boy at all, but one of my bossier friends was in charge of the game. She decided who would be married to whom and when we were to kiss. I wanted Dominic to be my pretend husband, because I knew him, liked him, and his mom and my mom were best friends. What I remember most about this particular day was when my dad saw Sammy and me kiss, I got in trouble. I thought my dad was angry because Sammy had cooties, and I might get them. So I told my dad that we'd put this clear candy wrapper in between our lips before we kissed. (Was I aware of bad breath or birth control at age six?) I was sure that would prevent the spread of cooties. I didn't tell Sammy I thought he had cooties, but I am sure I had some convincing argument for using the candy wrapper because I remember Sammy did as he was told. (He had the makings of a good husband!) Looking back I just have to laugh when I think of how serious my dad remained when he said, "No more kissing—I don't care what you put between your lips." I know he had to be laughing inside. I remember that as if it were yesterday. Back then it gave me a good excuse not to kiss Sammy. I said, "My daddy doesn't allow me to kiss any boys."

Maybe my heavenly Father is trying to teach me something about physical intimacy right now. It will be the excuse I use to wait until I get married: my Father doesn't allow it. I will in all honesty be able to say I want to, but I can't. I believe that is what God wants me to do, and, with His help, I pray I can wait if I ever have a serious relationship again. I just don't want to believe waiting will squash my dreams.

There have only been three men in my life that I would say I was attracted to in every way. That is why Adam has my attention, because he is one of them. My husband George was the second man I felt this way about. However, I could not write this silly fairy tale without mentioning my first love, Todd. Some would call it puppy love but, nonetheless, he was an important part of my life from the time I was thirteen until I was seventeen years old. I was so attracted to him, and I really cared for him. I would have married him if he had asked me. I loved to be with him, and when we weren't together he was always in the back of my mind. He was sort of my summer love. He lived in my neighborhood, and every summer we would see each other. He stopped at my house many nights. We would talk and talk—and yes, make out (Back then we called it necking)—in the front yard. My dad would keep coming to the door to check on us. One night he told Todd and me to come in the house. After Todd left, my dad had to explain to me that I was getting this boy excited. I was very naïve and didn't understand all of this. My poor dad was a little embarrassed because he had to tell me how he knew Todd was excited.

My dad said, "Didn't your mother tell you any of this?"

I said, "No."

My dad and I were very close, and he was very protective of his little girl. My dad told me not to tease Todd, even though he knew I wasn't doing it on purpose. It was the second time my dad had to tell me "I don't want you kissing a boy," but this time he added "for too long." It is a little different from the Sammy story, but it's a cute story about teaching a young woman about her responsibility in a relationship with a man.

This story about Todd has something to do with the Holy Spirit too. Years later, when George and I were first married, we went to Florida with two of the children. The night before we arrived at the theme park, we stayed in Daytona Beach. We took a walk on the beach, and we were gazing at the stars. George loved to do that, and so did Todd. Maybe that was what jarred my memory. I started to talk about my first love. I explained how I had been so crazy about Todd. I told George I never acted on it in a sexual way, even though Todd always said he wanted me to be his first. I confessed that when I had gotten divorced I'd thought about calling Todd because, at age thirty-two, he was still single. But I'd decided against it. I met George shortly after that, so I hadn't given Todd another thought. For some reason, that night in Daytona Beach I was thinking about Todd. I told George everything that had and hadn't happen between the two of us. George said he was so happy I hadn't called Todd.

The next day, we went to the Disney World theme park. We weren't even in the park an hour before I heard someone calling out my name: "Rebecca." I immediately recognized his gruff voice. I looked up, and there stood Todd. He said to me, "I thought I would see someone I knew here today, but I never dreamed it would be you." I just couldn't stop looking at him. I guess I was shocked. For a moment it was as if we were back in my front yard, and it was just the two of us looking into each other's eyes. The moment ended abruptly when George extended his hand and said, "I'm George, Becky's husband—well, Rebecca to you." It still makes me laugh when I repeat this story. George just had a way with words, using very few of them. We were the exact opposites. Todd shook George's hand and introduced himself. When Todd said his name, I know George was thinking, Becky was just talking about you last night. However, George never said another word other than, "Nice to meet you." (He knew when to hold his tongue.) Todd and I talked a little more, and then he said he had to go.

When he left, my daughter Ann asked, "Mommy, who was that man?"

Then my son Alan said, "Why was he staring at you that way?"

I honestly don't remember my reply. I was surprised that my own children could see what I saw too. It seemed I was still special to Todd. I believe the Holy Spirit was with George and me the night before so we would not be caught off guard when Todd appeared at the theme park and he and I couldn't take our eyes off each other. It was a very strange meeting, and it was the first of many times George would call me psychic. I know George didn't mean it in a satanic kind of way. He didn't know what to call it, but he believed knowledge was given to me supernaturally from God. I do believe that it was a prompting from the Holy Spirit, called foretelling. I think the Holy Spirit had gone ahead of us to prepare both of us for what, otherwise, could have been an awkward moment. It is amazing that it happened just that way. I know one thing for certain; I was given a great deal of attention from George that day. He couldn't take his eyes off of me. He acted like he never wanted to let me out of his sight. It wasn't because he didn't trust me; he was just so happy I chose him. It was my second trip to Disney World, and it was a special trip of its own kind.

When I think about meeting someone special and waiting to get married, I wonder what man will be willing to wait too. Seeing Todd's reaction to me helped me know that waiting didn't stop his desire for me. In fact, after seeing him act that way when he saw me, I think it might have increased it. I guess I was "the one that got away." Because he had constantly tried to entice me to give in to him, I'd had mixed feelings about him. It was always, "He loves me. He loves me not." I think that was why I never reconnected with him after my divorce. I didn't think I would have been able to resist him, and I didn't trust him or myself. I was afraid he just wanted me for sex, but seeing him that day in the park told me I was wrong. Sex before its time can complicate a relationship.

I know I married my first husband more or less on the rebound, because I still was in love with Todd. I know if I hadn't married, Todd and I would have seen each other again. Who knows how it would have ended. All I can say is I have no regrets. That day at the park, I saw his desire for me but I saw sadness in his eyes too. I think seeing me with George made him realize he didn't want to stay single, and he wished he could find a woman to love. Todd told me he had just come from visiting his college roommate, and his roommate was happily married to his college sweetheart. A few years later, Todd's roommate was killed in an airplane crash. I heard Todd ended up marrying that widow. The last I heard, they were still together. It reminds me that we don't know God's plans, but He has them nonetheless.

I trust God that even if I do get hurt because of this situation, He will heal me of that hurt. Right now I am focused on God and believing He knows just the right man for me. The right one who just can't get me out of his head, his heart, and his soul. He can't stop thinking about me, and he can't stop dreaming about us spending our lives together. It feels so natural, that he catches himself thinking about it frequently. But it really isn't about sex;

it is about the scent of a woman. I don't mean the actual way she smells but rather the whole package. I want a marriage created in a passion for me that is so strong that no other woman can satisfy him. That is how he'll know it is meant to be. Even if he'd previously spent his life trying to find a woman the wrong way, he will have a desire to do it God's way now. Deep down he'll think it might actually be best, and he will want to obey God too. I know our society doesn't think this way, but the way men and women are relating to each other isn't working. I've heard the divorce rate is around 50 percent for those that call themselves non-Christians and Christians alike. So what's the solution—abolish marriage because it doesn't work? I don't believe so. Maybe going back to trusting God and showing each other that we will humble ourselves before God is a good start. I want to obey God, and I believe when He knows that's my heart's desire, He will bless me by helping me be able to obey Him more and more. It is a process.

I titled the next chapter "Obey Is a Four Letter Word" because I think most people think of obey as a dirty word and not something desirable to do. We want to do our own thing—from speeding to getting into relationships that we know God would not honor. I ask God to help me want to obey Him, because I know on my own I cannot even do that. My sinful nature would win out every time. I surrender my will to God and pray for His help and strength. I believe when I desire to do what God desires, He will find a way to make those dreams of conquering sin in my life come true. It's all about being in a relationship with God when it comes to matters of the heart.

I think being in a close relationship with God is what is missing in so many marriages today. Couples might not really believe that God arranged for them to be together and will keep them together. Maybe they didn't seek God first and ask for discernment when getting involved. If they did, maybe they haven't made the transition to going to God in prayer together as a couple. I know I didn't seek God's advice the first time I married. I actually went against God. If couples are living together outside of marriage or having premarital sex, that sin may make them feel separated from God. They might not hear what God has to say about the arrangement—including the sleeping arrangement. It makes it harder to hear from the Holy Spirit too. I am not saying He isn't there; He just gets quiet. I know this from firsthand experience. Now that I am more mature in Christ, I don't want to recommit the sins of my youth. When I am hurting the Holy Spirit, in other words sinning, it makes it impossible to hear His voice and His instructions. I'm not saying this to convict people of their sins or pass judgment on them. That's not my job. That is the working of the Holy Spirit too. I just want to go before God in prayer with a clean heart. The only way I can really do this is to acknowledge that Jesus died for my sins and repent. That makes it so much easier to fess up to what I am doing wrong. I will admit to God that I sinned and then ask for help not to continue in that sin. Knowing there won't be any punishment and God won't hold it against me makes it so much easier to talk to God. I can go to God in prayer without the hidden agenda of just escaping punishment, because that is not the reason I confess. I confess so I can receive healing and direction, not forgiveness. I just want to interject that even though I know I won't have eternal punishment for my sins because I've accepted Jesus, there are still earthly consequences to sin.

If I ever marry again, I want a husband who wants to pray with me. Together we will ask God's blessings to keep our marriage strong and healthy. I pray we will always give thanks to God for bringing us together. I hope I will be married to a husband that tells me I was an answer to his prayers. For marriages to be successful, it requires couples to submit to God first and then to each other. That requires both individuals to pray by themselves too. Solitary prayer times provide opportunities for me to ask God to show me what it is I need to see about myself. I ask him to show me my sins or things I need to have changed in me, including my attitude.

If I don't go to God and admit I am sinful, that sin can become buried so deep inside me that the truth becomes harder to acknowledge. I run the risk of having a hardened heart. That's when God needs to use the sledgehammer on me. I sure don't want that! I have had it used on me once or twice in my life already. It can be an awfully ugly scene. There is a lot of mess to clean up afterwards, and it is difficult to put those pieces back together. I didn't lose heart in those situations, because in the end my heart became a lot stronger from the superglue God used to mend it. I pray to always be open to what God wants to change in me and be cooperative when I sense He has things He is prompting me to do. It makes life go much smoother.

God can take away our desire to sin. If we allow Him to, He will give us the power to resist even the biggest temptations. We will never be perfect, without sin, but God will make a way for us to not be fooled into thinking that sin will make us happy so we can resist giving in to sin.

Because of all the assurances God is giving me, if this relationship with Adam and me ends up working out, I will have confidence in it, just like George and I had in our marriage. It was the glue that held us together when times were rough. We believed God arranged for us to be together. I love this passage: "Then the servant told Isaac all he had done. Isaac brought her into the tent of his mother Sarah, and he married Rebekah. So she became his wife, and he loved her, and Isaac was comforted after his mother's death" (Genesis 24:66–67). God knows I'd love to be in that kind of relationship with Adam so he and I could comfort one another, because life can be difficult.

Obey Is a Four Letter Word

S ince I've been a widow—or, as I now refer to myself, single—I've had to be willing to drive myself if I want to go anywhere. Now I want you to know I had one traffic ticket when I was sixteen years old for driving on the wrong side of the road. I didn't think of it that way. I was merely pulling up in front of the movie theater to drop my friend off at work; only trouble was the theater was on the left side of the street. Being a young and inexperienced driver, I didn't realize I couldn't just cut across the traffic and pull up in front of the movie theater. This was considered driving on the wrong side of the road. I understand that now, but it was a hard lesson to learn. When I got that ticket, being a teenager who knew it all, I argued with the police officer. The police officer had to explain that even though I didn't go far, I was still driving on the wrong side of the road. I went over forty years with no other driving tickets. I would say I had an almost perfect driving record. And honestly, it wasn't because I never drove.

After George retired, I did less driving; we usually went places together, and George drove. After George died, I was driving all the time. I wanted to use that as my excuse for the string of tickets I received in 2010. I know a reason I received one of those tickets was because while I drove, I played praise and worship music, sang praises to my King, and I soared like an eagle. And eagles like to go fast. I would fly along the road, sometimes forgetting to pay attention to the speed limit or how fast I was driving or both. I believe God used the tickets to remind me that I am still here on earth in the real world. I have to keep one foot on the ground and keep my head out from above the clouds while driving. I serve an awesome God.

But I learned something else from this experience. Our society has found a way to work the system. It is a point-free solution. It is perfectly legal in Carolina, Virginia, and maybe plenty of other states. But "no thank you" I don't need to know through firsthand experience if other states will change a speeding ticket to a nonmoving violation that carries no points. The offender can hire an attorney to represent her at court to attempt to change the ticket into one for "defective equipment." I can see how that could still be a true statement, because the defective equipment is my brain. If I were thinking right, I would not have been speeding in the first place. In other words, I am guilty of speeding.

That much I knew as soon as I was stopped the first time, and I admitted it to the police officer. I did not doubt him when he said I was going 50 mph in a 35 mph zone. After I received the ticket, numerous letters from attorneys in the area arrived with offers to defend me in court. I got off with no points and only had to pay court costs and an extra fee to the attorney. When I was stopped the second time, I was going 77 mph in 70 mph zone. The police officer said "If you had been going under 75 mph, you could have escaped." I used this second speeding ticket as an opportunity to learn something. The first time, I merely went through the process without learning a thing. I made excuses to myself the first time: I was talking, not paying attention. George had just died, and I was talking about him at the time. This is what I told my daughter when she told me, "Mom, you better start paying attention when you are driving." I did not accept responsibility, and I didn't talk to God about it either. That is a scary thing to get used to doing. It took two speeding tickets for God to teach me this. I learned nothing from that first ticket, so I had to learn the hard way.

The second ticket really got my attention. Because my eyes were open and focused on God, I was able to learn from that experience. When bad things happen, I always want to ask God, "Why?" not "Why me?" meaning, "What do you want to teach me?" I'll admit sometimes this is not my first response. "What do you want to teach me" is the spirit I want to have, so I can learn God's truths. At times, I can be so opinionated. I am trying to be honest with God first, so I don't look like a fool. As I was complaining to God and to my police officer son about the court system, I thought this method of getting away with no points was just such corruption of our society and its laws. Once I admitted I was guilty and stopped making excuses, God gave me some insight into how I could use this to illustrate what He wanted us to know. So these tickets and the hefty fine I paid are now going to be used for God's purpose.

When I got the first ticket, I joked that I was the unlucky person who got caught and rationalized that it was a blessing I got the ticket instead of someone who could not afford it. God wasn't buying that lame excuse for speeding. I quickly realized that even though it was not a hardship for me, rather an inconvenience, it was a reminder that I am guilty of breaking laws and of being arrogant to boot. Whether points against my driver's license are involved or not, driving over the speed limit is serious stuff. It is dangerous! That experience was a little humbling and, I might add, embarrassing. I needed a correction. It is easy when you believe you have a friend in Jesus to take advantage of that friendship. I never want to take advantage of God; therefore, I needed what I will call a little spanking from my Daddy.

So I humbled myself before God, and He showed me what I needed to learn from this. Earthly judges will bend or change the laws to accomplish what they want—in the case of speeding, teaching us to slow down by giving us more of a financial penalty in exchange for no points. That is their right. However, God doesn't work that way. He is the same yesterday, today, and tomorrow. I find the earthly system confusing. To me it seems to send the message if you have enough money, you can buy your way out of trouble. I talked to God about that. He reminded me that all authority is under Him, including judges here on earth and, therefore, in a place of authority over me. I don't have to answer for their decisions about how they interpret the laws. I just have to obey the laws of the land because I am a citizen of the United States.

I'd like to think these tickets served as an opportunity to have a conversation with God, get off my high horse, and learn something that I am able to use to bring you knowledge of how God is a sovereign God, worthy of His high place and willing to give me wisdom when I seek Him. Here is the comparison I want to make. Yes, the judge could interpret the law in a way that meant I could pay an extra fine and get off without a speeding violation. The end result was I didn't have a four-point violation on my record from each of the two speeding tickets. It is perfectly legal. However, none of that got me off the hook with God. He wanted me to admit I was doing something wrong. I wasn't being obedient to the authority He allows to rule over me. As the Bible states, "Everyone must submit himself to the governing authorities, for there is no authority except that which God has established. The authorities that exist have been established by God. Consequently, he who rebels against the authority is rebelling against what God has instituted, and those who do so will bring judgment on themselves" (Romans 13:1–2). I know I am guilty of this sin. Thankfully, Jesus died for all my sins.

I am not always a bad driver, but when I don't know where I am going I can be a terrible driver. This is what happened when I was in town for First Friday. First Friday is a night when people come out and have a get–together. Part of the motivation for the event is to turn the city around and make it a place people will want to live, work, and serve. It's similar to a street fair. Vendors bring their crafts to sell, and some businesses set up tables and hand out advertisements. Many of the surrounding churches participate to witness for Jesus using various ideas to reach out and talk to people in a way they hope may eventually have long-term, positive influence on others' lives. It's a fun time. Some churches reach out and talk to people or give out bottles of water symbolizing Jesus is the living water. Some have a group of singers. Others do prophetic drawings. There are numerous other ideas churches use to reach out to people. I was there to observe the prophetic artists. I watched as person after person came up and sat with one of the gifted artists. The artist would be inspired to draw something, but she didn't know for certain that what she drew would have any significance to the person who was to be the recipient of the sketch. I watched in amazement because, invariably, these pictures were meaningful to each person. They provided a way for them to sense God was speaking to them. When people spoke about their interpretations of their own drawings, they often would relate important stories from their pasts. The artist didn't know what the meaning would be when putting the images to paper, but each person that came received God-given insight. I was amazed to watch and listen. That is what I did as I silently prayed in my spirit for each person that came.

At the end of the evening, I walked to the parking lot. I was still feeling close to God as I got in my car and drove away. I was talking to God, feeling His presence, and thinking about how much He cares for all of us when I realized I was lost. I tried to read the print out of the directions and reverse them in my mind. This is hard for me when I am totally concentrating, let alone when I am talking to God and driving too. I don't talk and work well at the same time. As I was driving, I unknowingly went the wrong way down a one-way street. Luckily, it was under construction and there was no oncoming traffic. Of course, maybe oncoming traffic would have been the hint I needed that something was wrong. So I was trying to read the directions and reverse them in my mind while looking at street signs that seemed hard to read and traffic lights that appeared odd to me too (I wonder why). That familiar-of-late red flashing light appeared in my rearview mirror. The police car just slowly followed me as I continued to drive a little more until my brain processed this, too, and said, *STOP*. I prayed, "Oh no! Please, God, not again."

When the police officer approached the car, I rolled down my window. He asked for my driver's license and registration. Then he questioned me, "Did you notice anything unusual while you were driving?"

I replied, "Yes, the street signs were hard to read. I am lost. I'm not originally from this area. I just recently moved here to be closer to my son. I am trying to find my way home. I don't know my way around down here." I held up the sheet of paper and said, "See, here's my directions. I am trying to figure this out in reverse."

Luckily for me, he was a very good and patient listener. He asked, "Do you know what you are doing wrong?" (A good question—I liked that! He's a wise man, a little like my Father.)

I replied, "I think I am going the wrong way on a one-way street."

He could see I was slowly processing all this. Then he said, "You *think*?" It's okay; you can laugh.

I said, "Oh, God have mercy on me."

"Have you been drinking alcohol?" he asked.

I replied, "No, but does drunk in the Holy Spirit count?"

His immediate reply was, "Were you down here for First Friday?"

I knew he knew. Let's just say that. I figured the Holy Spirit had just revealed that information to him. He asked, "Do you realize how serious this is?"

I said, "Yes, I could have killed someone."

Then, I got mercy. He said, "Next time you come down here for First Friday, make sure you know which way you are going before you even get in your car."

Now, I did not get what I deserved. And the police officer did not bend the rules to change what happened. He just, in his mercy, left me go free. I didn't have to pay my way out. This is similar to God's mercy. Mercy means you don't get the punishment you deserve. It cost us nothing. But God didn't stop there. He gave us grace, which is giving us what we don't deserve, such as eternal life and blessings on this earth. This all came at a cost to God. He watched His Son take on our sin to pay our justly deserved punishment, because He loves us that much. And because Jesus was willing to obey to that degree, I want to be willing to obey also. It is a loving response to let God know I am not taking His mercy and grace lightly. I understand just what it cost God. It makes me so appreciative and joyous. Sometimes I am tempted to just skip the thought process and go straight to joy. In a way that is okay, but I never want to forget in my heart that this is serious stuff. Someone could have died, and it could have been me. Or because of my bad driving, I could have killed someone else. In the spiritual sense, I would not be getting eternal life in heaven if it wasn't for God's gifts of mercy and grace, because it is not what I deserve.

As the police officer directed, I pulled into the parking lot to turn around. I looked up and saw a church. It was one of those beautiful old stone churches with the tall steeples. I took a moment to thank God for how things turned out. Then I prayed, "God, I need a husband if for no other reason than to drive me around." In a way it was a funny moment between God and me, because I was trying to plead my case for Adam to God. But as I reflect back, it shows once again the power of God to use all things for good for those He loves. This story brought me into God's loving arms. Even though I joke about a husband, I'm serious too. I know God is all I really need, but if I'm honest I'll admit I still want a husband. I am so blessed in so many ways, at times I feel guilty for all that God has given me that I don't deserve. I do thank Him for all that He has given me, and in a way, I am ashamed to ask for more.

The very next day, my grandson and I took a ride in the country. Robert and I had so much fun that day. As we were driving in the country to find the little schoolhouse that was turned into a winery so that I could enjoy hearing my girlfriend's daughter sing, we got lost. Nelly, my GPS, said to turn right, and I heard Robert echoing the directions from the back seat. He was four going on twenty-four.

He said, "Grandma, did you hear her? She said turn right."

To that I replied, "Yes, Robert, thanks for helping Grandma."

Then he said, "Turn right here, Grandma."

I made the right-hand turn. I continued to drive, but there were no house numbers even close to the one that I was looking for so I turned around.

"Grandma, I heard her. She said turn right, and we did. She was wrong. I heard her."

I said, "Thanks, Robert. You're my witness."

Now this four-year-old said, "Grandma, find someone and ask them how to get there."

I said, "Robert, that's what I am planning on doing." I drove into the parking lot of a shopping center.

Robert piped up, "Grandma, there's a man. Ask the man."

Robert is a so quick minded. I reassured him that I would ask the man. So, long story short, it seems we were to turn left instead of right.

Robert repeated, "Grandma, Nelly was wrong. I heard her. She said make a right."

It was such a sweet moment for me to have my four-year-old grandson defending me. We ended up finding the winery and got to enjoy hearing Rhonda's daughter sing. Robert ate some cheese and crackers. When Rhonda's daughter took a break, Rhonda's husband, Charley, did some singing and guitar playing of his own. He dedicated a song called "The Chocolate Ice Cream Cone" to Robert. It was so cute to see Robert blush and see his smile as everyone looked at him as Charley sang. If you Google the title, you can read the lyrics, about a little boy and his desire for a chocolate ice cream cone. How cool is that! It was a beautiful fall day. As we headed home, I received another sign that God was watching over me. It was just the night before that I had been given mercy by that police officer. But that day, as I drove on the road right at the spot where I had earlier made the wrong turn, a cute sports car approached me from the opposite directions. He flicked his lights. They were the kind that the whole covering goes up and down when the lights go on and off. It looked like the car had eyes. I thought, "Maybe there is a police car nearby." Sure enough, a few seconds later, a police car came down the road right behind the car that had just winked at me.

I thought of God once again. It was as if He said, "I am here. You have me."

I acknowledged how personally God works in my life. Then I said, "God, does this mean I'm not getting a husband anytime soon?" I like to think God laughs as He sees me trying to wear Him down.

In all seriousness, I thanked God for reminding me He was there and for helping me slow down. This all came together in my mind. It was just one more time God was saying, "You are free to live your life, but pay attention to what you are doing, too, and surprise me with something creative to give back to me." This story is my appreciation back to God for getting me off on that last ticket. I am having fun with it. And yes, I still believe God wants to give me a husband. There is no limit to the gifts God wants to give me. He knows I acknowledge Him and like to show off how good God is to me. You see, He allows me to brag about Him, and He is pleased that I love Him too. He knows I don't just want Him for the things He can do for me. He is my God, my Father, my creator, and everything to me. I just pray He keeps giving me a spanking when I need a correction, because I never want to be called a spoiled brat. Just call me loved.

I am in relationship with God, and I know there is no end to His mercies. It is all about how my heart has been changed. It is because I have accepted Jesus that I am changing, little by little. I want others to see that God is able to change me into a person who desires to do the right thing, even down to not speeding.

I had my own prophetic drawing done that First Friday when I went downtown. The drawing had two oval objects with lines extending from them. They almost looked like eyes, but not exactly. They were on a blue background. One was floating a little higher than the other, but they weren't that far apart. I sensed one represented me and the other one might have been someone important to me. I didn't interpret it that night. In fact, I left and forgot to take the drawing, but it stayed in my mind's eye. I remember thinking I hoped one day I would understand the drawing.

My grandson drew a picture at nursery school on a day when I was the one who picked him up. He gave the drawing to me. The teacher had written the title "Fireworks and a Moon" across the top. I knew Robert had told her that was what he had drawn. That picture was especially for me. It represented that Fourth of July night Robert, Marie, and I watched fireworks from my deck. I knew it stayed as a special memory with Robert. It was the night we put up the umbrella so we wouldn't get moon burns. I still have the picture hanging on my refrigerator. One day I walked past that picture, and I noticed the fireworks again. I instantly knew where I had seen shapes like those fireworks before. It was on my prophetic drawing. That was what those two objects were. It was a picture of two fireworks in the dark blue sky. It made me feel hopeful that I'm not the only one who experienced the fireworks. It represented love at first sight. It also reminded me that God made man in His image, but we are a little lower than God, meaning He has authority over us. I pray He helps me to submit to Him and shows me the places I have not surrendered to Him yet.

Believe in Make-Believe

I saw Adam in October 2010, and it was sure a surprise. By this time, I was working with one of Adam's colleagues, but that day the coworker was running behind schedule. Adam was aware of that, so he called me into his office instead. I had heard his voice behind the closed door, so I had known he was back to work. When I heard him laughing, I was thankful he seemed to be back to himself. I had been thinking about him a great deal since I'd learned of his mom's death. When he called me into his office, it was an answer to some of the questions I had asked God when I read the book *Cliff Hanger and the Giant Snail*. Adam's kind offer to take care of me that day when I wasn't scheduled with him helped me realize he wasn't mad at me for being there. I didn't think he would have called me into his office if he didn't want to see me professionally again. We took care of some of my business transactions and then we talked. That was the second time he mentioned the book I was writing.

He said, "I can't wait to read your book. I'm excited about it."

I said, "It is with the publisher now and being edited. It should be out before the end of the year."

I left there flying high. It was one more time God answered some of my specific prayer requests. That day I came to believe Adam truly did want to read my book. We seemed to be a little more comfortable with each other again, but we kept everything strictly business—there was no looks or flirtation going on between us. That was the day I told Adam I'd found the publisher I had finally decided to use. Though I told him I thought my book would be in print before the year's end, it didn't happen as quickly as I had anticipated. I had my first book edited three times, so that process took longer than expected.

In the meantime, thoughts of this second book were rolling around in my head. I started to write some of it before even returning to South Carolina. I wasn't feeling very hopeful that Adam and I would end up together. I was just writing the book for fun. It may have even started out more like for spite, instead of in spite of, if I am honest. After having second thoughts, I deleted what I had written. Shortly after being in South Carolina, I saw the advertisement for the writing contest sponsored by Women of Faith. That was when I became serious about writing this story. Since most of my work on the first book was finished, I now had some time to write again.

I was dreading the Christmas holiday. I talked to my daughter about going to Florida instead of staying in South Carolina, since there would be only the three of us. The thought of that was so depressing; I had gone from having so many family members to share the holidays with to being down to just the three of us. I knew my son and his wife wouldn't be coming, because they were not speaking to my daughter at this time. It was so painful for me—I could hardly stand it.

So in October 2010, I booked what I hoped would turn out to be a dream vacation. The closer the holidays approached, the more

Ann and I both were craving a different kind of Christmas. After George died, I quickly learned not to hold on too tightly to some of the old traditions, because nothing would ever be the same. I also learned some traditions are never meant to change. There is purpose in some of those traditions.

It was only a few days before Christmas 2009 when my son-in-law told Ann he wanted a divorce. Talk about poor timing. The news was so unexpected and devastating. But I learned that when my eyes were focused clearly on Jesus, no matter what was going on around me, it could be the best Christmas ever. No matter how I spend the holiday, when I celebrate the birth of my Savior nothing tarnishes that part of Christmas.

When I moved from Florida to South Carolina, I wasn't sure I would ever return to Florida, let alone go back to another theme park. I thought those days were behind me, especially after my husband died. But never say never. Life is surprising sometimes. It seemed Mickey and Minnie had other ideas, because my granddaughter Catherine, my daughter, Ann, and I went to Disney World for Christmas break. It was perfect timing to enter the world of make-believe.

Originally, Ann and I were thinking of taking Catherine to Disney World during spring break, but I felt it would be too much pressure to try to make that trip with only a week of vacation time. It seemed like there wouldn't be enough days to drive to Florida and back to South Carolina without being rushed. Plus, it would be so hectic for Ann and Catherine to start right back to school the very next day. One of my friends mentioned the idea of going to Disney World for Christmas. She thought it would be the perfect time of year for all the magic that the theme park has to offer. Considering everything that was going on in my family, I couldn't have agreed more. Since Ann works for the school district, she would still have more than a week off after returning to South Carolina on Christmas Eve. So we both agreed to go to Florida for Christmas. I made a few phone calls and was able to rent a one-bedroom condo right inside the theme park. The dates lined up perfectly. I was feeling blessed that this unit was even available on such short notice. It was going to work out perfectly for us. And we would be back home in time to attend Christmas Eve service at our home church, to celebrate the reason for the season for certain.

Ann mentioned to me that one of the highlights for little girls is to have dinner with the princesses in the castle. I called to book the dinner and was told it would be nearly impossible to get a dinner date inside the castle because those dates are booked 180 days in advance. The woman on the other end of the phone said she would check, and *lo and behold* she had a dinner opening on Wednesday, December 23, at four o'clock. I said that would be perfect! It would be the grand finale. I made the reservations. Even Grandma can dream about dinner in the castle.

I've been to Disney World theme park many times over the years. My first time was in August 1972, soon after the park opened. Ann was almost two years old at the time. We arrived there in the evening, and the castle was all lit up. I never will forget the sight of that castle off in the distance. It was like being in a fairy tale. I felt the excitement and wonder of make-believe. I was three months pregnant with my son, Alan, at the time. So I was not only expecting a baby but I had expectations of a wonderful life waiting for me back at home. What a contrast to what was actually happening back home in my real castle, where my husband was sleeping with a woman he thought was a princess while my daughter and I enjoyed the world of innocence that would abruptly end when I returned home from that trip to Florida. As much as I like to pretend unpleasant memories don't come back, they sometimes do. It doesn't tarnish this story; rather it makes me realize that God had His eye on me then too. Even though I would spend several weeks in another world of make-believe—hospitalized because of all the devastation that occurred before I ended up divorced—I survived. I started back on the road to recovery, and I conquered all those hurts with God by my side. That is because my God is mighty. He can change any situation to bring not only healing to His children but blessings too. So it doesn't hurt to remember things as they really were. That dose of reality in the big scheme of things only gives me another opportunity to thank, praise, and glorify God—for He is good all the time. Life is not this perfect, make-believe world where nothing bad ever happens. When I believe in God and His divine providence that He can take any bad situation and bring good from it, the storms are easier to weather. So I was looking forward to another chance to go to Florida and make some more good memories.

On Wednesday, the day before leaving for Florida, I asked God if my connection to Adam was just my imagination working overtime or if there was more to this story. You see, by now I was earnestly working on writing this book, and I had a deadline in mind. I kept asking God if I was meant to write this story. I thought if it became published that would confirm that I was the woman meant to write the Ruth and Boaz story. I hoped it would explain why Adam and I had this connection. I also prayed it would bring me one step closer to ending up with Adam as my husband. I was thinking this very thought, as I was about to enter one of our local breakfast eateries. A man and his wife were walking in front of me. The wife continued to go into the restaurant, but her husband dropped back behind me.

Then he said to me, "Redheads are in."

I replied, "I've been in and out most of my life, because I've had this red hair since I was sixteen except for a few years." I made my hair red even when it wasn't popular.

His reply was, "As long as you have the right brain."

His comment had me thinking, "What does that mean?"

When we entered the restaurant together, his wife was sitting at the table right by the door. She said to him, "What happened to you?"

I immediately told her, "He was out there commenting about my red hair."

They both laughed, and he said to me, "Gee, thanks. I give you a compliment, and you try to get me in trouble."

His wife said, "Yes, he's in trouble all right." I could tell they were a playful couple. We were all teasing, having fun, and no one was fooled.

The way the man spoke out to me did get my attention though, especially since I was in the midst of talking to God at the time. After I sat down by myself to have breakfast, I realized God had been speaking to me once again through the prompting of the Holy Spirit. I believe God was letting me know He hears my every thought and prayer. It was a personal message once again—reassuring me that God knows every hair on my red head. For an instant, I wondered if Adam was thinking about my red hair too. I do believe God was letting me know that when my brain is focused on God I have the right brain. I immediately had confidence that I was to write this book even in the midst of my preparations for my trip. Against my daughter's wishes, I decided to take my computer along just in case there was something else I believed I was to write about during our trip.

After that little revelation, I finished up the last minute packing in preparation to leave the next day for our vacation. We planned to leave right after school on Thursday, December 16, 2010, to start the drive to our halfway point. Wednesday evening, the school district announced there would be a two-hour delay on Thursday morning because of the ice storm that was predicted to hit our county. Since Catherine and Ann had spent the night, the plan was Ann would take Catherine to school, and then I would finish packing the car and pick Catherine up from school at three o'clock, meeting Ann back at my house so we could leave by four o'clock. We were going to drive to a hotel in Georgia. I had already made reservations.

I had so much to do that I didn't even allow myself to entertain the idea of driving in an ice storm. When I went to bed, I put on the weather channel. It predicted Georgia would be spared the ice storm and the rain would be stopping by afternoon. I thought, *This is a good sign. If I get out of town around four o'clock, heading south should be free sailing.*

The "two-hour delay" turned into "school closed" because the weather was predicted to be worse than expected. We were all awake by seven in the morning, so we continued to gather our last minutes items and pack the car, anticipating that by the time we were ready to leave we could reassess whether to venture out. By noon, we were packed and ready to go. When we headed out from my driveway, there was not a drop of ice or snow, but only light rain was falling. We stopped at a fast food place for lunch, gassed up the car, and by around one o'clock we were headed for "destination Disney." It was six o'clock in the evening when we arrived at the Best Western Hotel in Richmond Hill, Georgia. The chocolate chip cookies were all warmed up and waiting for us. I told Ann I took these as just another gift from God: an extra day of vacation, perfect weather, and cookies to start off a trip that some little girls only dream about—including dinner with the princesses! Sometimes, the storms that are predicted never even happen.

When we checked into the hotel room in Georgia on Thursday night, the first thing Catherine spouted was, "This room is great! It's on the first floor, so if there is a fire we can go right out that window."

I said, "Catherine, if there's a fire we can go out the door, because we are on the end and it is close to the outside."

Then Catherine informed me, "Grandma, we need to feel the door first to make sure it isn't hot."

This was too much reality and negativity for Grandma. I said to Catherine, "We don't need to worry. There won't be any fire, anyway."

Boy was I wrong. The next morning, we went to the breakfast area at the hotel to enjoy the buffet with all the wonderful extra specialties: my favorite flavored coffee creamers and syrups, eggs, sausage, biscuits, sausage gravy, French toast, waffles, bagels, and so much more. We were eating and talking away, and then the fire alarm started to ring. Everyone sat there as if they didn't hear a thing. I saw one of the employees and asked if it was a required fire drill.

As she casually walked away, I heard her say, "I really don't know."

I commented to my daughter, "This has happened to me once before. I'm amazed how no one seems to react to a fire alarm anymore. I don't know if it is because of denial or apathy."

I didn't smell smoke, but believe me I had one eye on the front door, which was directly across from where we sat, and the other eye on the employees. I watched them as they slowly embraced the idea that this might be a real fire. When the manager tried to shut off the alarm, it wouldn't stop ringing. That indicated there was at least smoke in the building, so we were told to evacuate. We calmly exited the building.

My car was parked directly in front of my room and too close to the building for my comfort. I told myself, *It might be a good idea to move the car just in case all hell breaks loose.* After I moved my car away from the building, I noticed I was the only one who took such action. Ann, Catherine, and I just stood by watching. Nothing seemed to be happening, so I called 911 just in case no one else had thought to do it.

The woman answered the phone saying, "Richmond Hill emergency."

I asked, "Has anyone reported the fire alarm at the Best Western?"

She assured me, saying, "The fire department is aware and on the way." That stopped me from taking my anxiety to the next level I call fear.

We waited at least ten minutes for the fire trucks to arrive. After talking to some of the employees, we learned there was indeed smoke in room 108. That happened to be three doors down from room 114, our room, which housed my pills, camera, our jewelry, makeup, toiletries, my daughter's purse and my computer with this unfinished story. Ann was amazingly calm about the entire situation. I was surprised because I know the panic a woman could go through at the thought of her purse going up in flames. What a nightmare it would be to replace credit cards, driver's license, vehicle registration, and insurance cards.

In fact, Ann told Catherine, "All that matters is our safety."

I was thankful I had my purse and the car keys. I commented to Ann, "We can still go to Disney World, because we each have half our houses sitting in the trunk of my car." Ann and I laughed at that idea because it was so true. I think we over packed, as usual.

I thought about my first book and the fact that it was safely with the publisher getting ready to have the design team create the cover. I was getting excited at the thought of the book coming to completion, and I felt affirmation that the book was pleasing to God. There are so many times I've felt God blessing my writings. "And we know that in all things God works for the good of those who love him, who have been called according to his purpose" (Romans 8:28). At these times I think things in my life reflect some of the messages God wants me to convey.

As I stood outside in the parking lot while the fire trucks arrived, all I can tell you is Grandma needed a correction. Things had been going pretty well for me. It was easy to get caught up in my own world, especially when writing and dreaming happy dreams. I told Catherine this was indeed a wake-up call for me, and I was wrong to tell her that a fire couldn't happen. I told her I was glad she was prepared. The situation reminded me of life and how some people pretend or deny the fire will ever come. They go through life unprepared. It so paralleled the story within the story that I was already writing. I just had to wonder how much of the material for the book God was really supplying or if this was all just a huge coincidence.

The smoke alarm was set off because a mattress was smoldering, apparently from a lit cigarette. The fire marshal had several of the firemen looking over every inch of the mattress for evidence. When I called my son, Alan, and told him about what had happened, he teased me. He said, "That is what happens when you stay in cheap hotels." I immediately corrected Alan and told him the hotel was inexpensive but not cheap; it was one of the nicer hotels I've stayed in. The wing of the hotel we were in was a nonsmoking section, but there is always someone who thinks the rules don't apply to him. I overheard one of the employees say they were looking for the person who had occupied that room. It seemed he had vanished into thin air. He knew he was guilty.

After the mattress was removed from the hotel and all concerns about a fire erupting were over, everyone was allowed back in the hotel but us. We were the only guests left who had stayed in that wing of the hotel. I approached the fire marshal, and he gave me special permission to enter my room. I went in by the side door; that reminded me of what I had told Catherine the previous night when I never dreamed there would be a fire. The rest of the hallway was blocked off because of the water on the floor and the mess that was in front of our room. I quickly gathered our things, took them out through that same door, and repacked the car.

I needed to go to the lobby to check out, throw away some trash, and get some ice for the cooler. There I met the owner of the hotel. I didn't know he was the owner at the time. I was teasing him because he was feeling the rug, which was now wet all the way from the far end of the hallway up to the lobby. As he bent down to touch the rug, I said, "Osmosis."

He replied, "I'll get a dehumidifier and get this all cleaned up soon. I've been wanting to make a room with a Jacuzzi suite, so that is what I think I'll do with room 108."

I love a man with a positive attitude and vision. I said, "Good! I'll be back. In fact, we're already booked to come here on December 23 on our return trip from Disney."

He said, "I'm sorry for any inconvenience the fire might have caused you."

I told him, "Oh, don't worry about it. I'm writing a book, and it's given me some good material for one of my chapters. I had already written about how God had given us a perfect start with the extra day vacation even though we never had any ice from that storm. I'm going to be writing about this too. I'll write about you in the book, and maybe one day when it gets published I'll bring you a copy." I teased him and said, "You can put me up free for a night in that new suite of yours."

After I mentioned I would put him in the book, he said, "Oh, good. I have dreams of this place getting so busy that I have to add a third floor."

There was something about him I could relate to right away. He was a man with a vision—a dreamer—and although lately I can relate to that, I don't want my dreams to end with just my earthly dreams. I plan on giving him a copy of this book one day. I hope it becomes more than an earthly blessing to him too. After I told him I would bring him a copy and he could put me up for a free night in that Jacuzzi suite, I started dreaming my earthly dreams. I hoped I wouldn't be alone. I asked God if he would tell me if I would have someone to share that suite with, and I giggled. I was having fun with God, and it was good.

On the serious note, the fire represented the fact that we truly don't know what is on the other side of the door; but if you believe Jesus rose from the dead, we know death has been conquered. We know Jesus came back from that place to tell us what He experienced. He conquered and rose victoriously. No one here on earth has been to hell and back, although life does seem like it at times. Some people have claimed to experience a taste of heaven when their hearts stopped for a while, but none of us knows with 100 percent certainty what waits for us after death. My eyes are opened. I believe in heaven and hell. I am prepared because I have Jesus and don't need a backup plan. He has prepared my way straight to heaven. And don't think I am leaving you an out because I said no one knows for sure. I am a realist. If I said I know what to expect for sure, that would be a lie because I haven't been there. If I told you I spent time with God (in thought, prayer, and in his Word), some would only doubt more. All I am saying is I believe God's Word. That is why it is called *faith*—believing in the unseen. If you read the rest of this book and come away from it saying, "That woman has quite an imagination," it is your choice. I am proclaiming I'm a real down-to-earth woman who just happens to believe God is writing this story through me because He wants us all to believe in heaven and hell. More than that, He wants us to believe not only in His Son, Jesus, but in the Holy Spirit too. I really am not smart enough to make all this up or to arrange my life to flow into a story that just happens to have all these correlations. That is why my faith keeps growing and so does my hope for all things good through God who strengthens me.

So all I can do is share my beliefs and let you know they come from a place of love in my heart and not from an "I'm right and know it all" attitude. I can tell you what I believe God shows me as truth, explain how He leads me to live in that truth, and share with you the true facts about my life and how these situations relate to telling the story. If you share my beliefs or not, either way, I respect you. But I don't want to live my life thinking I should have shared the story about Jesus and the Good News with you and feel regret for not taking the opportunity. It is a privilege to spend this time with you, even though I haven't met some of you.

There are times I believe God is getting my attention and letting me know He sees all, hears all, and knows my heart. If I end up on my honeymoon with Adam in that Jacuzzi, it is a bonus. My real dream in life is you. I want you to know I believe there is a hell, and I don't want you to go there. I want you to believe God's plan includes you too so be prepared by accepting His free gift of salvation through His Son Jesus. I want God to receive the honor, praise, and worship He deserves and the acknowledgement that He is a loving Father.

On Friday, we arrived safely in Disney World. Our condo was great. There was a bus that would take us to all the theme parks and also to downtown. I could just relax and leave the driving to them. We'd planned to go to the park on Saturday, but it poured down rain all morning. That worked out, because it gave us time to relax and finish unpacking. In the early afternoon, the rain slowed down to a drizzle. Even though more rain was predicted, we headed to the park anyway. As soon as we got off the bus, the sun unexpectedly came out. It didn't rain again that day. We were able to see eight attractions that day, which is remarkable—especially at Christmas time. We even saw the special light-up ceremony for the "decoration of lights" that would be covering the castle. It was a wonderful day. All three of us were enjoying the magic of Disney at Christmas time.

We spent Sunday evening at Hollywood Studios and it was totally lit up for the holiday season. It was an over-the-top magical time. It was such a beautiful night, filled with sights and sounds of Christmas. There were over five million lights on the buildings. When we entered that area as the Christmas music played, I could feel the atmosphere was filled with anticipation. It was more visual than I could handle. In a way, I was so caught up by the splendor that I forgot all about any thoughts about my life. I just enjoyed being among all the people sharing in the beauty of the Christmas season. It was chilly, and it reminded me of Christmases from my childhood. Hearing the Christmas classics from long ago didn't bring me to a place of sadness like it sometimes does. It felt more like what I think I might be experiencing someday when I am carefree in heaven, seeing so much light and hearing worship songs that I used to sing on earth. My daughter and granddaughter were with me, and I was happy. I stayed in the moment and just appreciated how very blessed I am.

Thursday, December 23, was our last day at the park. We ended it with dinner at the castle. When we arrived, we had a special surprise. We found out Catherine had been chosen to be the "Princess of the Day." This entitled Catherine to receive a special star to wear distinguishing her from all the other guests, a free photo with Cinderella, and an announcement to all the other guests stating, "Princess Catherine has arrived." We were seated at the best table by a window overlooking the ninety-three-year-old carousel. I couldn't believe Catherine was chosen out of all the guests—or could I? I just giggled and thanked God once again, because I believed He provided all of these blessings for me to share with you. I kept asking Him if He was trying to tell me something, and then I heard Him say, "I have my eye on you." It was the perfect ending to a wonderful, magical, dream-filled vacation that three princesses were blessed to enjoy.

While I was at the park, I shared about the two stories I was writing with several women. One woman asked me if I had an email address. She wanted to write to me after reading my book. I had thought about including my email address in my book or perhaps having a webpage so I could hear from people who believed the book had personally touched them. I asked God about my idea, thinking I could use it for book number three. Then I remember whose idea it really was. I think He was just confirming that His messages to me were coming through loud and clear.

I was just in awe of what was happening in my life. I wonder why I would be surprised. This was the very God who, despite numerous complications, allowed my husband to live thirteen years with a prognosis of less than a year. Did I think He would stop blessing me now? What was I thinking? And if He could do the impossible by having George live a dozen extra years, all these little blessings were just child's play. I was sure God had been blessing me so much more than I ever thanked Him for over the years. I realized my eyes were just beginning to be opened to all the wonders of Him.

When we went to see *Beauty and the Beast* that day at Hollywood Studios, it started me thinking about Adam again—but not because I thought he was a beast. I wondered, was I trying to have him fall in love with me or was I trying to change our situation by loving him just the way he was? I didn't think that would necessarily be a bad thing. I also didn't pretend he didn't confuse me by sending mixed messages. When I wrote to him asking for more clarity because I was confused about what had happened between us, he never acknowledged anything that transpired between us. I told him I was confused and felt stuck. He never did anything to clear up the matter. I wondered if he wanted me to stay stuck on him or if he was confused, too, and didn't honestly know what to say to me.

In some ways, I consider myself goofy for thinking that writing an entire book would make a man fall in love with me. I hope sharing my story clears up any confusion anyone might have about Jesus and it helps people accept how much God loves them. As far as the confusion about Adam, I don't know if that will ever be resolved. After writing this book, I realized how confused I still was. Maybe that is another reason God wanted me to write this story. When it comes to Adam, I am more confused than ever. It's funny—I thought writing this would help clear up the confusion. Maybe, eventually, it will. I am waiting to see Adam's reaction to the book. If after reading this he still continues to leave me in the state of confusion, I will clearly see he is not the man for me. Maybe after he reads it, both of us will have a happy ending knowing he believes he won't ever die, either. In a way, this story could relate to the beast's story in that fairy tale.

I will say there is one thing in my life I am not confused about: where I'll go when it is over. That is one thing I know without a doubt. Maybe that is why I am not afraid to take a risk and act goofy. And if I am in the state of confusion, it's okay; it's only a temporary address. I'll be getting a permanent one soon enough. It is called heaven.

But while I'm here on earth, my next dream is that I will be writing book number three. It will be called *Love at No Sight*. At first I thought it would be about us loving God without seeing Him first. I hoped it would be filled with stories that readers sent to me about how my books gave knowledge of God's love to them just when they needed it the most. Now, over a year after conceptualizing the book, I can tell you it is about all the times God shows up in my life and gives me insight about applying His Word to my life's situations. It is about how God is there for me, although I cannot physically see Him. It is also about how He connects me to others. I hope it will also be about how my dreams from this book came true and Adam and I did end up loving one another even though we didn't see each other, as in date. I'll just have to wait and see the material God sends me. Either way, I hope to have a website of my own and perhaps a blog. I haven't a clue how to make that happen. I did, by chance, see a guy on TV talking about this when I was channel surfing one evening after a day at the theme park. He was telling others how to set up a blog and get sponsors that would advertise on it. He mentioned Twitter and Facebook. I do go on Facebook, but I don't really know all the ins and outs of it yet so I get frustrated with it. While I'm figuring it all out, I am just enjoying writing, sharing my faith and my life with you. I don't know if I want to tweet, chat, blog, or just hear the sound of someone's voice. Sometimes I think I want to hear the sound of a familiar voice accompanied by the clicking of a pen.

For now, I will enjoy remembering the all sights and sounds of Disney and the time I spent in the land of make-believe. There is a little kid in me that just can't help but want to come out and play. Like this theme park that is for kids of any age, our relationship with God should be like that too. We really are all God's children and He wants us to enjoy Him too and be in awe of all He created. We just need to tell Him we need Him, and we'd like to come into the castle for the banquet. Jesus is the way to be invited in. He's gone to hell and back for you. All you need to do is believe and make-believe.

November 22, 2011, I went to my grandson's school to celebrate the Thanksgiving Feast with him. So many parents brought such good food. As I sat with many of Robert's five-year-old friends, I could tell the little boys were excited to talk to me. One boy told me he was a turkey. He said, "I ate your face all up. I ate your nose, your checks, and your mouth. I spit out your eyes, and you still have them." Then another boy looked at me with a big smile on his face and tenderly said, "You look like a princess." He just naturally had the confidence to flirt. I thought, "I guess I still have something that makes little boys see me as a princess. Thank you, God, for little boys who can still make me feel special." As I pondered the comment this little boy made to me, I felt as if God himself was calling me His princess too. I remembered I had called myself a princess when I wrote this chapter. I believe this moment at Robert's school was a sign from God that I was truly one of His princesses and He wanted me to recapture the experience of being loved by Him and add it at the end of this chapter. I can say it was a great day to be a grandma, and I am thankful.

Tiny Kisses

I accepted Jesus in my heart when I was little without really knowing what that truly meant. I didn't stop seeking Him. I continued to desire more knowledge about God so that I could understand Him. With this understanding came the ability to experience Jesus many times as I studied and read the Bible. I finally accepted the fact that God has authority over me. I understand now that even though Jesus died for my sins, I am to obey God. I surrendered, and I have to do that over and over again, too. It is a relationship between me and God, Jesus, and the Holy Spirit. It is fluid; I think of all three persons of God in relationship with me and me with each person of the Holy Trinity. It is back and forth over time, through seasons of my life. My ability to understand this came one day, not "the day I said my sinner's prayer," but the day I fell head over heels in love with this man called Jesus. It may have started with a desire in my heart, but it is now full-blown love.

This love I have for Jesus is hard to put into words. It is similar to the feeling I have when I think about Adam and me being together. When I think of my dream that we could live together happily ever after, as they say in the fairy tales, I know that is the dream I believe Jesus gave to me. When He hung on the cross and said to the man next to him, "Today you will be with me in paradise," that is what I am counting on will happen to me one day too. When I have moments in my life that are so wonderful, it feels like what I envision it will be like living with Jesus in paradise. Experiencing romantic love has helped me sense just the slightest comparison of what that life ahead of us might be like. I am sure that romantic love doesn't really compare to eternal life with God, but it is the closest things we humans can relate to when we speak of love. Anyone who has been head over heels in the state of new love might agree. There is something not only magical but beyond explanation when we feel such love and desire for someone else. Even though we can't maintain that feeling, we can remember it and strive to recapture those fleeting moments. This would be the ultimate explanation of "tiny kisses from heaven."

I like to call the times that someone touches my heart in such a way that it brings a little taste of heaven here on earth tiny kisses from heaven. I experienced one not too long ago when Robert looked at me and said, "Grandma, I'm going to kiss you right now." He does this every so often. He doesn't always want me to kiss him, but he loves to kiss me clear out of the blue when I don't expect it. I always smile and giggle. I think that is why he likes to do it so much. Just writing this makes me cry happy tears. I hope this gives you an idea about what tiny kisses from heaven mean to me.

It was hard for me to experience these after my husband died. I was so caught up in grief that it was hard to even breathe at times. I went through the motions of life for a while. But the day I met Adam, it felt like a tiny kiss from heaven. For a moment, it felt like a surprise from out of the blue. Then it continued to change from a tiny kiss into a longing desire to be kissed. That's what life is sometimes. It's the journey and the anticipation of a tiny kiss from heaven now and then. And, at times, it is the longing and the desire for eternity. We are made to desire "forever." We want to live and love forever. When I sense those tiny kisses from heaven, I know I am still alive and loved by God. One day I will live and love forever, for all eternity. I can't even begin to wrap my mind around that concept. I can only compare it to what it feels like when we are engaged and approaching the wedding. We believe we will be together until death parts us. Many believe even death won't separate us, because couples desire to spend eternity together too. Sadly, time changes that desire for many couples and the passion they had for each other disappears. One day, all will be the way it was meant to be and we will see God face-to-face. That is when the new heaven and new earth will meet. Until that happens, we have to settle for the tiny kisses.

When my children were little, I loved giving them raspberry kisses on their tummies and making them laugh. It was so fun for them and me too. I think in a way, God is doing that to me now. He is giving me those kinds of kisses. I can feel it, and sometimes I can't contain my laughter. It is almost embarrassing.

This leads me to another Adam story. I had come back to Indiana to help celebrate Marie's eighth birthday, January 24, 2011. I decided to stick around to take care of some business since I was in town. I usually don't come North during the winter months. It was for Marie, more than any other reason, I came. I hadn't spent one birthday with her except for the day she was born. It had been a rough winter, and there was a terrible amount of ice accumulated on my driveway. I found myself outside chiseling away at it. I became obsessed with wanting to rid my driveway of that ice. I wanted to break it up so it would melt on those days when the sun peaked out from behind the clouds.

Early the next month, I scheduled an appointment with Adam and prayed the roads would be good enough for me to get there without any difficulties. He and I took care of things that needed to be done at this particular time. As was the case lately, we always seemed to get around to personal conversations, but only about me now. Maybe it was because I was afraid to bring up anything about his personal life. I don't mean to give the impression that I didn't care. I did care, and that's the dilemma. I didn't want it to seem as if I was prying, going on a fishing expedition—but I sure would have liked to go fishing. Anyway, I was so excited because the cover design for my first book was finally finished. It wouldn't be long before the book would be in print. I had only a few loose ends to wrap up. Adam and I were talking away, and that is when I noticed the crow's feet by his eyes. My mind went totally blank. I couldn't think of anything else. I just wanted to give him tiny kisses right there on those little lines. I wondered what in the world I was thinking. I also started to think, *I don't know how much longer I can keep coming here.* We weren't alone in the office. I knew I would never act on those impulses anyway, but I wondered if the woman with us could tell what I was dreaming from the expression on my face or if she was able to sense my thoughts. I guess because Marie can tell when I'm thinking about Adam at times, it entered my mind that other people might be able to perceive my feelings because of how I acted around him. I also was feeling more than a little embarrassed at the moment.

Adam was talking about my book. He asked me when it would be in print and how he would know that it was out. He was asking a good many questions that day. When I was getting ready to leave, he held out his hand for me to shake it. I remembered when I had done the same thing with him, and he had rejected my offer. His gesture took me back to that moment and between me wanting to kiss him by his crow's feet and him extending his hand to me, I was feeling very emotional. I couldn't say anything, because we weren't alone. Even if we were alone, I don't know if I would have been able to tell him what I was experiencing.

I took his hand, and we just stood there. He was talking, but I honestly don't remember a word he said. I know I wasn't looking into his eyes the way I usually do. I was just looking down at our hands. I saw that they weren't shaking back and forth the way they were supposed to if we were doing the usual handshake. I just kept looking at our hands together. I felt like it was the moment of reconciliation. We had finally come to that point. It was the passing of the peace. After several moments, I realized we were still holding hands, and I immediately let go. I wondered how long we would have stood there with our hands together if I hadn't. I don't even remember the rest of the visit.

I left there with the assurance that we had taken another step closer together. I got in my car and drove away. I didn't even make it past the red light at the nearest corner when I saw that image of our hands together. I made a left turn onto the street that would eventually lead to the entrance of my neighborhood. I only drove a few feet more, and I started to cry. I cried the entire way home. At the time, I didn't understand why. I knew we were reconciled, but that wasn't the feeling I was having that day I left Adam's office. I just couldn't put my finger on it. I felt like Adam didn't want to let go of me.

It is October 19, 2011. I am editing this book that is supposed to be in chronological order, but sometimes I add to the story because I have more insight. Sometimes I delete things too. This chapter brought me back to that day in February when Adam extended his hand to me. I can still see our hands together. I still don't know how to describe it. I've talked about this with my sister and a few close friends. I told them I don't know what made me cry. I couldn't explain the feeling. It was reconciliation, but it seemed like something else too. There was something familiar about it, and I felt so comfortable with Adam when our hands were joined. I wished we were alone, because I was feeling an uneasiness knowing someone was watching us. I felt as if someone was invading my privacy and might sense the feelings I was trying to hide from Adam and myself. Oh my goodness, now I understand what it seemed like. It's the same thing you do when you get married. You join hands. I cannot believe this. I just had this revelation, and it was immediately followed by a loud crack of thunder. I kid you not. God what are you doing to me?

This reminds me of the time I wrote that one poem of mine, which I included earlier in the book. That day I laughed with God because I realized I couldn't hide my feelings about Adam. God knew all along what I was feeling. It was a revelation. I learned I couldn't do anything to rid myself of those feelings. I couldn't pretend, deny, or control them away—I could only admit them to God. When I wrote about blushing in front of God, at that exact moment, the electricity in my house went out for a few seconds. It was such a moment with God. That day in December 2009, I laughed. Even now I still smile, because I remember what I was thinking: that I couldn't hide from God. It was the day I got honest with God and said I couldn't stop desiring Adam and wanted him in my life. It was God's way of saying, "I made you that way, and you don't need to be embarrassed about it either." I wonder why I feel like I am about to lose it, at times. I honestly don't know how much more of this I can handle. And why is it thundering in the middle of October? It isn't supposed to thunder in Indiana in October. I know because of everything that has transpired that God is involved in this situation. I am at the point where I am sure this is the time God wants me to give Adam this book. I don't know what will happen, but I trust that it will all be for good.

Sometimes I wonder what Adam will be thinking as he reads this story. I wonder if he will be totally afraid of me afterwards, or if he will come to believe, like I do, that God has a reason for us being connected to each other. I know God is involved, but I know God gives us choices too. God doesn't hold a gun to our head and make us do things. I just need to trust that God knows the outcome, and He will turn it to good for me no matter what happens.

Sometimes I think maybe, just maybe, Adam is experiencing some of these same things and he will understand me. Maybe he will recall this day when there was a loud crack of thunder at five o'clock in the afternoon. I know he is close enough to hear that thunder, and maybe this is meant for him too. Sometimes, as Adam knows, I just do what God tells me when it comes to writing things. So this I know he will be quite used to. Maybe this is meant to calm him down after he finishes reading this chapter—or scare him away. I am just joking with you, Adam.

I have totally lost all thought of what, if anything, more I had wanted to write about, so I guess this chapter is finished. The conclusion sure wasn't where I thought it was headed, but that's okay. I know, in the end, it will all connect. I just trust God that this is what I was meant to write. When you hear the thunder, only a fool would argue with God. And I am no fool.

The Wedding Invitation

I believe love at first sight can happen when God makes the arrangements. I had already experienced this once before, when George and I met and eventually married. We immediately sensed that we were meant to be together, so this idea is not a new one to me. George and I were happily married for thirty-one years. Considering this was a second marriage for both of us, this was quite an accomplishment. Second marriages have around a 60 percent chance of ending in divorce. I not only believe in love at first sight, I also believe sometimes God arranges those marriages. When we first met someone and hear our inner voice tell us we are going to be married to that person one day, it's one of the methods God uses to get our attention and bring this about. It certainly does something to the person hearing this; it drives you to do almost everything in your power to see if this is really true. George and I were each praying for God to bring someone to us, and we both had turned our love lives over to God. We believed God answered our prayers when He brought us together. I just thought it wouldn't happen to me again, especially since I wasn't even praying for someone. I do believe God answers prayers. I see this desire for me to even want someone again as an answer to George's prayer for me. I think the Holy Spirit knew what to pray for me even when I wasn't aware of what I wanted or needed. "In the same way, the Spirit helps in our weakness. We do not know what we ought to pray for, but the Spirit himself intercedes for us with groans that words cannot express. And he who searches our hearts knows the mind of the Spirit, because the Spirit intercedes for the saints in accordance with God's will" (Romans 8:26–27). This is a good explanation of how the Trinity works on our behalf.

God is sovereign. He can do what He wants, even in the love department—from arranging for us to recognize our intended mate to putting a burning desire in us to be with that person. Aside from choosing Christ, choosing a mate is the most important decision of all in life, so why would God have us just make it on our own? When we have that moment, that connection, and hear that inner voice speak to us, it is shocking. I think that is the way God gets our attention. When we start to admit that we have a desire for that person and the pieces begin to fit together, we instinctively know that something is brewing. Sometimes we have confidence that this is God's plan, and we know it is His doing. When we go to God in prayer, inviting Him into the situation, He begins to instruct us and test us until we become willing to allow for this possibility. Logically it may make no sense, but when God uses numerous circumstances to convince us of His involvement it becomes clear that this could only come from God.

Today, the world is so scary. I know I need to trust God above all else. I believe when I trust God He will be there to let me know He is hearing me and watching me. He is a living and active God. He can find a way to help me become more confident and let me know that He has not left me to fend for myself.

Even though I tend to be impulsive at times, God was with me all along. I believe He protected me from rushing into this relationship He knew neither of us was ready for because He knew what was ahead for both of us. God's timing is always perfect, and that is why I wanted to wait for Him to let me know when, if ever, I should act on my feelings.

God is grooming me for the life He has planned for me. Whether I find out that both Adam and I have this desire to be together or I learn it is not in my best interest to be involved with Adam, I trust God. I have learned not to rush into things. I have spent much time with God. I continue to seek His will for my life and for this relationship. God has not closed the door, and He is using so many coincidences and God sightings to let me know I am on the right path. I realized I have to go through this spiritual battle of doubts and remember that I am an overcomer. I know this dream might just be a fantasy, but I believe in fairy tales or, shall I say, God connections. I am willing to see this through to the end. I am confident I will know when the end has arrived. My God is not a God that leaves me stuck, and He doesn't leave me with unanswered prayers either. He just leaves me waiting for His timing.

I will just simply say I believe in love—the love God has for me that ensures He will meet my every need. It wouldn't surprise me if He would give me the most unusual engagement story. I know that is what our life here on earth is with Jesus: it is the engagement time. If this time with Adam doesn't end the way I hope, to some people I might look stupid, naïve, or foolish. I know I won't look that way to God. That is what matters the most. I feel certain that I can trust God, and I believe He wants me to write this story and give it to Adam. I feel like Noah, sometimes, especially when no one seems to understand my faith and trust in God. I do trust God with this relationship with Adam. I believe God will show me why He put Adam on my heart and wouldn't take those feelings for him away. I am building the boat. It may not rain, but I heard the thunder. And, coincidently, it never did rain at my place that day I heard that one loud crack of thunder. I heard it rained like crazy in other parts of town. God knows exactly when and where to send the rain. He is God, and He has a purpose for everything. He is all-knowing and all-powerful. I am learning that about Him. I don't question Him about why He does the things He does. I do question Him about things that are relevant to my life. I do ask Him for discernment so I can proceed with confidence. In those cases, I ask lots of questions with a purpose. I ask for guidance. "God, show me where you want me to go and what you want me to do." God knows I desire to trust Him. He is standing with me during this time and encouraging me to trust Him and trust my heart. Since Jesus is in my heart, that isn't that hard to do either. I am going to hold on to the hope that I will get my miracle. However, I realize that during the time Jesus walked the earth, Jesus did not give miracles to everyone. He did it for a purpose, so others would know that the Father had sent Him. Through the Holy Spirit and the power in the name of Jesus, the apostles were able to do some miraculous signs and wonders too. It was all for the purpose of bringing others into the body of believers. When I receive my miracle, I believe it will be to point to Christ as the risen Lord and to the power of the Holy Spirit to bring the gifts of love, joy, peace, patience, kindness, goodness, faithfulness, gentleness, and self-control to believers. It is up to the Trinity to do a work in me and through me. It really has nothing to do with me. All I am doing is acting out my faith. And believe me it would be a real miracle if I get married again, because everyone knows the saying about the chances of getting married after the age of thirty—let alone sixty. My chances of getting struck by lightning are better. I'd say that already happened long before I even heard that thunder. Was it love at first sight? It was for me; it just took me a while to see it. I am now waiting to find out if Adam sees it too. I know I was struck and stuck on Jesus. That is the most important love-at-first-sight relationship of all. I would love to be blessed to have that kind of love with another man. God created us to be in relationships with others too. We were created to desire relationships and be in community with others. We were meant to be in relationships, because that is where we can learn to love one another.

I want others to believe that, even though God is spiritual and there is a spiritual world in addition to this earthly one, the two worlds do meet. Once I accepted Jesus, I was able to know that this physical world is not the only one that exits. That is my reality. I see myself as set apart, but not separated from either world. Maybe because I have my eyes wide open I can see things differently. I see both worlds at the same time. I see God with me and sense His presence. I talk to Him as I go about my day. I am not good at multitasking, but I am able to do this. God's presence is in my mind most of the time, especially since my husband died. I think that is why the Bible refers to widows and children so much; we see God more during those times in our life if we have faith.

I know that since I am without a husband, my bridegroom, Jesus, is here comforting me and loving me. I don't have an earthly husband to distract me. Maybe that is why I can sense God's presence so much now. I think my ability to see God work in my life comes as a result of my need for Him. I am alone, and I need God more than ever before. Without Him, I would be in a place of despair. I want to believe that if I ever marry again, I will still be this close to God for the rest of my life. I want to believe He will still give me all this wonderful material to write, the material that is my life right now. I desire to have God use me to reach others, even if it is in what may seem like a weird way to some.

If Adam is my Boaz, then our hearts have already been joined and we have that spiritual connection. I am waiting to see if we are to have a physical connection too. Don't get all excited. I am not talking about sex. What I am trying to say is that if Adam is meant for me it will really happen in the physical sense, too, in what we call reality. Is this story going to end with Adam and me actually becoming an item? If so, sex will happen in the right order too. I am writing about romantic love, and sex is a natural part of that type of love. God created sex, and in the right order it is, well … yea, God! That is all I am going to say on that subject, other than I want guiltless sex—the kind I can have only after I am married. I don't want to joke around about my sex life, past or future. I don't want to embarrass my grown children by talking about it either. I guess no matter what age your children are, the idea of their mother having sex is just beyond the boundaries. I will say one thing: I know if Adam is single, I have permission to flirt. One of my pastors preached a sermon about this. I believe he would not lead me astray because he is a good shepherd. He remarked, "If you are married you need to be flirting with your spouse and no one else. You singles can flirt with each other all you want." He also said if you are living together as if you were husband and wife waiting to see if it works out before marrying, you are hanging on a dangerous cliff. If you do get married, you are at the greatest risk of having your marriage end in divorce. I'd like to add that if you are just living together with no intentions of ever getting married, you are just playing house. Even my earthly father knew the dangers of that, and he never wanted that for his precious little child.

Since God has brought so many coincidences into my life that related directly to Adam, I like to think He would not tease me unless He has a really big surprise waiting for me. Maybe this is all a test or it is going to be God's fun way to answer my prayer. In the end, I may just be that fish that got away. Maybe this book is the surprise and it is going to be used to help other singles who are waiting and wondering if they will ever find true love. However, I am hoping I will get both. It really is up to God and

Adam. God can do only so much. He gave us all free will. God would never force Adam to love me, the same way He didn't force me to love Adam. It was my choice, but I do believe God put the desire for Adam into my heart. I am the one who made a decision to act on it by admitting to it and praying about it too. I could have just denied it or buried those feelings. God just set the bait. I fell for Adam—hook, line, and sinker. I am waiting to find out if Adam fishes just for sport or if he thinks I am a good catch. All I know is the wait is killing me. I'm hoping Adam will cut me off the hook and jump on in to be with me. We can swim free, and neither one of us has to die.

Well, what do you think? Am I a woman with a love addiction, a lady in waiting, or am I just obsessed? It seems these days more men are getting addicted to pornography and more women are addicted to the idea of love. The world seems to be obsessed with sex even more than romance but, as the song goes, "What about love?" Some women believe "If only I had a husband, my life would be fulfilling." No, your life would be different, that's all. I know, at times, I want my life to be different too. I don't want to be alone so much. I want someone to share things with and someone to go places with.

I was grocery shopping the other day and thinking, *If I never grocery shop again in my life, I wouldn't miss it.* It's not that I don't like to cook, but with all those choices of brands and all the different varieties of things—such as ten types of mustard combined with ten brand names—I just about have a meltdown. There are too many choices. Just give me Heinz ketchup, because I'm from Pittsburgh. But that isn't simple anymore, either. I bought some hot and spicy ketchup by mistake one day. Really, do we need to have ketchup with a kick? I started to laugh when I went to buy toilet paper and there were so many choices within those brands too. Just make it simple, please. I want soft and lots of tissue on the roll so I don't have to keep changing the dumb thing. I live alone, and there is no one to hear me yell, "I need toilet paper." That's really why I want a husband. I tried to teach the dogs to fetch me toilet paper, but forget it. And then there is this business about driving. We won't even go there. I told my son if I don't get a husband soon, I will get a chauffeur and we can call it "driving Miss Becky."

In all seriousness, I know having a husband won't simplify my life. It probably will complicate it. In the end, this is not really about having a husband at all. It is about Adam. I want to know if this feeling I have toward him is because we love each other and we are destined to be together. Who can explain love? I just know when I think of him the feeling I have for him is familiar. I have felt this before. In spite of all I have done to rid myself of this feeling, it won't leave. That is why I have to follow my heart now and send out the invitation.

I took the Beth Moore study on The Book of Revelation in the winter of 2011. One day I was preparing for class by doing my homework assignment. During that time, I was given some insights and felt God's presence so strongly. I had told Him I was regretful that I had not studied His word more intensely over the years. Because I am getting older, I knew I would never have time to make up for all the time I had wasted. I wanted to know Him more. I wanted to really know and understand so much more of the Bible too. I wanted to dig in and learn—not just the facts, but also all the details—and have God speak to me through it. I decided to read the introduction to Beth's workbook, which I had been using for almost ten weeks. She wrote, "My worst nightmare is that I'd diligently study the Scriptures but somehow manage to keep them in my head and never let them get to my heart. The sign of a true disciple of Jesus Christ is that the study of Scripture enlarges the love of God in his or her heart. If God seems to get

smaller and our hearts colder in our Bible study, something is
grossly amiss. Thankfully God is merciful to us in our pursuits
and more than willing to revive our waning, wandering hearts"
(Beth Moore, Here Now...There and Then: A Lecture Series on
Revelation). Those words gave me such comfort. If Beth Moore,
who I admire for her commitment and her thirst to know God's
Word and share her love for Jesus, can have that fear, then I could
have my regrets. I knew that even though I have not studied the
Word as much as she has, what I have studied was enlarging the
love of God in my heart. For that one moment, I had the blessed
assurance that God sees that too. And because God loves me so,
He spoke to me through this poem that I immediately wrote
down on my homework assignment paper.

Regrets

> I said to Him that I was
> Running out of time to know Him more.
> He said, "How silly! Look at what's in store.
> You'll know all of me when we meet face-to-face.
> You will see firsthand, you'll be in this space.
> Then, to the throne room, you will come.
> You'll be free, and I'll watch you run.
> I will sit here and enjoy you.
> We will celebrate that all trouble is through.
> I know, for me you will dance and kiss my feet.
> That will make our joy complete."

That was such an awesome moment with the Lord. We had our
talk after that, and I asked him about Adam. It seems somehow
Adam's name still managed to come into our conversations at
times. I asked God to give me some clear answers so I could put
all this aside. He whispered this: "I am not going to reveal all to

you. I want you to have that excitement and anticipation about this world, as well as the next." I thought, *Okay, I will have to be satisfied with this answer.*

That very night, I went to the class I had been preparing for that day. When Beth spoke on her session ten video, she revealed a great deal about her relationship with her husband and her extended family. She talked about how she loves her husband, Keith, more than anyone in the world, and how she hates him more than anyone in the world too. Of course, it was meant to be humorous, but I understood her meaning. I, also, knew I still wanted that kind of closer-than-all relationship with a man. Beth talked about romantic love and its three stages; the first was lust, the second was attraction, and the third was attachment. In the attraction stage, it is more than carnal, physical attraction and even more than hormonal dopamine. In the attachment stage, you want to spend time remembering over and over again. It is this euphoric stage that Beth describes as when, "You are stupid." I loved that she described it that way.

I remember thinking about how many times I was acting stupid over Adam. I also thought about how he was acting that way too. I wondered how this could be. Was I really in romantic love with Adam? Had this gone beyond fantasy and infatuation? Was that why I'd been struggling so much? Did God want me to understand that relationship for some reason? Or was this just taking place so that I would be able to understand Beth's comparisons that being in heaven with Jesus will be similar to the euphoria we feel when we are in the beginning stages of romantic love—but, unlike romantic love, this feeling will last for eternity. I wondered if God had me feeling that euphoria so I could understand Beth's study and be able to easily relate to what she was saying since this feeling was so fresh in my mind and soul. She made a remark that took my breath away. She said when she first met her husband, there was an attraction—oh, what an attraction. Then she said he was engaged. She didn't say anything else, but she just repeated that there was this attraction. It was the tone of her voice that said it all. I thought of my situation. I had to wonder why God would allow me to hear these words on the very day I questioned Him again about Adam, even after I thought I'd put all of these questions to rest a few months prior. God knew how much those words would speak to my situation. Then I wondered if He purposely arranged for me to hear them exactly on this very day. God, why do I feel like every time I'm getting over Adam, something keeps this dream going? That is what I do not understand. God, why would you tease me? I do think this chapter of my life is not completely over, but I sense it is getting closer to the end … or to the beginning.

I hadn't been thinking and obsessing over Adam as much. I mailed him a signed copy of my first book. I actually included a little note I'd written, and I was feeling a sense of closure and calmness about it. Just for fun, I did spray my perfume on the page where I talked about the stranger, referencing the first time I meet Adam. I did it, too, I guess as a reminder—as if he needed to smell my perfume to remind him of our first meetings. I admit I debated about doing it and felt a little naughty. Then I asked God to forgive me if it was wrong. After I did, I just laughed and had no sense of guilt in the matter. It was just my fun way to get sweet revenge, or maybe it was more like a prompting. Either way, no harm done, because I trusted God would be there with Adam when he read page 192 in that book.

In the afterword of that book, I wrote that I hoped people would take a second look at Jesus and fall in love with Him. Maybe, in some small way, I hoped that Adam would take a second look at me when he read my first book and fall in love with me too. Maybe I wanted to drive Adam a little crazy wondering if he really smelled my perfume or just imagined it. I laughed because I believed he would get my drift that I was teasing him and being playful. It was just meant for old time's sake and not in any way as a mean-spirited gesture. Part of me thought, *If he really can't forget me, then this will give him a little encouragement that I still can't forget about him either.* I believed God saw it that way too. Maybe, if nothing came of it, I would finally get it through my head that the boy had indeed made up his mind that I was not in his future plans. I told myself to not look into his eyes when I went to see him and just look at his nose. I laughed as I thought about his nose, but somehow even the thought of his nose doesn't stop me from dreaming about him. Only God could take this desire for Adam out of my heart, because I truly believe God is the one who put it there.

I prayed that if Adam and I don't end up together, God would at least restore my reputation. I hope to be seen as a woman who brought her every want and need to God. Then again, I know God sees me that way—and, in the end, that is all that matters. For those of you who may be experiencing a similar fate, I want to encourage you to bring everything before God. That is what I believe God has shown me through this time of struggle. I heard him say, "Surrender all of your life to me. I want every part of you. Hold nothing back." When I do this, I never feel alone. I know God is with me, and all will be well.

Tick Tock

*T*t was early in the month of May 2011. I had returned to Indiana from my winter home in South Carolina. This would be the first time I was to see Adam after sending him my perfume-laced book. I told God I was not going to ask Adam anything about the book. I wasn't going to ask if he had read it or what he'd thought about it. I wasn't even going to ask if he'd received it. In my heart, regardless of whether he said anything or not, I believed he would like the book. I just wasn't sure if he would be comfortable discussing it with me. I said to God, "If Adam wants to talk about it, he will have to bring up the subject." I told myself, *If he doesn't talk about it, I'll be fine because I'll consider this to be the closure I'm expecting. I'll know that the purpose for Adam and I meeting is complete. I will move forward.*

I stood in the exact same spot where one year before Adam had waved his hands high in the air to get my attention. This time I was looking down because I was signing a copy of my book to give to the receptionist.

When I heard his voice, I looked up and saw Adam briskly walking toward me as he announced for all to hear, "It's a good book. I read it. I bought one." I knew he had heard my voice, and that was why he came from what seemed like out of nowhere to start this conversation. Then he accompanied me back down the hall like he had done so many times before. He directed me to his office, as if I didn't know my way. He still didn't say my name. I noticed he had stopped saying it after things became awkward between us. I always loved hearing the way he said Rebecca. Even though he doesn't say my name anymore, I know he hasn't forgotten it.

I don't know why it shocked me that Adam would make such a loud announcement for all to hear, pronouncing the book good. As we walked down the hall, I was processing what he had said. I had noticed that he made three distinctive short statements. I thought, *He wants me to know he bought a copy of my book.* I had thought perhaps he might mention the book and would simply thank me for the copy I sent him or he would say something favorable about a part of the book he liked. I never anticipated this reaction. He was over-the-top talking about the book in this steady voice that sounded unfamiliar to me. He let it slip out that he had just met a woman who, coincidently, knew me. He kind of mumbled to himself, saying he needed to remember to give her a copy too. Although, I heard every word he said, I couldn't believe he was saying this.

We talked about how I might know her, and I finally said, "I have no idea who she is."

Adam said, "Well, she knows you. She knows all about you."

I pictured him talking to her and thought maybe he was talking about me to other people too. That is when I thought he was not only sweet, but perhaps I was right that he was, also, smitten by me. I think the woman who accompanied us into the office might have sensed that too.

Adam was going on and on about the book, and we interacted to the point of, well, nausea. Adam talked about ways I could promote the book. He listed who he thought would be my target audience. At one point, in the middle of all of this, he interjected that we better take care of business by stating, "That's why you're here." It was only half true. I think all three of us could agree on that. So we took care of the business at hand, which only took a few minutes. Then, the conversation was off and running about the book again.

Adam said, "Some people say they are writing a book but never do. Some write a book, but the story isn't even true. Some people actually steal another person's idea and pawn it off as their own work. And then there are those books by famous people that end up selling, and some of those stories aren't even that good. Your book is good."

He went on to imply that he believed every word of it too. I had another copy of the book in my purse, so I got it out to show the woman who was listening and watching us. That is when Adam grabbed it from me. I'm used to him doing these things with me, and it is what lets me know how comfortable he is with me.

As he held the book in his hands, he said, "The cover is so good—the picture, the color—and what you wrote on the back cover is good." He rubbed his hand over the front cover as he pronounced it good. Then he turned it over and rubbed the back of the book. The book does have a rather silky texture. I can understand why a touchy person might like to rub it and enjoy the feel of it. I was giggling inside as I watched his hand go across my face—well, the picture of my face that appears on the back cover. I felt as if he was caressing me. I felt the excitement. Hopefully, I was able to hide this in my expression.

Adam continued on, saying, "Everything is good, the cover and every word is good." He ruffled the pages and repeated, "Every word is good, really," and he emphasized the word *every*.

I remember thinking, *Does this mean he loves Jesus, too?* I knew the most important message of the book was my love for Jesus and my belief in His power to heal both physical and emotional wounds.

At this point, I showed Adam some letters I'd received from a few professional people who had read the book. One of the letters Adam read was from the judge who presided over George's malpractice lawsuit. Adam took his time reading the judge's letter that was sent to me in response to me sending her a copy of the book as my way to say "thank you." After reading her comments about not only my testimony at George's malpractice trial but also her compliment to my writing style being as warm, sincere, and compelling as my words were on the stand, Adam simply said, "Beautiful." It was the exact same word I had said out loud as I sat in my study all alone and read that letter for the first time the day it had arrived.

Adam also read letters from two of my husband's doctors. One doctor wrote that he remembered George as a person who battled cancer with such dignity. The other letter was from a doctor who is a professor of medicine at this prestigious university where George received some of his medical treatments. In the book I referred to this doctor as a "special person." That doctor wrote me a letter and stated, "Thank you for sending me a copy of your book and your accompanying note. A very touching and lasting way to acknowledge a special person and the gift of faith." Adam's responded to the letter by saying, "Sweet." I agreed that this doctor is just that, and I was thinking, *Adam, you are sweet too.* When I first read the letter all I could think was George's doctor referred to himself as a "special person," so I know he had read the book. I might have shared that thought with Adam. I don't remember. I was too rattled to remember everything that I said that day. I do remember thinking the doctor understands the spiritual gifts too. When he pronounced the book a gift of faith, I was pleased because I sensed he knew the Holy Spirit had given me that gift. It is the gift of faith that points to God's power and the belief that He is the living and active God.

By now, I would say I wasn't in what I call "the garden" with Adam anymore; I was floating on a cloud. It was the pinnacle moment for me. I had all the earthly and spiritual recognition I ever needed to know that writing that book was indeed good. I had the acknowledgments from the judge at our trial and two of the doctors who were so special to me. Now I also had this encouragement from the man I believed God gave me, pronouncing the book good. In that moment, I felt loved. I could tell I was starting to lose control of my ability to remain calm, but I wasn't prepared for what would eventually happen.

Adam talked about how to promote the book. He mentioned he thought my book would make a wonderful Hallmark movie and suggested I try to send it to someone at Hallmark. He stated he thought that Christian bookstores would be another good place to have my book available. He also mentioned I might want to do a book signing at our local Borders Bookstore. While he was making these suggestions he looked at the printouts of my promotional materials that I showed him. I told him that I was in the process of editing them. I shared how overwhelmed I was feeling now that the book was in print. He said, "Just make your list." I was in the process of doing just that, and I wondered how he knew that. It was just another one of those moments when we connected without saying much. I know he could sense that I hadn't a clue about what to do next to launch that book or even where to start to promote it, for that matter. I told him it had been a while since I had written the text for those promotional materials, and I no longer even remembered what I was ordering. He was helpful and explained that he thought one was for bookmarks, another looked like my business card, and the third was for postcards. He thought the fourth one might have been a display poster or banner, but later I realized it was just the picture for one side of the bookmark. That did give me an idea that I might want to invest in some type of a board to use for the display table at the book signings. As Adam looked over these printouts, he even noticed the tiny letter "a" I had added at the end of my name. I had corrected the spelling with a black pen. I was surprised that it stood out to him among all the other words on the pages, because I didn't think it was that noticeable. It reminded me about how Adam hadn't notice my age on that paper that clearly stated it. This entire exchange reinforced in my mind that Adam does have an eye for details. It confirmed my theory that God hid my age from Adam. After looking over all my material Adam said, "Don't forget to go back on the computer and fix that before you send it back." I was able to see how much Adam wanted to help me with this book.

I thanked him for his suggestions and mentioned that I didn't want to keep any profits from the sale of the book. I sensed that he believed me the very first time I expressed that to him. He said not to worry about whether or not the book sold at retail. I was working up to offering to give him a book to give to the woman who, coincidently, already knew me, so he wouldn't have to buy another book. I told him I had bought one thousand books at a good price using the author's discount. I think that was when I shared my idea of promoting the book by giving away one thousand books. I didn't get a chance to tell him directly that I would be more than happy to give him some books to give out to others, but I was trying to get that across to him. Even though I wasn't saying this clearly, I thought Adam knew what I meant just as much as I understood his previous comments about him promoting my book. He knew why I wrote that first book. He understood it was to get the message out there to encourage those battling cancer or struggling with other trials in life. I thought perhaps he understood it was also to let people know what to pray if the Holy Spirit moved them to accept Jesus as Lord and Savior. He said, "Wouldn't you rather make one dollar on one million books than five hundred thousand dollars on one book? I know what I want." I believe I understood what Adam was saying. He was saying, "You want a million people to read this story, don't you? I want the same thing." He also was saying, "I am trying to help you by telling people about your book."

At this point in the conversation, I told him I wanted to start a nonprofit and name it "Love One Another." He held two of his fingers close to my lips, and I understood his gesture. Even though his fingers never touched me, I felt as if he had tenderly touched my lips as he said, "We'll talk about that later." I just thought, "Someone pinch me." His comment also made me wonder if he was seeing us together in the future.

The woman in the office with us kept looking at Adam when I did and then she'd look back at me. She was smiling from ear to ear, and every so often she was laughing a little too. I know she saw how Adam and I related to each other and how we connected in this bizarre way. I know she could hear me dropping some hints to Adam about my dreams, and I wondered how much she sensed that I wanted him to be included in those dreams. What I noticed most was she was getting a kick out of seeing Adam remain so steady even in the midst of some of the funny things I was saying. I made a joke about going to Las Vegas to launch my book and said the headlines in the newspaper would read, "Christian Woman Comes to Vegas for a Quickie—a Quick Way to Get Her Book Noticed." Adam never cracked a smile. At first,

I wasn't sure if it went unnoticed, but later I doubt that it did because of the comment he made about all the pornography that is so deeply piled up on the streets of Vegas. When he said that and motioned how high the literature was piled on the sidewalks, I had already had a vision of him doing that exact same gesture. I told him I had already thought about that, too, and I didn't want my book about my husband to be thrown on the sidewalks with all that pornography. I didn't dare tell him about my vision or the fact that I thought he was the one who would accompany me to Vegas to promote my book. I told him I would love to give the book out and compete with all those who were passing out pornographic literature. In all honesty, if any book would be the one to pass out in Vegas, this would be the one that would be most suited for such a launch. Vegas is known as a place some people go to look for sex, but true love is really what we all want.

I eventually had the uncontrolled giggles that day. It was another time I experienced holy laughter. As Adam was talking to me, I was talking to God. I said, "Yes, God, Adam is sweet and steady."

A while back I had taken a seminar at my church called "The Leaders Potential." We were learning about personality types. I had wondered if Adam was an "S" personality. Some characteristics of type "S" are stable, shy, servant, security oriented, conservative, reflective, good listener, patient, empathetic, loyal team worker, and friendly. "S" types also are resistant to change. I had asked God if that was Adam's personality type and if we would complement each other. The more Adam spoke in that unmistakably steady voice as he encouraged me and gave suggestions on how I might promote my book the more I was laughing with God and letting God know I understood the answer to that question was yes Adam is an "S" type, sweet and steady. It was as if God was answering so many questions I had previously asked him—from Adam liking my book, to him being someone that would help me promote it, to seeing his "S" personality features surface—I was just in awe. It was a moment God showed me that He could reveal whatever He wanted me to know about Adam. I could see how honestly interested Adam was in what was going on for me. I was so excited to tell him all about the coincidences that led me to believe God was involved with my writing. I knew, in that moment, that Adam shared in my dreams for my book to be used to reach others. I knew when he read the book I was about to give him, *When God Winks at You* by SQuire Rushnell, how the book would tie it all together. Adam would understand and see the coincidence of the coincidences, so to speak.

When I finally gave Adam the book by Rushnell, which explained the term godwinks (God sightings), he asked, "Did you read this?"

I answered him, "Of course, I did. I have one too."

As he walked away reading the note I had written inside the book, he simply declared, "Good."

He said it in a way as if to say, "Things are moving along according to the plan." I knew he would find joy in knowing we both had the same book. It was just one more piece of paper that would bind us together. I couldn't help but wonder if he still had the three letters I'd sent him. It didn't matter. I knew he held every word on them in his heart.

When I was in Adam's office, I watched this scene all play out. I felt so out of control because I felt so much that God was in control. That is why I eventually could only giggle. I watched the expression on the face of the woman I affectionately referred to as "Green Bean." She is tall and slender, built the way I long ago wished I looked before I accepted myself as being the way God designed me. I watched her watch Adam and me together. I saw her smile. It was another one of my dreams come true. She was every woman seeing Adam and I together and seeing us interact. It was a preview of my dream of the day Adam and I would stand on the stage of the Women of Faith. This book would be the catalyst that brings us there. Adam and I would tell our story, but in the end, we really would just talk to each other. Everyone would see our love for each other and how we are so well matched. We would share this unique story of how God brought us together through the books He called me to write. The audience would see how it all fit into God's plan. Women would see that when God destines you to be together, it happens. It would provide hope for all the women longing for that romantic love that God created them to desire too. It would be obvious that when God destined it to be, nothing could stand in the way of his plan. The message would be that God provides everything. All you need to do is pray, walk in faith, and believe. If you have faith that God arranged it all and rest in that belief, God is pleased. What seems impossible—even when it seems as if we are star-crossed lovers or unlucky—with God what is meant to be will be. Nothing can stop His plan. If God destined for Adam and me to be together, God will make the arrangements. He will also make his message clear if that is what He wants accomplished. I believe God is saying, "You just need to do it my way, the right way, and not manipulate, use sex, trap, plan, or deceive in order to find love. All you need to do is love, and love will find its own way."

I see that God had this planned all along. Because I now understand the way He uniquely designed me, it helped me believe I was made for such a purpose as this. He made me in such a way that this would all fit together for me to not only document what happened between Adam and me but also for me to use my gifts as a means to accomplish God's purpose. I only needed to be willing and to trust that this is a God thing. He supplied everything to help build my faith and trust in Him. He prepared each step.

I don't think Adam is going to be that surprised by this either. I'll bet God is working on him too. I know Adam knows me pretty well. He knows I was destined to write. He knows I am bold when I believe it is something God wants me to do. Adam also knows when I am around him I get tongue-tied. He'll understand I had to write what I couldn't find the words to say. Besides, if I took up all his time at work to tell him all that's in my heart, he would surely get fired. He may actually be wondering why it took me so long to get this book published, because I told him before that I don't like to waste time. He also knows I have the tendency to be a little impulsive, which is part of my "I" personality type: interactive, influencer, and a creative problem solver. When added to my spiritual gifts of faith, encouragement, and giving, it's the perfect combination to be a writer. I take no credit; it's the way God created me to be.

My first book is about the dream that came true when George lived such a long and blessed life because God destined it. I couldn't tell Adam that I believe this book is a foretelling of the life God has destined for me for the second half of my life. I couldn't explain how I want to live a life of significance, and that I hope Adam will be that person of significance in my life too. I couldn't share how I believe God presented Adam to me, but that doubt and fear interfered with the natural progression. How could I ever tell Adam I see us as the Ruth and Boaz of the twenty-first century?

I showed Adam the business cards I was carrying and explained that I believed they were signs that God was making the arrangements behind the scenes. The business card from a woman that works at the Women of Faith was on the top of the pile, which was held together with a heart-shaped money clip. Adam grabbed the cards out of my hand and took off the clip that held them together. He began to read each card in the group. What man does this with a woman he hardly knows? Adam took his time and read each card, one by one, as I explained their importance to me. I told him about my dream of being a published author with Thomas Nelson. As he looked through the business cards I explained the connection I had with the woman who works for the Women of Faith a division of Thomas Nelson. I shared that it was just one more coincidence that keeps me believing God is going to promote my book. Then I told Adam how I had gone to a church in South Carolina to see the Christian singer Mandisa perform and that this woman who's business card I now had was working behind the scene at the concert that night although I didn't know it at the time. She actually used to be a member of that church where Mandisa performed but now she belongs to my church. I explained that someone at my church introduced us and that was how I ended up with her business card. Next, Adam read the card that has my favorite Bible verse, Jeremiah 29:11, on it and I told him about the connection between those cards. Then Adam saw the card from my therapist, and he carefully studied it. I was quiet, but I couldn't help but think about how I had blurted it out that I was in therapy just a few minutes earlier. It was a good thing I had already told him that or it could have been a very awkward moment for both of us. Somehow, when he saw the card, I knew God had prepared the way for that too. I didn't feel embarrassed, and I didn't feel the need to explain it to him either. I knew if I ever gave him this book I was writing, he would understand it all. And besides, how could I explain it, especially under the circumstance. I did tell him I was overwhelmed. It's a little overwhelming when God keeps showing up in all these coincidences. I just wanted to be sure I was sane and in reality.

Could I tell Adam that my therapist's first day at the agency was the day I went there the first time too? Could I tell Adam that Ralph is a Christian, although the agency is a secular one? I knew this the first time I saw him, because of the cross that hangs from the chain he wears around his neck. I wanted to tell Adam that Ralph said, "God is providing all these coincidences because He is encouraging you with this relationship regarding Adam," but I couldn't. I couldn't tell Adam that my therapist thinks Adam left me stuck because he doesn't want to let me go.

I wanted to tell Adam how my therapist had jokingly said, "Give me Adam's number. I am going to call him and tell him, 'For therapeutic reasons, I need to know if you have feelings for Rebecca. I need to know the truth so I can treat her.'"

My daughter was right when she said, "Going to a therapist is really just like paying a friend to listen and keep your secrets."

I don't think I would have chosen to go to a male therapist, but now I see that God truly planned this all out too. My therapist gave me a man's prospective on the situation. He suggested that perhaps Adam isn't saying anything because I do see him professionally, and he realizes he can't mix work and personal relationships. My therapist offered up that he, himself, is single but wears a wedding ring just to keep boundaries with some of his women patients because he isn't allowed to date his patients. Then, he asked if I was sure Adam knew how I felt about him. I said, "Yeah, he should. I wrote to him three times." It made me stop and think, *Maybe Adam doesn't know how I feel about him. I have been sending him some mixed message. How could he know how I feel about him when I am still trying to figure those feeling out myself?* I wondered what my therapist thought my feelings were for Adam. I do love him with a Christ like love, but am I in love with him? Doesn't it take two to really be in love?

I gave my therapist a copy of the manuscript and told him, "If my dream comes true, I'll sign a release of information form so my records can prove it was a foretelling. If not, we could coauthor a book about a woman obsessed." We do get silly, but Ralph also gives me encouragement to take charge of the situation. He tells me that I have great analytical thinking skills too. That reminds me, I need to schedule an appointment. I have several more God sightings to share with him. He just loves to hear about them. I think he is even a little jealous that God winks at me so much.

I told my therapist about my plan to send the invitation to the book signing to Adam. I thought that would be a way for us to meet and talk outside the office. I said, "If he doesn't come, maybe I will finally get past this feeling that there is more to this relationship." I was backsliding on the idea of giving Adam the book.

After I left the office, I went home and wrote a little note inviting Adam to my first book signing. He was the one who encouraged me to go to Borders, and that led to the opportunity to do my first signing. I mailed the invitation, but I honestly didn't think he would show up.

I received a text from someone a few days after I mailed the invitation to Adam. The text simply read *Yo*. It reminded me of the day Adam came out into the waiting room and said "whoa or yo." I wasn't sure which, but "whoa" went with the idea of "hold your horses," so I used it when I wrote that into the silly story about the day I knew Adam was surprised to see me. Remembering what transpired that day helped put me into a playful mood. So I sent a text back to the person who, coincidently, had a Pittsburgh 412 area code. I wrote, *Do I know yo?* A text was returned saying, *Dis Deja*. I thought that meant this is Deja, but later I realized the person was asking me if I was Deja. I just thought, *Yes déjà vu*. Of course, that was more of a connection to Adam. Then I laughed because I thought about how this text, obviously sent by mistake, was one more thing God arranged so that I would lighten up and enjoy this adventure. I totally forgot all about these texts I'd been sent on June 11, 2011, until I rode passed my church on Wednesday, October 26, and spotted the signage in front of my church that read "Who sent the text?" Although the sermon was about the text of the Bible, the signage prompted my memory about my text messages. I took it as a personal message from God to me. He was confirming the idea that He was personally involved in helping me write this book. I still had that text saved on my phone too. I kept it as a reminder of how God can do the impossible, even down to a silly little note that would remind me not only of Adam but, more importantly, of how God is encouraging and guiding me. God was sending me a silly little love note He knew would mean something special to me.

This leads me right into the reason I titled this chapter "Tick Tock." This God sighting happened soon after Adam failed to show up at my book signing. Adam being a no-show led me to vacillate all the more over giving him the manuscript. Regardless of my decision on any given day or moment, I continued to work on the book because I wanted to get it published. It is written for Adam, but I thought Adam might see a selfish motivation behind me writing it. I theorized it might be seen as a form of manipulation too. That is when I realized that this was stinking thinking. God had been involved all along. Besides, telling Adam I have feelings for him isn't manipulation.

When I researched some information about fairy tales, I happened on a book titled, *Kurt Schwitters Lucky Hans and Other Merz Fairy Tales*. Peter Read's review written for the *Times Literary Supplement* and found on the Princeton University Press website stated, "Schwitters's *Merz Fairy Tales* are lies that speak the truth." I thought that was quite an ironic statement considering my situation with Adam and my desire to know the truth in his lie. I found the title and the introduction to the book intriguing, so I ordered it. As you follow along, you will see why I have no doubt God wanted me to have this book.

It is Schwitters who came up with the name Merz and describes its meaning this way. "Merz is a standpoint that everyone can use. It is from this standpoint that all people can consider not only art, but also, all things, that is, the world. For me, Merz has become a world view." (Kurt Schwitter, *Lucky Hans and Other Merz Fairy Tales*) This is true for me too. When Schwitters goes on to explain his three requirements to the Merz standpoint, I was in total amazement because I was in total agreement. The fact that I had been thinking these same concepts prior to reading the Merz philosophy was utterly astonishing to me. It was my confirmation that God wanted me to have this fairy tale book because He knew exactly what it would mean to me. Schwitters goes on to say that "Human beings cannot create anything in accordance with the spirit of the almighty divinity. They cannot create nothing out of nothing, rather they can merely create out of definite givens, out of definite material. The act of human creating is only a process of forming that which is given." (Kurt Schwitters, *Lucky Hans and Other Merz Fairy Tales*) That is the exact philosophy I have about my writing. I cannot write what God has not given me. He supplies all the material, especially since I write about my life and my relationship with Him. I cannot write anything new that God does not already know. I will take this a step further and say, I am not the creator. I merely report what God has given to me. In other words, I take dictation and then get it into print. This is so funny because when I went to school for my degree in secretarial science, I was not able to write in shorthand or type that well either. When I went for my degree in health information technology, it was only by the grace of God that I passed my transcription class. I was blessed when I took an evening class. That part-time teacher was so lenient; I never would have passed otherwise.

The second point Schwitters writes about is "Perfection (completeness) cannot be attained by human beings." (Kurt Schwitters, *Lucky Hans and Other Merz Fairy Tales*) Considering I had already written the chapter about Adam and Eve, this statement just confirmed that I was on the right track. I was indeed following God's lead about what He wanted me to share with you when I wrote this book.

The last point Schwitters made was this: "In his work the artist seeks to strive only for that which he can attain. Added to that comes the serious striving to make everything so good, so honest, so open and so logical as possible. The result from all this is Merz." (Kurt Schwitters, *Lucky Hans and Other Merz Fairy Tales*) I knew God wanted me to read this because it described me to a T. When the fairy tale book came across my path, it provided one more concrete, tangible way for God to show He really is personally involved in my life. I knew the instant I read this, God has been with me every step of the way. This book has the power of the Holy Spirit in it for me; it is personal and affirming. "Merz is the smile at the grave and seriousness on cheerful occasions." (Kurt Schwitters, *Lucky Hans and Other Merz Fairy Tales*) I had the opportunity to smile at my husband's funeral service when I read a poem I had written and dedicated to him. I experienced the seriousness on cheerful occasions each time I saw Adam at his work and had to wear my "poker face." Several times the song "Poker Face" by Lady Gaga came on the radio at the exact time I pulled into my parking spot at Adam's workplace. It helped me get all my laughter out before I had to go in and act serious.

I don't know if you will be able to understand the depth to which the book *Lucky Hans and Other Merz Fairy Tales* connected me to God and Adam. Adam would because he knew from reading my first book that I was inspired by God to write it. He knew I would not have been able to write it without God. Adam understood I wanted that first book to be so good, so honest, so open, and so logical because I wanted it to give glory to God. It is the same for this book. Adam knows the connection we had through not only my first book but also all of the books that were brought to us along the path. I gave Adam a copy of the book *Lucky Hans and Other Merz Fairy Tales*; I knew it would touch his heart in a special way too. It was written in Germany around the time his parents lived there. The fact that is was translated and introduced by Jack Zipes in 2009, the year Adam and I met, is purely just another coincidence—along with the fact that the author of the fairy tales died in 1948, the year I was born. It is just one more set of things that have a special and silly meaning. You know, 1948, the year Adam never noticed on those papers I gave to him. I included a note with the book when I gave it to Adam. I shared my two favorite fairy tales with him. Of course, I have a copy of this book too. My grandchildren enjoyed it when I read some of the fairy tales to them. Robert's favorite was titled "An Old Fairy Tale." It began, "This is a gruesome fairy tale, but it also happened very long ago." (Kurt Schwitters, *Lucky Hans and Other Merz Fairy Tales*) It is gruesome, and that was exactly why Robert and Marie laughed when I read it. I was surprised they didn't have nightmares, but they understood it was not a true story.

One of my favorite fairy tales is titled, "The Swineherd and the Great, Illustrious Writer." (Kurt Schwitters, *Lucky Hans and Other Merz Fairy Tales*) The characters are the swineherd, the illustrious writer, and the peasant maiden. The writer asks the swineherd if he is indeed happy. He replies, "I am indeed, serene and also content, but I'm not happy. Oh, if only I were a fairy-tale prince! Just think how many swineherds are the children of royalty! How many!" The swineherd points to his Bible, and the swineherd reads about the children of royalty. The writer is so moved, he puts the swineherd right in the middle of his masterwork, his very best fairy tale. Though now a prince, the swineherd still isn't happy, so the writer gives him a lovely little woman, a peasant maiden, to help him tend the pigs. It isn't enough just to have her with him; the Swineherd is still not happy. He falls in love with the peasant maiden and can't take his eyes off of her. He was happy at the first kiss. Now he decides he wants to marry her, but she isn't royalty. She is just a peasant girl, so he cannot marry her. The writer and the swineherd argue, and the swineherd wants to give up being a son of the king. The writer says to the swineherd, "How can I let the king, your honorable father, become a beggar at the end of my masterwork and reduce him to the father of a mere swineherd?" The swineherd not only lost his happiness, he was no longer content or serene. He no longer had any peace of mind. In the end, the writer not only takes the peasant girl out of the story, he writes the swineherd out of it too. Then the writer and the swineherd go off to tend the pigs together. The swineherd says to the writer, "Come, sit down beside me. We'll tend the pigs, you and me. We'll eat, drink, sleep, lie in the sun, and our entire concern will be the welfare of the pigs. That's not happiness, but it is serenity and peace of mind." When I read this fairy tale, I wondered if I was trading my serenity and peace of mind to chase after a dream about living happily ever after with a man. That was why I wanted to have a husband who not only knows Jesus but also believes God arranged for us to be together because he wants to bless us and have us be a blessing to others too.

After I read this fairy tale, I said to God, "I have to give Adam my manuscript. It is the only way I am going to be set free." It is just as the fairy tale "The Swineherd and the Great, Illustrious Writer" implies: "'Swineherd,' said the writer, 'you are wiser than I am. Why should a man run after happiness? There's no happiness that lasts longer than a moment. Give me some of your serenity, something from your peace of mind, and I won't want to be happy anymore.'" (Kurt Schwitters, *Lucky Hans and Other Merz Fairy*

Tales) I concluded that maybe God gave me that answer through the words in this fairy tale. I just need the courage to do what I believe He is telling me to do. Then I will have serenity and peace of mind. I may not be happy, but that is the risk I think I need to take.

I had so many questions: Is this the place I'm at in my life? Are serenity and peace of mind what I need most? Is giving this book to Adam my pathway to peace? Is that the way to let go and let God? I had thought letting go meant doing nothing. I began to realize that maybe letting go means not holding on to this book and the past. Maybe it was time to release it and move forward. The rest would be up to God. Was this one of those times I was to act? Maybe my idea of doing nothing was wrong, and God was telling me it was the opposite of what I had been thinking. Just the thought of giving this book to Adam helped me feel at peace. Did I have the courage, strength, and security to do just that? With God's help, I knew I would be able to do this, surrendering all to God, knowing He will be there for me no matter how things end.

Another of the fairy tales inspired the title of this chapter. I found "The Little Spirit Clock and the Lovers" fascinating. This one was about lovers in a bug-ridden garden where a large clock lived, far from the city. "A pair of lovers, a young man and woman, came there, and they didn't hear the ticking: 'tick tock' and 'tick tock.' They loved each other very much in the month of May when the lilacs were blooming and a thousand smells perfumed the air." (Kurt Schwitters, *Lucky Hans and Other Merz Fairy Tales*) Eventually the man noticed the clock ticking. He used his long cane to send the little clock spirit to flight, and the pendulum stood still. The fairy tale ended when the young woman gave the young man a long kiss.

This fairy tale spoke to me too. Adam didn't notice the clock ticking. He did nothing to move forward, and I was stuck in time too. I was no closer to knowing the truth. I was still confused and longed to move forward. I still hoped that one day I would be able to give him that kiss I was longing to share.

I looked at these as fairy tales and wondered if my life for the last several years had been the same thing, nothing more than a fantasy or fairy tale. I thought of the Bible and how some don't believe it either. That is the difference. I do believe in the Bible and in God's promises. "Delight yourself in the Lord, and he will give you the desires of your heart" (Psalms 37:4). I can live a life of peace and serenity knowing I do the will of God. I have found my purpose: to write and share the Good News that Jesus died so we may have life and have it abundantly. I can have happiness too. As long as I have a husband who also wants to do what he trusts God destined for him, I will be able to have it all. I want a husband that has royalty in his bloodline. I want him to be the son of the King. If I have that, I will have the whole field—just like Ruth. Adam, are you the son of the King, and am I the woman you long to kiss? I know the garden is bug ridden and sin happens. We don't live in a perfect world. We surely aren't perfect people. But when we have the love of Christ that forgives, we can defeat Satan and live in that garden and playfully work together. We can fulfill our destiny.

There have been so many more godwinks lately; I'd like to share some of them with you to show just how relentless God can be. I went to Border's Bookstore one Sunday after church to see what books I might find at their going-out-of-business sale. I was looking in the religion section, and I started to talk to a couple of women there. I told them a little about doing my first book signing at the store. I joked and said, "Now, Border's is going out of business."

One woman asked me what my book was about, and I told her a little about that first book. Then I told her about this book. I spoke a little about how I had written it last year but was working on some finishing touches. One of the women was very interested in this story. She wanted to know how I came to believe I was meant to write it. I told her some of the details of why I thought God wanted me to write this story. I shared that I believed it was meant for other women who were obsessed like me—they think they have met their Boaz and want to know how to discern if it is true. I told her I was waiting on God and didn't want to act on my feelings without knowing what God wanted me to do. I also told her I'd been praying about this for some time.

She smiled and said, "I am a pastor of a church in the area. I'm here, coincidently, because my church had no electricity this morning."

We found out why: the power was at Borders. We joked that we were having church here today.

Then she said, "I believe God has an anointing on you to write this book. I have many women at my church who could benefit from reading this book. Many are seeking to find their Boaz and going about it in the wrong way."

After stopping at my car to get a few copies of my first book I followed her back to her car and handed her some of the books. I signed copies for both the women and gave a few extras to the pastor to give to those she believed were meant to read the book.

The woman who was with her said, "I don't believe this—I saw someone reading your book just this week."

I asked, "Are you sure it was this book?"

She replied, "Oh yes, I'm sure. I recognize the cover. I am positive it was your book."

We ended our time together by praying, and the pastor laid hands on me and prayed this second book of mine would soon be finished and be published so other women could be helped by it. I left them and reflected on how God had destined our time together too. This was just one more amazing piece of this puzzle. I forget just how many pieces have appeared so far. As I write this story, it helps me see the big picture too.

After the two women left, I went back into Border's to look around. That is when I found the book *Captivating*, written by John and Stasi Eldredge. I took my new book and went out to lunch at Panera Bread café. It was fascinating to read Stasi's description of how God designed women to desire romance. I also read her reference about little girls and their love of fairy tales. I thought about what I had written in this book and how we had both referred to Adam and Eve and also the use of fairy tales to show how little girls love romance and want to feel beautiful. This book confirmed that the Holy Spirit is working in others besides me and that God does indeed want us to share what He places on our hearts. It reinforced the idea that God placed this desire for Adam in me, and it was an indication that my heart was healed. When Stasi wrote, "God gave Eve a beautiful form and a beautiful spirit. She expresses beauty in both. Better, she expresses beauty simply in who she is. Like God, it is her essence." Stasi goes on to say, "Beauty may be the most powerful thing on earth. Beauty speaks. Beauty invites. Beauty nourishes. Beauty comforts. Beauty inspires. Beauty is transcendent. Beauty draws us near to God." (John and Stasi Eldredge, *Captivating, Unveiling the Mystery of a Woman's Soul*). It longs for heaven and the eternal. When I read how she described beauty, I could relate. Adam makes me feel beautiful when he looks at me. I know I am feeling the way

God created me to feel. Even though this feeling may only be a glimpse of what it will be like one day, it has been wonderful to have this experience, if only for a brief moment. George helped me feel this way too, because I could see his love for me when he looked at me. We can only imagine how it will be when we see God face-to-face and have Him bring out all of our beauty when we are with Him for eternity. There are moments when I sense God wants me to know that I am His beautiful creation, and I look for the day when I will be with Him forever.

This book just confirmed that no matter how things end between Adam and me, these good feelings I have about myself are the way God intended for me to feel. He wanted me to know I am lovable. Being in touch with that part of myself is healthy. When a woman's heart is not hurting or hardened, her natural desire is to feel beautiful and have a longing to be known and be in an intimate relationship. It was so amazing that I found the book *Captivating* among all those books in the store and that God would present it to me in His perfect timing. I think I was meant to read it. It was no accident that it was still there, sitting on the shelf, even though many of the books were already sold out. I knew God wanted me to have it so I would know He sees me as His beautiful creation. I know I am a new creation in Christ, and I am that much closer to being the person I was meant to be from the beginning of creation. So even when I feel sad because I am alone, I know all those desires will be satisfied in the life to come. It gives me hope that some of them might yet be satisfied in this life too. I just have to wait and see whom God has for me. When Adam told me I looked really good, I believed Adam saw me as being beautiful. If I am right and God placed that desire for me in his heart, we will both know God arranged it for the two of us. Whether more develops between Adam and me or not, it has been wonderful to be awakened to the possibility of love. That confirms to me that I am indeed past my grief and feeling joy.

As I sat at Panera Bread alone reading my new book and eating my salad, I looked up and I couldn't believe my eyes. Across from me, I saw a man reading a book titled *Tick Tock*. Of course, I started to giggle. I thought of my favorite fairy tale. It was as if God was saying, "Enjoy all that I have for you, because you are my beautiful princess. I want you to know I am here with you." Yes, God had joined me for lunch. He listened and knew all that I was feeling in my heart. He was that attentive lover. I was enjoying every bit of this romantic adventure I was having with Him.

Some of you may think this can't get any stranger. If you believe that God will find a way to reach you and supply all, it just seems natural. All I could think when I saw the book *Tick Tock* was, *What are the chances of this?* Like my grandson Robert might say, one in a gazillion. I knew, without a doubt, God did it for me.

A few weeks later, I took Marie and Robert to see the movie *Spy Kids*. For those of you that haven't seen it yet, I'll explain the connection. There is a character in the movie named Tick Tock. I kid you not. I was in the show, fortunately with only a few other people, and I don't think I need to tell you what happened next. Oh yes, the holy laughter began. I couldn't stop laughing. This guy appears over and over with a head in the form of a clock. These identical men just keep coming; there is a row of about twenty of them, I would venture to guess. Each one represents a time Tick Tock goes back to try to change his past. In the end, the moral of the story is you can't go back in time and change what happened. No kidding! So I told myself, *Rebecca, get over it if that is where you are stuck.* The conclusion pertained to me. It is now my motto: "Keep moving forward." Giving Adam this book · is my first step in moving forward.

One night while I was out for a drive, I was yelling about Adam to God. I realized I was full of rage. I hadn't admitted until that moment just how angry I was. I thought I was merely frustrated. So much for moving forward, I'd say. I asked God why He let this happen to me. I asked Him, in all seriousness, "God, do you really want me to give Adam this book? Is that what this is about?"

I heard this inner voice say, "It isn't all about you." Now that would certainly be something God would say to me. I felt as if I had the answer. God really does want me to give this book to Adam. I instantly felt a peace come over me. I went a few miles and came to a traffic light. There was a car sitting to my right at the red light, and I noticed a Steeler emblem on it.

I giggled and said, "Okay, God, I see the sign. The Steeler emblem is for me, isn't it?" Then I looked at the car again and noticed a small white emblem with "Pgh" in black letters. I said, "God how do you do this?" It was so specific to me, the Pittsburgh girl. (Remember, I now live in Indiana.)

Then, I heard God say, "Back up and look at the license plate."

I said, "God, are you kidding me? If it's you then you know I have bumped into three unmovable objects with my car while backing up this last year."

I heard him say, "Just do it."

I looked very carefully to make sure no other cars were behind me. I made sure I turned around and looked to the sides and behind me not just in my mirrors but actually looked directly with my own eyes. I stopped backing up after a few feet. The license plate was in full view. It read "KTPEACE." I immediately thought, *Key to peace.* A few days later, as I relayed the story to someone, I said, "I think I'm cured. I didn't think keep the peace. That is what I would have thought before. Now, I think I can celebrate recovery."

I am such a slow learner at times. Only a few days had passed after having this wonderful encounter with God when I became so overwhelmed with emotion again that I went to bed and cried. I was feeling confused and scared. I didn't want to give Adam this book and appear foolish. I started to doubt every God sighting, and I told myself I was just making something out of nothing. I really was sobbing. After all my tears were spent, I curled up next to my dog, Rocky, who always seemed to be by my side when I needed him. Then I heard that still small voice, only this time it wasn't encouraging me. I heard God say to me, "You don't trust me. You don't trust the discernment I am giving you. You need to learn to hear my voice." I wasn't laughing, and I could sense the seriousness of this encounter. I knew God was speaking the truth to me. I felt a stillness come over me. I told God I wouldn't doubt Him anymore. After that I knew that even though this had been fun, it was serious stuff too. I knew I had to stop going back and forth about this. I had to do what I believed God had been coaching me to do. So I promised Him I would do it no matter how scared I sometimes get.

I just want to add that on October 16, 2011, I was at a singles group retreat when God again spoke directly to me. I know it was Him because of the name He called me. It was printed up on the board for all of us to see. He called me "Perfumed Risk-Taker Ruth." That was, in all honesty, the moment of all moments for me. I knew God was letting me know that He had heard my promise to Him and that I was not alone. He is with me, and I do not need to be afraid. Dot was leading the session and discussing the book *No More Christian Nice Girl.* This book is a testimony to all of my sisters in Christ that we can step out in faith and we don't have to be stuck in the role of an image of a sweet and nice Christian girl. During the discussion, Dot called on me to explain the story of Ruth and Boaz. I explained how Ruth was told to perfume herself up and let Boaz know she was interested in marrying him. The book also pointed out other women of the Bible who were bold and didn't fit the mold of sweet and passive women. I bet after reading this, Adam might tell you I am not that nice or sweet, but I am a good girl, meaning I obey God. Seeing those words about Ruth was just one more example of God's impeccable timing. So I said to myself, *You go, girl. God is blessing you. In fact He put it in writing up on that board just for you. He is giving you permission to not follow tradition or convention when relating to Adam.* It is okay to make my move in this most creative way that God has given me to let Adam know I am interested in him. I know God intimately. He is an awesome, all-inspiring, wonderful God, who doesn't want me left hanging. Yea, God!

I thought about this book and how much I hoped, not just for my sake but for all of my readers, it wouldn't end as a cliffhanger. It leaves people frustrated, and believe me—I know that feeling. Then I thought about my coauthor. I remembered His credentials. He is the author of the number one best-selling book of all times. Now, He knew how to end a book. It is called Revelation!

I mentioned earlier that my granddaughter Marie knows I have a crush on someone. She told me that she likes a boy too. One day when we were out on a lunch date, we made a pact that we would tell each other the name of the person we like. I told her the guy I like is named Adam. Then she told me the name of the boy she likes. She waited a minute or so, and then she giggled. She went on to say, "Grandma, that isn't really his name. I tricked you." I told her I had done the same thing too. We laughed so hard; people around us were just looking at us and laughing too. It was just one of those moments I know we will never forget. Two peas in a pod, I'd say.

When we finally sat down to have lunch, she got very serious. This is what she said to me: "If you ever become more than friends, I need to check him out. He better be like Poppy." (That is the pet name she called my late husband.)

"Marie, he doesn't need to be like Poppy. He can be different. He is his own person," I said.

"Oh no, Grandma. He needs to be like Poppy. He better love kids, dogs, and chocolate cake."

I said, "Well, what about me and God?"

"Grandma, of course—that is for sure. Oh, but one thing I forgot to tell you. He needs to like to travel back and forth from Indiana to South Carolina."

I laughed so hard my face turned beet red. I just couldn't stop laughing and blushing. I knew Marie didn't have a clue why I found this so funny.

Marie got so concerned, she said, "Grandma, why is your face so red? I've never seen it like that before."

The next time I saw Adam, I had my grandchildren with me. I was very nervous because I thought Marie might see my face when I was with Adam and realize he was *the boyfriend*. She had her DS, as the kids refer to their electronic game system, and she was so wrapped up in the game she hardly noticed Adam. I know God was there, because if she would have heard me say my dreamy "Hi" to Adam and heard him say his dreamy "Hi" back to me, Marie would have known something was amiss. All I could think was, "Adam is so me." I couldn't believe how we sounded so alike. Then when we were in his office waiting for my grandchildren to move their games off the table, Adam stood close to me and rested his hand on my arm. It was the same hand I had held this past winter. I wondered if he even realized he was doing that. I wanted to reach over and put my arm around his waist, because it felt like it belonged there. I quickly put that thought out of my mind. It was then that I realized what a good thing it was that the kids had their backs to us as they played their games. My grandchildren are more outspoken than my children were at that age. They might not have waited to ask why Adam and I stood there so close together with his hand resting on my arm. Like I said, I know God was there in that moment. He was controlling the situation. Even though Adam tried to engage in conversation with Marie, she ignored him. I didn't insist she put her game away and talk to him. I was thankful for what appeared to be her rudeness that day. God knows it's true that out of the mouth of babes comes the truth, and He knows there is such a thing as the right timing too.

All of this made me appreciative of the fact that there are some things we have no control over. We can't always hide our feelings. Sometimes they show on our faces. We certainly can't control it when we blush. I never would have thought that at my age the thoughts of a certain man would show all over my face and make me blush. That is another way I know Adam is the man God presented to me. Now, I just need to know if I am the woman God presented to him. If he believes I am, than maybe we will finally go out for that cup of coffee. If not, God just used Adam for another purpose. Either way, there is a connection between Adam, God, and me.

October 22, 2011, I received an email with the subject line *how fairy tales really end*. This was followed by an email with the subject *chocolate cake for 1*. As usual, I found this ever so timely, and I smiled. I'm not going to read too much into them. They were a reminder about how God keeps me levelheaded, but He still encourages me to dream. The next day, I received an emailed article from Women of Faith that talked about Isaac and Rebekah and how their marriage was divinely arranged. The article went on to say God gives us choices, but He also wants us to trust and obey. I didn't have a doubt this was meant for me. I made a copy of it and put it in the envelope for Adam to read along with the manuscript. I hoped he would see it as a God sighting too.

When I wrote this poem on August 6, 2010, I had no idea it would be in this book I planned to give to Adam.

A Lady in Waiting

I am a lady in waiting this much is true.
I am waiting on God to see what He'll do.
I have followed all the things He has placed on my heart.
Now, I am just waiting for Him to do His part.
I have things on my mind that I hope will come true,
Promises or dreams of all the things He will do.
I feel the anticipation of His blessing
And, at times, I am sure I feel myself wrestling.
No matter how stirred up I sometimes feel inside
His great love from me I know He never will hide.
Even though I am still a lady just waiting
All good things from Him I am anticipating.
Often times I wonder, how can this really be?
Then I am reminded of all He has done for me.
That is how I know there are more blessings to come.
I see so many with the rising of the Son.
The only problem I really fight now and then
Is waiting to know exactly what, where, and when.
I hear Him softly whisper something in my ear.
I want to surprise you the time is drawing near.
Then I feel so excited about the short wait.
I can almost picture him, the man, my soul mate.

I know that this longing I have inside of me
Was placed in my heart by the Lord above, you see.
For who honestly knows me much better than Him?
He knows I'd be faithful it wouldn't be a whim.
So, as I live my life and each day passes by
I talk to my Lord and Savior and sometimes cry,
I want to share my life with someone so special.
He hears me when I struggle with thoughts I wrestle.
Then He brings a peace as I softly hear Him say,
"It will be very soon. I'm glad you came to pray."
He desires me always to talk to Him you see.
And if I have a mate, I still to Him will be
The child he made, He cares for, and He loves so.
This is most important for me to always know.
Even if I marry and have my lover near,
My Lord wants me to turn to Him and never fear.
As I learn to live my life with God by my side,
I am learning to banish all my sins and pride.
As days turn into months and slowly tick away,
I pray I'll be so faithful, never ever stray.
For God above is where my heart truly belongs.
I feel that for sure when I praise Him with my songs.
As I worship the God of all eternity,
I pray I'll be worthy to sit upon His knee.
When I go before His throne, I will know for sure.
Because of the Lamb, I am seen as truly pure.
I can come before Him to plead for all my dreams.
It is because He loves me, always has it seems.
When I think that this is all very, very real,
Thoughts of a wonderful man lose their appeal.
For I have everything the Lord above will give.
I will be with Him, and forever I will live.
Now I have my right focus on the Light of Day.
Everything in earthly terms vanished fast away.

So thank you again for bringing peace to my heart.
You always seem to find a way. You're so very smart.
You know me better than I know myself I'd say,
And I will live to serve you yet again today.
You are a mighty God, and I believe it's true
You have loved me always, before I even knew.
With this last line of my poem, I wish to say
Thanks for being there for me and listening when I pray.

When I gave Adam the manuscript, I included this little note to him.

> Dear Adam,
>
> I'm waiting to see how this book will end. In the meantime, I am wondering what pet name I should call you. Let's see, will it be Boaz, Bozo, or the Big Red Dog? Or maybe I'll just call you Adam. I like the sound of that name too.
>
> As always,
> Rebecca

Remember those Cliff Hanger books I wrote about? Since I no longer had possession of them, I had to verify the information I'd written about them on the Internet. While looking them up, I discovered how the Cliff Hanger series really ended. Cliff was rescued. He finally let go of his tight grip and started to fall. He then landed on a blast of water from a whale, and the waves took him to, of all places, the beach. Later, he was seen at the beach, reclining on a chase lounge—just the way I pictured him when I met him, all alone, as in single. Heavenly thoughts! This tied into the very first conversation Adam and I'd had about our mutual love for not only Siesta Key Beach but also for all the great beaches in Florida. I think I can safely say, Adam won't look at the beach the same after reading this either. Hopefully, the beach will remind him of just how much God loves him and how God has done everything in his power to let Adam know. I prayed Adam would feel that God has done everything to answer his prayers and take away any confusion he might be experiencing too.

If you are hanging over the cliff, waiting for "someone" to rescue you, all you need to do is let go and trust God is the only one who can really rescue you. He truly loved you at first sight. He is waiting for you. All you need to do is say, "I believe in love at first sight too." When you do this, the fairy-tale life you are living will change and the reality of a life with God will begin. You will live happily ever after with the King of Kings. I'll see you at the wedding feast. It will be quite a celebration. And who knows, maybe we will all have a beachfront home. Wouldn't that be paradise?

Stepping Out on a Maybe

A fter I gave Adam the manuscript, there was no maybe about me being certain I was supposed to do this. I told him, "I finished the book."

He said, "Already! You are just a writing fool," as he inched his way a little closer to me. The word fool confirmed that we both were on the same page, once again. The entire exchange was rather strange because I couldn't recall ever mentioning I was writing a second book, but he seemed to be expecting it. I watched his face as I passed the manila envelope to him. It contained the manuscript along with the Women of Faith article and the Cliff Hanger book, which I now had possession of since my copy arrived in the mail that very day. Our eyes met, and we stood close together taking in the moment. When he removed all the contents and saw the book titled *Cliff Hanger, the Lap Dog, and the Riddle,* a soft smiled appeared on his face. I watched him as he quickly ruffled through the pages and then handed the book back to me. I said, "Oh no, you have to read it because it is the reason I wrote the story." That was my way of saying, "This thing between us is a God thing."

He said, "I've already read it. I have it at home."

I was shocked that he had the book and questioned him, asking, "Are you sure it's this exact book?"

"Yes, I am sure."

I said, "There are four in the series. Do you have the other three?"

He replied, "No, I only have this one."

I drilled him again, saying, "Are you sure it is this same book?"

"I am positive it is this *exact* book, and I have the stuffed animal, the Big Red Dog at home too." I was amazed because I ended the manuscript suggesting that might be the pet name I call him if he and I get together. Now, with eyes wide open, I can see what he was trying to tell me between the lines. These were some of the God sightings that were given to him. I don't know how I could have missed it—but, then again, I do. I was too busy trying to control the situation to see what this meant. If I would have had my eyes open that day, I would have kissed Adam right there and then. I believed more than ever that God was writing this story and every detail was the way He intended it to be. In all seriousness, I was pretty certain I wasn't meant to kiss Adam that day in his office. I do, however, believe God wanted me to see things with a new prospective.

I saw Adam several times shortly after I gave him the manuscript. I hoped he would share his opinion about the book. More importantly, I wanted his blessing to get it published. I prayed I would have answers to those two questions I'd asked him. Basically, I wanted to know if he was saved and if he was single. I was a little disappointed, because we were never alone. It didn't stop me from finding a way to let Adam know what I'd been up to lately. And I was able to give him some more of my writings too. I had an opportunity to tell him about my attempts to witness to many Jewish people God had brought into my life. When Adam heard the great length I went to in order to convince people to accept Jesus, he said, "Save your breath, because some people just don't get it." Adam rightly sensed that I was trying to force others to believe. After that day, his words echoed in my head whenever I tried to convince or control someone's thinking about anything. I appreciated what he told me.

Even when I tell parts of this story to some people, there are those who get it and those who don't. The ones who don't understand or believe in my dreams don't understand that this is about walking in faith instead of by sight. Some close friends and family aren't really that supportive of my newfound writing career. God gave me Adam, and he is one of the most encouraging people when it comes to my writings. I suppose that is one of the reasons I have such strong feelings for him.

I sensed that he liked to hear my stories. Recently I had so many to tell him, I rambled on trying to get him up to speed with all the encounters I was having while giving away my books. There were so many stories about other things God was doing in my life that I wanted to share with him too. I started to write them down, and each became a new chapter for my next book. That was one reason I call Adam my muse. Although I was able to give Adam some of the writings, I would love for him to read everything I wrote. Our time together at his workplace was so limited.

This particular day, I told Adam part of a story about a couple at the mall who had a kiosk and sold skin care products made from minerals found in the Dead Sea. The story is complicated and meant for another book, but the part that is relevant was that I ended up getting what I termed "Estherized." As I walked past the kiosk, this young woman said, "I love you," and then she mentions the dark circles under my eyes and, almost in an instant, she dots them with some cream. I ended up trying all the products, including the facial mask. Just like Esther, I believed God was preparing me for the day my man would have to make a choice about who he wanted for his wife. (Of course, I didn't tell Adam and his coworkers that part.) If you are familiar with that book in the Bible, you'll remember Esther was chosen. In the end, she saved her Jewish countrymen from extinction. It reads like a great soap opera. It is the only book in the Bible where God is not mentioned, although God is there in the circumstances. Along with the book of Ruth, Esther is another one of my favorite books in the Old Testament, because Esther was a very confident and brave woman. She stepped out on a maybe and took some huge risks. Her risks could have ended in her death, but God was with her. She and Ruth are great role models for me.

This was also the day I showed Adam my ring finger and told him I was wearing my engagement ring. A part of me hoped his stomach would drop when he saw the ring on my finger and thought I really was engaged to someone else. But his immediate response after I showed him the ring was, "Good." In my heart I believed Adam remembered what I'd written about him and I sharing a most unusual engagement. That was why he pronounced it good. It is the reason why I refer to the ring as the "hope diamond."

I told Adam and his two coworkers the story of why I put my engagement ring on as an act of faith. I proceeded to tell them about the products made from minerals from the Dead Sea I was using and the Jewish fellow who sold them to me. I explained that he was from Israel and that his American wife worked at the kiosk with him. I found out she was Christian and he was Jewish. The Israeli and I immediately hit it off, and we started to talk about our perception of God. When he would say things about God, I would point up and say, "Yes, Jesus." His new bride was trying to force him to believe in Jesus. I told her to just pray and let me convert him. He laughed and hugged me. I told Adam about the imaginary swordfight the fellow from Israel and I'd had. I even had my picture taken with him and his wife while I was wearing the facial mask. I continued to share with Adam details of the conversation I'd had with the Israeli and told Adam what would transpire when I won the battle, when the Jewish fellow admits that Jesus is God. My winnings were to be that he would find me a nice Messianic Jewish husband. I said, "I heard Jewish men make good husbands. He knows a single one around my age, but he lives in Naples, Florida. That's okay because, like I told the guy from Israel, I like Naples." That was my explanation for wearing my engagement ring, although I really hoped Adam would read between the lines and understand I still believed he and I were going to end up together. At the same time, I was letting Adam know I was keeping my options open and trusting God to reveal what was to come. I put on my engagement ring as an outward sign that I was keeping the faith and as a reminder that I was holding out until the wedding day. Since Adam had already read this book except for these last two chapters, he knew I trusted God to work this all out. I wasn't one bit surprised about his immediate reaction to my engagement ring, made before he heard my fable. I call it a fable because I am not interested in meeting the guy from Naples.

The funniest part of this particular encounter with Adam was that I showed up with no makeup on and Adam was sporting his five-o'clock shadow. It looked like he hadn't shaved for days. My appearance was no accidental occurrence. In all honesty, I wanted Adam to see me without any makeup so he could realize I was no longer hiding behind a mask. I had no idea what caused Adam to appear with his shadow that day. I found it so humorous that, once again, we were the same—presenting ourselves to each other au naturel. I explained to Adam and his two coworkers that

I was getting "Estherized" and that was why I wasn't wearing any makeup. After my appointment, I just laughed with God and acknowledged that He had arranged that entire coincidence to let Adam and I know we are always on the same page.

That was the day I brought copies of my first book to give to Adam's two coworkers. The previous time I'd seen Adam, he had found a way to let me know we weren't going to be alone the next time either. That was when I felt prompted to bring them each a copy of my book. I told them I believed I was to share my faith through my book. In front of them, Adam found a way to share his confession of faith too. He let me know he was saved not by works or by being good. He mentioned he understood that now that he was mature. I took that as meaning mature in Christ, a believer, a friend of Jesus, and a Christ follower. In between the lines he said, "Like you, I was confused at one time too." He elaborated enough that I understood that he and I had very similar experiences that led to some confusion about Jesus. That was when he looked down with an almost bashful look on his face because he knew what this would mean to me. I'll never forget that look or that day. I was so happy because I knew we were the same—we were both saved. I was relieved to know I didn't have to worry about him anymore, even if I never saw him again. I found comfort in knowing he believed in Jesus as Lord and Savior. Although we never spoke in what I call "plain English," he found a way to let me hear some of the things he knew I wanted to know. He told me why he raised his daughter in a nondenominational church. I was somewhat familiar with the church he attended. We both now knew we were the same, not only in our understanding of Jesus, but also in our familiarity with walking in faith and being Spirit led.

I knew in an instant that the purpose for giving him this book wasn't to bring him to Christ—he was already there. This confirmed what I thought was true from the first day we'd met. I sensed there was more to come too. That day I started to have confidence that the visions I'd had about us being together were not just my vivid imagination. I was so excited that he was in a right relationship with Jesus; that was the most important thing to me no matter what. Adam was the son of royalty. Good. Unlike one of my favorite fairy tales in the book *Lucky Hans and Other Merz Fairy Tales*, I don't have to write Adam out of the story. In fact, just the opposite is true. I believed Adam found a way to keep himself in my story.

That day I slipped Adam an essay I had written, which had been prompted by this quote by author, graphic designer and cofounder of New York Magazine Milton Glaser: "It's not the absence of restrictions but rather the restrictions themselves that produce the most creative results." (Milton Glaser) I related how this book was a direct result of the restrictions placed on us because of our professional relationship. I wasn't able to openly talk to Adam and find out if there were other things that restricted us from ever having a future together. Once again, I asked Adam in the essay if he had any restrictions on what I wrote, because I wanted to have the book published. I suggested maybe he could find a creative way to give me his okay. I wrote, "Speak now, or forever hold your peace."

In a playful way, we learned a little more about each other that day too. I shared a little more personal information about my plans to go on a cruise with my daughter. I said, "I booked a room with a balcony. If I don't come back, you'll know why. My daughter and I are like vinegar and oil."

Adam asked, "Did you ever see the movie *Man Overboard*?" That told me he got the drift. I couldn't remember if I had seen that movie, so when I went home I looked it up on the Internet. It was quite a strange experience because it led me to the singing group instead. Here is the poem inspired by that conversation and the songs I heard on the Internet.

Man Overboard

Here is what he said to me,
"Did I ever that movie see?"
I thought a minute and then said no,
But later to the Internet I did go.
That's when I saw the lyrics to the song.
I said, "Oh no. This is wrong.
I don't think this is the site where I belong."
As the song began to play
I wondered, "What did they say?"
As I listened while the words I read,
I started to laugh when it said,
You're my favorite fantasy girl.
Then my head began to swirl.
The words I read in the songs said
I think of you when I go to bed.
I think of you at eleven thirty each night.
Something like "You're my very favorite sight."
I was astounded, you see,
Because that same thing happens to me.
I wondered, is this honestly true?
Is this something that he does do?
Then, I prayed, God, how can this be?
Did you want me these lyrics to see?
Is this how he really feels about me?
Am I really his favorite fantasy?
Another coincidence, it is true,
I read these words and thought of you.

I asked God why did this come my way?
I know you hear me when I pray.
I gave Adam the manuscript, thinking this would end.
I no longer want to live in this world of pretend.
For a few days, I giggled about the lyrics to all the
songs I heard.
"I Like You," "Fantasy Girl," and "World Famous,"
I read every word.
It looks like we are holding hands these words were there.
Then I read how he looked at her and could only stare.
I thought of the words I wrote in my story.
I wonder is this from God and part of his glory?
How can this happen again to me?
That is all I really could see.
The words fit all that had taken place in my mind.
How these songs did I ever find?
I couldn't believe my eyes.
I was in awe of the surprise.
For a time I just let it go.
I said it's funny but so …
What am I to do about this happening?
I hadn't yet decided about my engagement ring.
This story is so crazy, I know.
I was having such fun, so I said to myself, "Just let go."
I decided a new poem I'd write.
I'll give it to Adam. I'd love to put it on my website.
I wondered, would he go to my blog to read my poem?
Maybe this is another omen.
I'm single and free to play.
I trust God, that's all I can say.
And if my crush is not single and free,
He'll have to be the one to tell me.
I asked him to pray to God above.
I know now Jesus he does love.

I have my one answer, my crush made it clear.
I was so happy I knew God was near.
I want this guy to pray, you see.
I want him to ask God about me.
If it's not right and I'm making him stray,
I want him to tell me to go away.
For now, I'll continue to believe he is free
And that he is honestly considering me.
If he doesn't give me my answer for sure,
I will go back till I know the score.
I believe the Lord's leading me down this path.
I am being patient and not feeling wrath.
Rather, I believe that God is so near.
He knows I trust Him. He chases away my fear.
One thing I know for sure,
God knows with Him I can endure.
He also knows my heart is true.
He knows I'm waiting to see what He'll do.
Sometimes I wonder, how will this fantasy end?
Will my crush someday be my best friend?
That is what I ask God each day
As I think of him and pray.
So Man Overboard led me to hope.
I hope I am not a dope.
I know that I am a writing fool
And I break every dating rule.
If I followed earthly advice,
This might not seem very nice.
But I trust that God is guiding me,
So I'm waiting to just see
Where this will finally go.
God is the one who does know.

Lifetime Treasure of Destiny

On another occasion, I had a chance to watch as Adam read an article I'd written, titled "Before I Was Born." I was blessed to be with him while he read it. I experienced firsthand his reaction to my words as he read each one and actually spoke a few of the words out loud. I watched his face as he read, and I heard comments like "That's good," and "I like that." Even though I didn't know exactly what part of the text he was reading when he made those remarks, I sensed that my work broadened his way of thinking. At first, when I mentioned it was about abortions, his comment was something like we don't always know why some women choose abortion. I think he might have thought I was sitting in the judgment seat, but that wasn't what I wrote about. Being pro-choice myself, the article was more about how I was guilty because I was apathetic about the entire subject of abortion. Prior to this awakening, I wasn't doing anything to help women make the best choice. Adam said, "So this is your new passion." Hearing him say that helped me realize I wanted to be connected in some way with the ministry that gives free image clear ultrasounds to women, saves babies and shares the gospel. At the time, I didn't see how this book was meant to connect me to that ministry.

I replied, "Yes, it's one of my passions. I have many of them, and writing is still my favorite." I wanted to add "because it connects me to God and you."

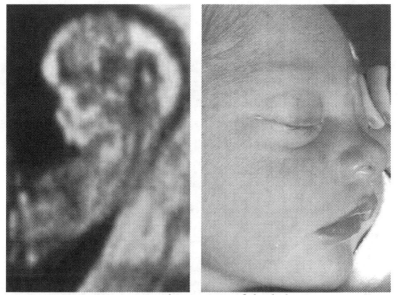

Mom sees this image of the baby

Here is the article Adam read:

Before I Was Born

I believe God loved me before I was even born. He knitted me in my mother's womb. Those words have started to penetrate my heart and brought a new meaning to me in this season of my life. In His perfect timing, God used another man named Paul Adam to bring those words to life and also to convict me of a sin. I was sure Paul Adam had no idea he would be the person in my life whom God would use to show me I needed to have a change of heart.

In one moment, Pastor Adam had changed my heart as he'd talked about his work with this ministry that is the pioneer and leader of mobile pregnancy center ministries. Mobile units or what I call motor homes are used to take a pregnancy ministry to women rather than wait for the women to come to a pregnancy center. I like to call it a home, because God has found a home there. He is there along with the volunteers who wait for that pregnant mom who might just be willing to see a picture of the love that is growing inside of her before she terminates her pregnancy. A "love at no sight" might be easier to abort, but the moms that step inside the unit are brave and courageous; they are willing to see that unborn child and face the reality that, as little as it may be, it is a person. Hopefully, with the help of the volunteers, the mom will be able to look upon that face and see a love so real that she can only say yes to life.

These mobile units can be seen parked in strategic locations, areas where the highest number of abortion-minded women might frequent. God is using this vehicle, and I mean it in both senses of the word, to reach out to save the lives of the unborn children He has made. For we are His masterpiece and we are made in His image. Many babies are now living because their moms saw God when they looked upon the faces of their unborn children. This ministry performs these ultrasounds free of charge so any mom can see the child within.

Isn't this what Jesus does? He helps us look within ourselves. I know He has done that for me. He has convicted me of my sin, apathy, but He did it in such a loving way. Jesus put it on my heart to have a desire to help this ministry reach out to moms and their unborn children. He gave me a vehicle to help the lost. Jesus showed me my sin, but only after He made a way out of it for me. That is what I love about Jesus. He makes a way. He didn't leave me stuck in my sin.

I had been studying the book of Acts at Bible Study Fellowship. I wanted to share that Scripture with you and show how God has used it to apply to my life and, hopefully, to yours too. Maybe you are familiar with Acts and the mission trips that some of the apostles took to spread the good news. I had read Acts several times before, but studying it this time opened my eyes to see what God really wanted to show me. To set the scene, it was Paul's second mission trip. "One night the Lord spoke to Paul in a vision. 'Do not be afraid, keep on speaking; do not be silent'" (Acts 18: 9). Paul stayed for a year and a half and taught the word of God. That was what finally led to him coming under attack. "'This man,' they charged, 'is persuading the people to worship God in ways contrary to the law'" (Acts 18:13). Then, Paul was brought to court. Gallio was the proconsul of Achaia so Paul was brought before him. "Just as Paul was about to speak, Gallio said to the Jews, 'If you Jews were making a complaint about some misdemeanor or serious crime, it would be reasonable for me to listen to you. But since it involves questions about words and names and your own law--settle the matter yourselves. I will not be a judge of such things'" (Acts 18:14–15). These words reminded me of my words when I said I was pro-choice. I believed that abortion was not what I would choose, but those women who chose an abortion will have to answer to God and nothing they did was illegal. I saw that being politically correct was really a hidden sin for me. It was the sin of apathy that I was committing. It was the sin of omission. In a way I had agreed with Gallio, since abortion is not a crime in the United States. God also showed me that He is able to bring something good out of everything. Because of this law some women are not only choosing life for their babies, they are choosing life for themselves; they are accepting Jesus as the way to eternal life. So God found a way to convict me of my sin, provide a vehicle for me to become involved, and personally answer my cry to have a passion for something beyond myself. Beyond that, God is using this ministry as a way for us to love one another.

I was so thankful that God used His Word to show me how I was acting like Gallio when I didn't want to get involved. I had stood on the sidelines too by not getting involved with finding a solution to the abortion crisis. God showed me a new way to think about it, and I believed it was His way. I knew I didn't want to murder doctors that perform abortions. I didn't want to march and carry a banner, either. But I wanted to save the life of an unborn baby and help a mom in crisis to see her choices more clearly. I just didn't know how to do it. If the money I donated or, perhaps, my writing this article saved one baby's life through this ministry, I knew I would be able to stand before God and not be found guilty of the sin of apathy. I cannot change the world. I cannot feed every hungry person. I cannot stop AIDS or prevent its spread. I cannot stop malaria. What I could do was partner with God. I could admit that I had not wanted to see all the ugliness in this world, because I was apathetic. I hadn't really cared. God opened my eyes, little by little, to the suffering occurring around me, and He provided a way for me to look at the suffering and still have hope. I can pray, and I can do my part. It might not be grand in the big scheme of things, but what I do matters to God. It made a difference, because God sees that my heart has changed. I was willing to look at the injustice in the world and ask the right question. The question isn't, "Why, God?" The question is, "What do you want me to do?" I was so grateful that now when God saw my heart, He saw a heart that was willing to do the part He asked of me. I prayed He would continue to show me where I have been guilty of turning my eyes to look away from what He wanted me to see. Sin abounds, and I am a sinner too. I am just as guilty as every mom who had an abortion while I looked the other way and didn't find some small way to show I cared not only about her unborn child but also about her. I was forgiven too, just as every mom who had an abortion was when she accepts that Jesus also died for all her sins. Jesus had found a way to save that mom's life too.

I learned all God was really asking me to do was look within. He asked me to not be afraid and not be silent. He wanted me to see His face. He wanted me to partner with Him to give water to all those that thirst. Come, drink and be refreshed, for the water is pure. It will bring life to all those who thirst.

After Pastor Adam helped me to identify my passion for this ministry, I knew this article belonged in the book I was writing. It goes together because God loved us at first sight. "For you created my inmost being; you knit me together in my mother's womb. I praise you because I am fearfully and wonderfully made; your works are wonderful, I know that full well. My frame was not hidden from you when I was made in the secret place" (Psalm 139: 13-15).

I believed God wanted me to financially support this ministry through the sale of my books. I remembered the day I told Adam about my vision to start a nonprofit and call it "Love One Another." I recall his response, too. When he said, as he almost touched my lips with his fingers to silence them, "We'll talk about that later," I knew this was the *later*. I had my answer to the nonprofit God chose for me to bless. In my first book, I joked with God and told him I'll keep ten percent of the profits and give you the rest. It was the reverse of the tithe. I knew I did not want to make any money from the sale of that book. I have that same desire not to profit personally from the sale of this book either. God has been so good to take care of me in every way and this is my way to thank him.

In August, I saw Adam for what I now know would be the last time—at least, professionally. As soon as I was in the room that day, I wasted no time preparing the way to give him three more pieces of my work.

I said, "Do you remember the last time I was here I told you about the couple who sold the skin care products made from the Dead Sea minerals?"

He laughed and said, "Yes, I remember." I was sure he was telling the truth, because I have no doubt he remembers everything I say and write to him. As we stood staring into each other's eyes, just the way we had the first time we met, I told him so much more had transpired that it would take too long to tell him everything; he would just have to read all about it in the rough draft of the chapter that was going in book number three. My mind, and hopefully his, recalled that March day when I arrived for my appointment wearing no makeup and an engagement ring. The fact that Adam read this manuscript and has never tried in any way to dispute or restrict anything only increased my faith that my dreams are going to come true.

I upped the ante by sneaking him the poem I wrote titled "Stepping Stone." I hid it between the two other articles I had written: one the chapter "The Dead Sea," the other a poem named "The Rhythm of God." Adam browsed through the three writings. I saw that he chose the "Stepping Stone" poem to read first. As he walked out of the office, it confirmed it was meant for Adam's eyes just as that still small voice said. I wasn't sure if I should include the poem in this book, and I questioned God about that, too. After reading the poem to my therapist, he said, "You need to put this in the book. It is really good." He was a godsend to me. Through all of this, he helped me stay balanced—especially in the midst of all these godwinks.

Stepping Stone

Is he just meant to be a stepping stone,
God given so I wouldn't feel alone?
Healing for a broken heart,
I thought he meant a brand new start.
If a stepping stone he is meant to be,

Why won't he please just tell me?
What do I mean to this man?
Does he see this as part of God's plan?
Stepping stone, I try to see
That is what he is to me.
But for now I'll only say,
Right now I don't see him that way.
I see him as the one I love,
Sent for me from God above.
Until he tells me something more,
I will hang in there and endure.
Stepping stone, one day I may say,
Yes that's why you came my way.
But for now, I cannot step out.
I call to God and I shout,
Please bring this man to me.
Help him to see this is meant to be.
So, stepping stone, if you are not the one
Please find a way to make me run.
Don't keep me hoping for this to come true.
Help me see and know the real you.
Let me know what's in your heart today.
This is what I always pray.
And then to God I always ask,
Please Lord let me see behind the mask.
I know God is here with me
And He wants me the truth to see.
So, stepping stone, listen to your heart.
Let go, let God, and do your part.
Release me from this pain I feel.
Let me know if this is real.
If you have no feelings for me,
You have the power to set me free.
And if your heart is united to mine,

Speak for now may be the time.
This is not a silly game anymore.
It is not fair if my heart you continue to lure
By being silent with nothing to say,
Especially when you look at me that way.
Please find your voice and speak.
Don't leave me feeling oh so weak.
All you need to say,
I'm sorry I don't feel that way.
Then I will be able to move on
Knowing you were the stepping stone upon
Which my writings were inspired this season,
And that was the part of the reason
God brought us to this place.
Will we ever this embrace?
No matter how this ends, you'll always be
Someone very special to me.
Stepping stone, maybe a new love I will get,
And I will never think of you with regret.
Just let me know how you feel.
Right now my life seems so surreal.
What kind of heart beats in you?
At times, I've sensed that you were blue.
Please don't feel pity for me.
I just want the truth to see.
Stepping stone, I just want to move away.
Take a step in a new direction I pray.
I want to know God's path.
Because of Jesus there is no wrath.
And you mean too much to me,
Please say it isn't all my fantasy.
Maybe I must find the strength to flee.
Will I ever see the reality?
Stepping stone, at times I want to say good-bye

And say I'm off to a new adventure and I'll try
Not to look back, to finally just walk away.
This is what I sometimes pray.
But when things happen that bring thoughts of you,
Then I know this is not yet through.
And this is when the circle I am unable to break.
I talk to God, and I'm not fake.
He is really the only one who can change my heart.
I guess I knew that right from the start.
So maybe this poem is all in vain.
I just wanted you to know of my pain.
Seems I am here, once again.
Is this going to go on until, when?
Are you retiring soon?
I hope so, because I am becoming a loon.
Well, my dear, I hope my poem you did enjoy.
If I am fun and you think of me as a toy,
It is really okay; you see,
There is no harm you can do to me.
I willingly allow my heart to feel.
I rather be like this, even if this isn't real,
Because no matter how you feel about me
I still am here for healing you see.
So as long as you enjoy this dance,
I will smile and think of it as romance.
For I am single, I am doing nothing wrong.
I am flattering you and writing my song.
All I can think is you are enjoying this too.
If not, there is plenty you could do.
Her name you could just speak,
Or are you just so weak?
But I think, by now, I know you well.
I am not the one to make you fail.
You have the power to control things too.

So this is also partly on you.
And I won't allow myself to think
I mean absolutely nothing but a wink,
Someone to flirt with and just play,
But if you're single, even that's okay.
Like I said to you before,
I like to flirt and to lure.
I'd like to catch a fish one day,
But not for sport, but to stay.
All I know for certain, you see,
Is God keeps bringing thoughts of you back to me.
I'd like to think God is smiling on us.
He is saying enjoy this do not rush.
So maybe one day when I am old and gray,
He will bring you to come my way.
Now, don't you think I'm old right now?
I bet that line made you smile.
So seriously, I wish you would know
Parts of my life are a mess, so I am enjoying this so.
You are my outlet to laugh and cry.
Thank you for that, so it is not good-bye.
Maybe one day I'll come running in,
I'll tell you I finally did everything win.
My life is everything I want it to be.
My books are selling, and God brought someone special
to me.
My children aren't hurting and blaming me for their pain.
Yes, and I am truly not insane.
But until that day comes true,
I will hold on to Jesus and you.
One thing I believe more than ever before,
God is the one who will make me soar.
And it is not revenge I seek.
I just want to learn to become mild and meek.

Do you want me to walk away?
If so, God, give me the strength to do this, I pray.
If you think God has given me to you,
I will continue to write my poetry and this will do.
Just know it is hard for me to write
And not dream of you at night.
The last thing I want to do
Is ever hurt or confuse you.
But you do confuse me at times,
When you ignore all of my rhymes.
One thing I do know
Is God sees because of Him my heart does glow.
Maybe He is arranging a love for me,
And for now I am just using you, you see.
God wants me to have an open heart.
He is preparing me for a brand new start.
Is it foolish for me to look to the future and see
You there holding hands with me?
If you are a stepping stone,
I am thankful because I did not feel alone.
I picture you with thoughts of me in your head,
Then I get silly and think one day we will wed.
Maybe God has so much work on us to do
Before any of these dreams could ever come true.
For now, you are part of the motivation I find
To help me write and not feel blind.
It is sometimes hard to see the path ahead.
Maybe I will not ever end up in your bed.
But I hope I have made you smile.
Yes, we have traveled together, if only for a little while.
I pray that you do see
The purpose was not all just about me.
I wish I knew just what I was to you,
Maybe just an author God used too.

If I brought God closer to you at this time,
I know that was part of the purpose of my rhyme.
I believe God wants to give me the desires of my heart.
I pray you will listen to His voice, and please do your part.
I know God is wise and my life is under His control.
I am willing and trust I will understand my role.
Each day I ask Him to bring someone special my way.
Bring that person who is meant to read my book, I pray.
I get so excited when He answers that prayer.
I look to heaven, and I am thankful that God is there.
That is when I know He brings all His children under
His wing.
I get so joyous, and I want to praise Him and sing.
So I know you and I connect in that way,
Spirit and soul I think I can safely say.
It is just that I want much more.
I dream that we could be together, that is for sure.
Until the day you take that dream away
I will live in hope, that is all I can say.
I just do not want you to think I am a creep.
I know what I write about can get awfully deep.
If you are married or have a love with you,
Just let me know I should not try to pursue.
If I am honest, this is so fun to do.
I think from the beginning that you knew
I am not trying to get you to bed,
But I am trying to mess with your head.
It is only fair, since you know you mess with mine.
And I wonder, are you having a good time?
Should I consider this our courtship, dear?
Sometimes I've sensed you think of me and feel so near.
I hope my poetry is a way
To show what's in my heart today.
I hope that reading this poem brings

You some happiness, joy and it rings.
Maybe the bell will finally go off in your head.
You'll say, "She's the one I want to wed."
Hey, it went with the rhyme.
Maybe it is only a matter of time
Until the day you tell me,
I'm already married, don't you see?
Are those rings you wear on your finger
A true sign if so, why do you linger?
Am I messing with your head?
Yes, I have dreams that you aren't wed.
This is really what I want to know.
With that line I will finally go.

I struggled with wanting immediate answers. I was not in a peaceful state. God knew I was getting impatient again. I had many questions, not only about Adam; I even began to doubt that I should get this book published. I saw God encouraging me through all his sightings, but I will admit I was feeling extremely frustrated. I was working on my third book, and as the chapters began to unfold I thought, perhaps, it was the one I should get published next. I wondered if this second book was just meant for Adam and me. I actually decided that unless I received some clear sign, I was not going to get the book published. I wanted to be sure this was God's idea, not mine. I thought about sending out query letters to other publishing houses, but in my heart I wanted it to be published by Thomas Nelson. I still hoped to one day become a writer for them and have them sell my books at the Women of Faith Conferences. Since the day I gave the manuscript to Adam, I have never wavered again about that decision. However, I was debating about whether I should get this book into print.

In October, I took my grandchildren to see the movie *Hotel Transylvania*. Naturally, I was happy to spend that Saturday with my grandchildren and give my mind a rest. When we decided to see *Hotel Transylvania*, I thought it was a safe movie for me because it wouldn't be a fairy-tale like *Beauty and the Beast, Ella Enchanted, Tangled*, or any of the other romance fairy tales that caused me trouble. When I least expected it, God once again found a way to let me know He knows exactly what I've been thinking about at any given moment.

As I sat in the movie theater, the love story started to unfold onscreen. I was getting a little nervous, but I wasn't prepared for what was about to take place. Count Dracula's daughter had come of age, so she was given her birthday gift from her now-deceased mother. It was a book that the mom had written for her daughter. The book was up on the big screen. I saw these words, bigger than life: LOVE AT FIRST SIGHT, THE ZING. I started to cry right there in the movie theater. Fortunately, my grandchildren didn't notice. Because Adam and this book of mine are so intertwined, it was hard to separate my love for him from God's purpose for this book. I didn't see this as a sign to have the book published. I'll admit at that moment I was rather angry with God, because He was relentless. I wasn't in the mood to be teased either.

All that changed Monday; that was the day I sat down to watch *How I Met Your Mother* (*HIMYM*). I had recorded the premier episode. With one spoken word, I regained my sense of humor. I laughed almost uncontrollably. Then I said out loud, "God, I am sorry I was mad at you." As I watched the TV show, I knew the word *Lebenslangerschicksalsschartz* was the one that captured the heart of this book. All along, since the first day Adam and I looked into each other's eyes, I sensed I was his Lebenslangerschicksalsschartz. It was the reason Klaus left Victoria at the altar, because although she was *wunderbar* she was not his Lebenslangerschicksalsschartz: his lifetime treasure of destiny. Hearing Klaus speak in his German accent made me laugh all the more. When I watched that show, I giggled thinking, "God, you sure outdid yourself this time." Then, in all seriousness, I asked God if He was letting me know I am Lebenslangerschicksalsschartz to Adam. When I heard Klaus say that "you know instantaneously she is the one because it courses through you like the water of a river after a storm—filling you and emptying you all at once. You feel it throughout your body: in your hands ... in your heart ... in your stomach ... in your skin." I know my heart's desire was that I would be that to Adam. God knows that is the only reason I would ever consider getting married again. Oh, how blessed I would be to have a relationship like that.

No marriage is perfect, and no two people are either. When I finally believed Adam and I were destined to be together because God had arranged it, I didn't see writing this book and giving it to him as a risk; it was an act of faith. I trusted that if God didn't mean for this to happen, He would find a way to put an end to it. Instead, He provided all the material for me to write this amazing story. No matter how things end, I know Jesus is our lifetime treasure of destiny, and we were destined to be together for all eternity. I knew that the instant I accepted Jesus into my heart. I had that same sense about Adam, and that was why I followed my heart.

After seeing *HIMYM* and discerning God was using it to get my attention, I agreed to make an effort to get the book published by entering it in the Women of Faith writing contest. I told myself, *Maybe the third time is a charm. If I win, that means I am meant to get this published.* When I went to the Wednesday night church service, I met Tracey at the welcome center. After we spoke, my confidence surrounding this story increased. I agreed to get this book into print and not depend on trying to win a contest. Besides, I still need help with some mechanics of writing and word usage, so I honestly didn't think I was worthy of winning a writer's contest. If the contest was about who had the most courage to write about her every thought concerning her crush and put it all on the line, then that would be one trophy I'd take home.

Talking to Tracey helped me see I was to continue on the path with the decisions I felt God called me to make. One of them was to join the church I called my sister church. I talked to Tracey about that process. I prayed about this decision for quite a while and was torn because I didn't want to hurt my former pastor or anyone of my friends at that church. I now know this is a necessary part of me moving forward—letting go of the past and embracing my new life. Tracey and I talked at length, and she helped me to see things about my faith walk a little clearer too. We walked to the parking lot together and realized we were parked fairly close to each other. As we walked to her car, we talked a little more. I told her about my first book and shared my idea to give books away as part of my advertising campaign. I explained how God used this practice as an opportunity for me to discern and trust Him to make the connections. After saying good-bye, I walked to my car and unlocked the door. That's when I noticed that I had just one more book sitting there. It reminded me of what my friend Lisa said to me. "You always seem to have just one more book in the car."

Immediately, I ran back over to Tracey's car. When she saw me holding up a copy of my book, she rolled down her window and said, "I was just sitting here hoping I would be able to read that book you wrote." She experienced what I prayed would be my future relationship with all my readers.

In the beginning, it seemed I couldn't even give my first book away. Lately, God arranged some awesome appointments that certified that He was involved with the connections I had with total strangers. Some of those people truly believed God chose them to receive my book. It wasn't just a random coincidence. I do believe God will do this on a bigger scale with this book, because

He has a heart for the ministry I want to bless through the sale of my books. I told Tracey about some of the personal connections God helped me make that showed me that "yes indeed" that person was meant to receive a book. God proved to me that He is making the arrangements. Sometimes I have a sense before I met a person that I am to go to a particular place. That helps me press on. Those connections have encouraged me to be bold and confident when approaching strangers that I sense God has put in my path. Those are two qualities I will need if God is going to promote me.

I had brought a bag of coins to church with me the night I spoke with Tracey, because I wrongly thought that was the night our spare change is collected. When I'd spoke to one of the girls at the café earlier in the evening, I asked her if it was coin collection night.

She answered, "No, coin collection is the last weekend of every month."

I was disappointed. I showed her my large ziplock bag of coins and said, "I won't be here then because I am headed south until spring."

She said, "Maybe you are meant to give them somewhere else?"

As I pulled out of the church parking lot, I heard an advertisement stating Dunkin Donuts was collecting coins. It grabbed my attention, and I giggled. Once again God came through "on the radio." Isn't there a song with that title? Anyway, I joked with God, "Are you telling me to go there because you are going to make the arrangements for Adam to be there and we finally will see each other outside of his workplace?" Then in all seriousness, I asked God if Adam and I were really going to get married. When I pulled up in front of the donut shop, I saw something sitting on the bench. It was wet from the rain, but, nonetheless, I knew God had it sitting there just waiting for me. It was a toaster oven box.

When I saw it I just blurted out, "Toaster oven! God, how do you do this?" I knew God was being playful with me again. He knew that back in my day that was the most common wedding gift. It wasn't unusual to receive two or perhaps even three or four toasters. Those were the days before bridal registries. I once again felt like God was dangling the carrot, teasing me about Adam in that most playful and humorous way. I was so excited at the thought that God finds so many ways to give me confidence by letting me know He was winking at me. I know God has the biggest crush on me and he loves me so very much. I entered the donut shop with a huge smile on my face, but not before taking a picture of that toaster oven box to document this God sighting. When I went in to give my coins, I asked, "Did I hear it correctly that you are collecting coins?" My cheesy smile must have been contagious, because the two workers behind the counter looked back at me with huge grins on their faces too. I sensed they were almost expecting me. I continued to say, "I didn't hear all the details of the commercial."

As I pulled out my gallon-size ziplock bag filled with coins, they both started to laugh. That was when they showed me this rather small by comparison box designed to contain the customers' change from their purchase, I suppose. They both laughed at the idea of all my coins going into the box and possibly filling it up. That is when I foolishly asked, "Do I get a free donut or something?"

The young man laughed and said, "No, all you do is get to put your coins in the box. You don't get anything for it."

I thought, *Oh, if you only knew. What I am getting is priceless.* I happily handed the bag over to them. The young woman smiled and started to put the coins in the collection container for me. I could tell by their smiles, I'd made their night. I ordered three manager special donut holes and a cup of decaf. As I turned to look for a seat, I caught a glimpse of him. This guy was all decked out from head to toe in a high-quality Steeler outfit. I sat down a little to the right of him and put my coffee and donuts on the table. I wanted to take his picture, so I got the courage to go over and talk to him. I said, "I see you are a Steeler fan like me."

To my surprise, I heard him say, "No, I won this entire outfit when I was in Las Vegas."

I couldn't believe my ears. I don't remember if I told you that I claim Jesus is a Steeler fan and also about my fantasy to run off to Las Vegas with Adam and get married. We would drive out to Vegas together, get to know each other a little more on the way (of course, we'd have separate rooms when we stop for the night), and decide we were meant for each other. When we arrived in Vegas, we would marry before giving away one thousand copies of this book as our publicity stunt to promote this book. So, of course, I was remembering all of my silly fantasy. God knows how my mind works, so it was most assuredly a connection of sorts.

I ended up sitting with Douglas, and he told me all about his love of computers and his trip to Vegas to attend a geek convention. He shared how that trip to Vegas was a dream come true for him. It was so fun to hear his story. I understood him and could relate to how exciting it is when dreams come true. It was funny because at first he thought I was a geek. He was so excited to have someone to talk to who had the same interest. Later he learned I was what we both decided to call a twit—you know, clueless. We came up with that name after he suggested I might like some of the things on a site called Twit.TV.

I told him, "Even though you are a geek and I am a twit, we still are able to relate." We had a great time together, although we really aren't that similar at all. I finally told him a little about the book I wrote. I asked him if I could take his picture for it. He was more than excited about that. That night, I envisioned this book with the pictures of the toaster oven and Douglas on the same page. As I already said, I am documenting my God sightings. This way I know it's not a hallucination. Besides, I love to show my pictures to others and tell my silly stories.

November 1, 2012, I went to the second annual ministry review and dinner for the ministry that gives free ultra sounds to abortion minded women. In my heart, I wished Adam were there with me to hear firsthand about all the miraculous things God was doing.

During dinner I sat next to the Chairman of the Board and had the opportunity to recall how she became the founder of this ministry. It all started when God gave her the idea to go out on the road and offer free ultrasounds to women instead of waiting for them to come to the pregnancy center. God helped her in many ways by providing not only the idea, but also the first donated mobile home that eventually would be converted into an ultrasound machine on wheels so to speak.

I was thankful God brought me into this relationship. I sensed that God wanted to use my gifts, the unique way he designed me, to connect this ministry to others. He didn't expect me to give up my dreams. He just wanted to connect me with others who share some of the same dreams. And more than that, God wanted to expand my territory, my sphere of influence. When I first learned about this ministry I knew I was meant to connect with it in some small way, but I didn't see this coming. I didn't see how God would make all the pieces of the puzzle fit together through this book. When I started to write this book, I hadn't met Adam Paul or known anything about this ministry. I could only surmise how the founder of this ministry felt that evening seeing the expansion from its beginning with just one unit to over fifty vehicles throughout the country projected to be operational by the end of 2013. It was so awesome to see God's handiwork.

After dinner, the Executive Director spoke of the sense of urgency to get as many "fleets for tiny feet" out there as possible because babies are dying. When he showed pictures of a few of those most darling children who had been saved, I knew in an instant I wanted to do my part to get as many of these units as possible out into the 'burgs—as we Pittsburghers would say—and help moms and dads choose life. When the Executive Director said, "There are fifty-five million people who are not with us today because of abortion," that's when it hit me that, although I already had the desire to raise money for this ministry through my book sales, I needed to finish this book quickly. I trusted God would open doors and use it as a springboard to spread awareness about this ministry and raise funds to help save babies. Besides saving babies and serving women, this ministry shares the Good News of Jesus Christ with everyone that comes onboard the vehicle.

Prior to the dinner, I hadn't thought about the dads who accompany the moms into the mobile unit. The Executive Director shared a story about one young man who accompanied his girl friend to get an ultrasound. After the volunteers told him about Jesus this young man accepted Jesus as his Lord and Savior. Instantly the young man was filled with hope and believed with God's help he could provide and take care of his family. I knew God was saying this ministry is not just for women; it is for families. As I sat down to finish this book and share the Executive Director's sense of urgency with you, I trusted God to put the pieces together as He so miraculously does. I knew He would come through and help me end this book in a way that will bring hope to all of us. God's heart is for all His children. It wasn't hard to figure out that God does not see the men as villains. He sees them as victims, too, of a fallen world that has men believing they aren't good enough either. It is the human condition, but that is the heart of the gospel. Without a way out of sin, none of us are good enough. God wants us to help others realize He is able to restore them and change them into the person He intended them to become.

I still don't have all the answers about how my story will affect this ministry, but I have a vision. It was something like the big bang theory. I wondered if my story, my walk of faith, would bring together my passions for not only this ministry but also for Celebrate Recovery and the Women of Faith and unite them for the purpose of saving babies. I hoped Rick Warren at Saddleback Church would play a part in spreading awareness about this ministry too. I know Rick is passionate about helping lower the abortion rate because he had been writing about this issue on his Facebook page. I wrote and told him about this ministry and prayed he would read it. He and I have a connection of sorts through Celebrate Recovery (CR). That ministry was started at his church. God had brought me to some CR meetings because I relapsed into some codependent behavior over the last few years, even prior to my husband's death.

As I said before, all three of my children had divorced since my husband died, and, frankly, my family was a mess. I am happy to say that God is in the restoration business and my family is starting to heal. My stepson, Tim, is now engaged. My other two children are seeing restoration too, as they experience the joys of parenthood even though they are also struggling-single parents. Little by little, God restored my life and brought me joy in the midst of so many changes too. CR reminded me of how only God can restore and heal us from our hurts, habits, and hang-ups. Years ago, I had attended Al-Anon and Overeaters Anonymous. The twelve steps were part of how I naturally lived my life. But some of my recent hurts were so painful that I relapse into some stinking thinking. I tried to control what others thought and tried to fix them. I carried burdens that weren't mine. Going to CR reminded me to give those to the Lord and pray, pray, pray. I have recovered from not only my grief after the loss of my husband but also from many of the past hurts that resulted after relationships with others dramatically changed after my husband's death. Through this program, I once again had great expectations about all the miracles God was able to perform. Hearing about the restoration he had done with others at CR was the reminder and encouragement I needed when I was dealing with my issues. I can't help but think that God chose me to write this story because He knew how brokenhearted I was when my entire family was crumbling after the death of my husband. God blessed me and gave me a reason to go on when I wanted to die. He gave me the first Adam, the guy I refer to as my crush, and then He gave me the second Adam too, Pastor Adam. Each one has a special place in my heart. Those relationships helped me to not only write this book, but also to move forward knowing my life has purpose.

I dreamed that God would find a way for me to speak to the church about my faith walk and encourage others not to give up on their dreams. I cannot help but think back to the book *Lucky Hans and Other Merz Fairy Tales* and how I happened upon that book. I believed it connected me to my crush in a way I'd never dreamed possible. I know when I gave Adam his copy of the book he agreed it was quite a miraculous find. I wondered if God knew when those fairy tales were being written what meaning it would have for us. Then I thought, "Are you kidding! God knew that before He even created the world." He knew I would write this story too. Isn't it mind-blowing to think that God knows everything that goes on in each of our lives? And more than that, when we surrender our life to Him, He will work out all things for His purpose. What better way is there to live than to have God use us?

I hope you have already experienced this close, personal relationship with God and have learned to hear His voice. He really is able to find a way to confirm that we are on the right path. Whenever I start to get anxious about tomorrow—what I should eat, what I should wear, or what I should do—I am reminded of the words of Jesus in Matthew 6. He instructed us not to worry, saying we should look at the birds and how God cares for them. Talk about scripture coming to life.

God is a loving Father and will take care of His children. He has made a way for each of us to come under His umbrella of protection. That way is through the life and death of His Son, Jesus. He gave up His Son's life so we are able to become family. It is the family of faith that will change this world, one person at a time.

I knew when I met both Adams, we were kindred spirits. I just sensed it somehow. According to *Webster's Pocket Dictionary and Thesaurus*, the word *kindred* means a person's relative by blood, having a like nature, similar. It is because of the blood of Jesus that we are related. Wow! God was showing me the bigger picture. One of His missions is to connect all of His believers and give us a heart to save each precious child He created.

The night I attended the dinner for this ministry, Adam Paul said, "Rebecca, you are an enigma." He meant I was unique, different, and special. I looked up the word *enigma*, and its proper meaning is one that baffles, anything puzzling, a riddle. In a way that is true, but yet I like to think of myself as an open book. Does that description fit the first Adam? I found him baffling. I didn't have the answer to this riddle yet because, despite all my efforts, he had remained silent. I think I know why. If he had spoken, I never would have gotten to the end of this story. So thank you to my muse; I couldn't have written this without you. And, by the way, I have found my compass too. Right now it is pointing south, because I moved to my condo in Florida. Now, like Cliff, I won't be hanging on, waiting to be rescued. I will be hanging out at the beach relaxing and telling others I meet about my book!

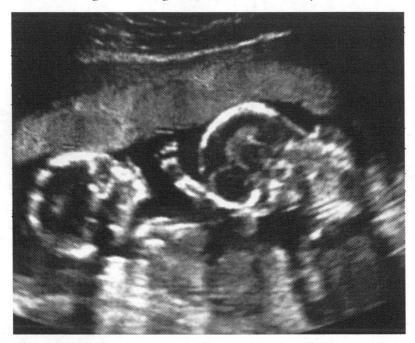

Twins seen by means of this ultrasound.

One Friday, I finally decided to start the process of getting this book published. When I looked at my calendar, I realized it was November 5, 2012. Had George lived, this would have been our thirty-fifth wedding anniversary. I certainly didn't plan this. I had honestly forgotten all about my wedding anniversary because I don't celebrate it anymore. But I believe George's prayers for me were being answered. He didn't want me to be alone. No matter how this story with Adam and me ends, I am not alone. God finds so many ways to let me know He is with me. Jesus is the funniest husband a girl could dream of having. He is quite the tease, but He comes through and takes care of me always. He wants to give me my heart's desire, so I am pretty confident He will make all my dreams come true.

It was hard to believe so much time had passed since I had given Adam the book back on December 2, 2011. It was even harder to believe that when I gave him the "Stepping Stone" poem that would be the last time I would see him professionally. I did see him one more time at his place of employment, but I was scheduled with one of his coworkers. When I checked in, the receptionist said, "We were ... I was so surprised you weren't seeing Adam today." She had a huge smile on her face, and it made me wonder what exactly she and others at the office knew. I replied, "I was surprised too." Just as the last words left my mouth, God abruptly turned my head to the left. I saw Adam standing at the door. He wasn't there a few moments prior, when I'd walked into the room. I am pretty sure he was hiding on the other side of that door, and he slipped out as I approached the receptionist. Maybe that was why she had a hard time keeping a straight face. He stood directly in front of the "closed door," the same door he *always* held open by leaning his back against it. I was shocked to see him there, and I attempted to get his attention by saying, "Hi." When he heard my voice, he quickly turned toward me and said a very quick, "Hi," back to me because he couldn't be rude and not acknowledge me. He is always such a gentleman. He immediately went back to staring at the closed door. He just stood there staring at the door while I stared at him. I was thinking, *What in the world is he doing, and what is he trying to tell me?* I knew he was playing charades. In my mind, I tried to guess his meaning. At one point, I even envisioned that picture of Jesus standing in front of the door. After a few seconds, I reasoned that wasn't the message Adam was sending. He stood there for the longest time facing the door and staring at it. I was pretty sure at one point he actually touched the door with his nose. I started to giggle, inside. As I stood there watching him, I saw him dramatically fling the door open. I was dumbfounded. He stood at the opening for what seemed like an eternity. Finally, he walked through the doorway and down the hall. As I stood at the reception counter, I could see him walk toward the coworker I would be seeing. They were both smiling, and they exchanged a few words.

When I finally was called in for my appointment, things started to make a little more sense. That coworker gave me a few messages that had come directly from Adam. The one that meant the most was when he said that Adam had wanted him to ask me what number visit this was today. In my head, I quickly did the math. To my surprise, I heard myself answer, "Number seventeen."

He immediately broke out in a huge smile, and I knew Adam had told him that number meant something special between us. I knew Adam had found a way to give me his okay to get the book published. When I sent the message to "speak now or forever hold your peace," I encouraged him to find a creative way to let me know if he had any objections to what I wrote. Like Isaac, I know Adam willingly allowed himself to be sacrificed because not only did he look foolish standing at that closed door acting out his charade but he gave me permission to write this story and expose him. I believe Adam prayed, and he trusted God. I also believe he is doing this as an act of love for me.

If I am perfectly honest here, the biggest obstacle I had about writing this book was I wanted to protect Adam. I didn't want to do anything to ruin his reputation. I didn't want to do anything to jeopardize any possibility of a future we might have together, either, by betraying what was between the two of us. When Adam swung the door open, I sensed he was telling me, "It's all clear." I believed he meant, "Do what you need to do, and write the ending using all the clues God has provided for you along the way."

When I think back to the day I first met him, July 17, 2009, I never imagined he and I would connect in such an unusual way.

When I think of the small still voice that went off in my head, it said, "Maybe." I sensed from the moment I met Adam that he and I were the same. I knew I should not have flirted with him. When I later looked up his lake, it was out of curiosity. When I went to see him that second time, I'll admit I felt flirtation. I took the risk because I thought I'd like to date him, and I sensed God in the moment. I wanted to send Adam the message that if he was attracted and interested in me, I was open to it.

I see that God had some work to do on me. He needed to teach me the right way to attract a man and how to use the right gifts He'd given me, not my body, to lure a righteous man. I think I used those good gifts to make an impression on Adam. I want to do all things God's way. Even though I am tempted to do it my way, God showed me He is faithful. He won't let me fall into the same old sins. Some rules are man-made and have a purpose, but the rules that I don't want to break are the ones God made.

The way I see it is simple. God is growing my faith not only in my belief that He will provide a good husband for me one day, but God is also growing my faith that He will always be here for me. God is testing me but more than that He is teasing me. The test is to see if I trust Him and if I am able to hear His voice above the crowd and obey it. I think I have passed it and that is why He knows He is able to tease me too. God is being playful with me.

I will use Sarah from the Bible as an example of how God tests our faith in Him. Had Sarah been of childbearing years, it wouldn't have required much faith to believe she would have a child. Both Sarah and Abraham heard God's promise to Abraham, "I will surely bless you and make your descendants as numerous as the stars in the sky and as the sand on the seashore," (Genesis 22:17). Would they believe it would come true? The fact that they were well past childbearing years was the test they were given by

God. They had to believe in the impossible, believe by faith—something they could not see. For me, the test is Adam said he was single but later, when he learned my age, added that he had a fiancée. My test is do I trust what I believe in my heart is from God and that Adam and I are meant to be together. Simply put, maybe my age is Adam's test, and maybe Adam's eligibility status is my test. I don't have these answers yet, but I trust God won't leave me hanging. I believe Adam is not talking for a reason, and I trust God is behind it all. Maybe Adam isn't the man God has for me, but I do believe God has a perfect union in mind for both my husband to be and myself. It will be for God's purpose and to give all the glory to Him. It's just a matter of time, His time of course.

Since the professional relationship I had with Adam has ended, it *may be* only a matter of waiting a little longer for us to be able to see each other outside the office. I was always torn because I wanted him to take care of me professionally. I didn't want to give up seeing him. Besides, I wanted a chance for us to get to know each other a little more. I wanted to go back to the first day in the garden and have a redo. On one occasion, he told me I could come back as much as I wanted; he said it with a wooing tone in his voice. I knew he looked forward to being with me too.

To be honest, I wasn't ready for anything more back when our eyes first met. I was scared of getting into a relationship. It was too soon. And besides, in order to write this story, I had to live it first. Over these past years, Adam and I have been together enough to know there was something special between us. I think other people who saw us together were able to sense it too. If you remember, the day I met Adam I went home and asked God if he had presented Adam to me. All the signs seem to be pointing to yes. I believe with all my heart that God gave me the signs to encourage me and help me not give up on this idea.

I believed Adam sensed when I gave him the "Stepping Stone" poem that I was ready to give up our professional relationship in order to have a chance at something more. He knew I was at the end of my rope. I wanted things to change. He and I communicate in ways that may be hard for others to understand. We are both a little goofy, but we know each other very well because we are the same. The Holy Spirit guides us both, and we are able to communicate with each other without using words. I know Adam wanted to make sure I was all right because my poem led him to believe I could no longer continue seeing him professionally. That is why his coworker asked me how long I could hold out. When I said I could hold out for quite a while, his coworker smiled. I have faith that this will come true.

I learned many lessons from this experience. One is you have to make room in your life to receive your blessings. In the Bible story the Widow's Oil, found in 2 Kings: 4, a widow needs to rescue her sons from slavery. All she has is a little oil. She is told to ask the neighbors to borrow empty jars. She already has the oil; she needs to make room for what she already has. God presented this chapter to me three times in one week, from three different pastors, and all three times the message from it was interpreted exactly the same way. I knew God was telling me I needed to make room in my life for all His blessings.

It was shortly after this that I bought my condo in Florida based on a gut feeling. I believed God showed me that I needed to have my own life, separate from my children. I needed to make room for someone first so that when that person comes into my life, my children won't see him as the person who changed our relationship. I had to make choices about my life based on where I believed God was calling me to be.

Now that Adam closed the door on our professional relationship, I believe another door will open. I think that was what he was saying when he acted out the charade. He was telling me he was opening the door that he had closed on D-day. I haven't given up that dream. I am expecting something good. Without words between us, Adam read between the lines of my poem and knew that was what I'd hoped he would do. No matter how this ends, I know for certain Adam does not want to squash my dream about being a successful author. That is a quality I want my best friend to have.

I came north to Indiana in February for some follow-up visits with my doctors, and as a bonus I was able to spend some quality time with my grandchildren. While I was in town, we went to see the movie Wreck-It-Ralph. That was the first time I saw Disney's animated short film *Paperman*. It was another "love at first sight" story about two people who's eyes meet after a piece of paper belonging to him flies in her face leaving a kiss on the paper. Later, he coincidently sees her in the window of the skyscraper directly across from his office window. That is when he begins shooting paper airplanes toward her. The paper airplanes are at the mercy of the wind and do not make it to her. After all efforts to get her attention fail, he leaves work hoping he will find her. As he is running through the city streets, the wind blows all his paper airplanes causing them to stick to him, but one makes its way to her. Naturally, it's the one with the kiss on it. She recognizes it and begins to look for him. They meet again at the train platform. That is when they experience their first kiss. Not only did this win an Oscar for best-animated short film, it reminded me of my situation. I hoped Adam was watching the Academy Awards that night and thought of me when the film was shown in its entirety. It was only seven minutes long. There's that number seven again.

The grandchildren spent the night with me after we saw the movie. That evening, I received a phone call. I was talking and not paying any attention to Robert. That's when he said, "Grandma, do you notice anything is missing?"

I replied, "No. What did you take?" He went behind the love seat and popped out with a stack of my Bibles and some of the other books I had been reading. He had gathered them from the other rooms and set them before me. Then he said, "Grandma, who do you love more than me?" I was still on the phone and trying to listen to two people at once. The caller was feeling frustrated and hung up. Robert repeated his question, but I was still distracted because of the phone call. He repeated his question once more. I answered, "I don't know." I was thinking he wanted me to list other family members whom I might love more than him.

That is when he said, "I'll give you a hint: G-O." I was still puzzled. He saw the look on my face and said, "Grandmaaaaa, you know who! G-O-D!"

I saw this as his way of saying, "You don't love anyone but God more than me. I feel loved by you."

I later told the story to my Bible Study Fellowship leader, and she said, "Wow. Your grandson sees that the love you have for God is first. How old is he?"

I said, "He is six."

She said, "He already has learned from watching you."

I believe this was a message from God letting me know that it is okay to have these intense feelings for Adam, because it is clear that God is first place in my life. I had been struggling with this. God found a way to answer that doubt too.

February 13, 2013, I went to my Bible Study Fellowship class. That day we studied Genesis 24, the story of Isaac and Rebekah. As I sat listening to the lecture, I knew this was no coincidence. God had arranged every last detail. I was hearing these words directly from God. The servant went to find Isaac a wife. The servant in my life is the Holy Spirit. He intercedes for me when I pray. The servant's prayer was made in the name of Jesus. He prayed concerning everything; his prayer was specific; and his prayer was expectant. God answered, confirming the answer through coincidences, but coincidences alone were not sufficient proof. Another important factor was that basic principles concerning the marriage were given. Do not marry a nonbeliever was one. The other was Rebekah was a virgin. It made me think of what conditions I had already expressed to Adam from the get go. One was "Call me if you are no longer engaged." The other was "I want to get married, and I am waiting for marriage before I have sex." Basically, if a suitor isn't willing to meet these conditions, he shouldn't waste my time or his. I was going to be a "virgin again." Some people think once you have had sex you are no longer a virgin, because they think in terms of the physical body. When we abstain from having sex outside the marriage, in the spiritual sense our bodies are pure and holy again. It is the same concept as being born again is spiritual, not physical. The last sign to confirm that God is guiding you is there is an inward peace. I believe God was giving me this as a measuring stick. Everything I've done has passed the test. I know this is God's answer to each of my prayers. God has been relentless to encourage me and give me that peace. He is in control. When our lecturer said, "When Isaac saw Rebekah, it was love at first sight," I knew God was answering me.

Just the day before Bible study, I was riding in my car and doubting all of this. A car pulled in front of me. The license plate read "WACO 1." I thought, *Yes, I am a number one Waco to believe this will come true.* Later, I thought back to that moment and how I was full of doubt prior to seeing the license plate. The Holy Spirit found a way to let me know that when I doubt I am a Waco. I laughed the way I always do after the Holy Spirit reassures me God is with me every step of the way on this marvelous journey. Do I doubt? Of course, in my humanness, I do. But the message I heard above all the noise was this, "You must believe and not doubt."

I have seen God in all the details. I know this is all His doing. Sometimes it is hard to believe He chose me to bless with His favor, but I'd like to believe He sees my faith. I have the faith of a little child who believes dreams come true. When God kept my husband alive for thirteen years in spite of all those strikes against him, I knew God was there in those circumstances, controlling every detail so that He would be glorified through our walk of faith. That is why I have confidence He will give me so many more blessings—because He knows I will boast about Him.

If you are disappointed in this ending, pray that God will find a way to let you know for sure if I get my man. I believe He will answer that prayer. You see, God hears our prayers, and nothing is impossible for Him. Just like the servant found Rebekah, the needle in a haystack, for God it was a piece of cake. God answered the servant's prayers. I know that is how I felt about finding the book *Lucky Hans and Other Merz Fairy Tales.* If God wants you to know something, He is able to reveal it. That book confirmed so much for me besides helping me identify myself as an artist. That is what writers are too. We draw using words and, hopefully, create a beautiful picture for others to appreciate. Perhaps by doing this, we bring others a little closer to the creator himself.

I had my nails done the other day. I chose the color *Suzi & the 7 Düsseldorfs.* It is one of those purple colors I like so much. The other two are called *Louvre Me Louver Me Not* and *Purple with a*

Purpose, both great names that encouraged me with my faith walk. It is like reading tealeaves, but I read nail polish bottles. Is it just me, or do these things remind you about my crush too? I asked the other ladies getting their nails done if anyone knew what the name *Suzi & the 7 Düsseldorfs* was referring to, and one of the ladies said, "I think it is a city in Germany." Another woman at the nail salon said, "It is like *Snow White and the Seven Dwarfs*." I thought, *Oh, like me. I'm Snow White because I am going to be pure for my husband on my wedding day.* When I thought of the names Sleepy, Sneezy, Dopey, Grumpy, Happy, Bashful, and Doc, Adam seemed to fit some of them to a T, especially Dopey because he seemed to be clueless at times—or maybe he was just Sleepy because God hadn't woke him up yet. Then I thought how some of those descriptions would fit me too, like Grumpy, Happy, and Sneezy. I had this uncontrollable sneezing attack because I was fighting a cold. It was a pretty funny moment.

The lighthearted moment didn't last, because I ended up in the hospital. Not to worry, God took perfect care of me while I was in there too, and He uncovered some things that were hidden. It all worked out just fine.

When Adam wouldn't speak to me that day in his office, I suspected he was luring me by being silent just as I wrote in the poem. Even before he did that gesture, I had another poem I'd written with me to give him that day. I titled it "Treasured Destiny." I'll keep that one between us for now. It was pretty much based on all that has happened in this last chapter I hadn't written yet. Sometimes I think, *It's not fair. I have the hard part in this situation.* Then I realized that if Adam really does want me as much as I want him, he would be going through some struggles too. Maybe he is thinking, "Is she ever going to get that book published? What's taking her so long?" My answer is this: I am a perfectionist. I wanted to get it right. God is just using one of my character defects to get this out in His perfect timing. I surrender to you, God. My work is done. It really is all up to you. The pressure is off of me. That is why I am smiling.

When I went back to my local church up North I told my pastor about finding an awesome church in Florida too. I asked him if I remembered his words correctly when I thought he said, "I am praying for Bishop T.D. Jakes to come and speak here. I'm praying for a miracle. Do any of you know how to get in touch with him?" Pastor's words stayed with me.

He smiled at me and answered, "Yes, he is the one I'm praying will come to speak here."

I told my pastor I was going to be at a conference at my newfound Florida church, and that Bishop T.D. Jakes would be speaking there at the last service during that conference. I said, "I hoped I am the one God uses to make this dream come true by making the connection. Wouldn't it be awesome if he comes here." We both knew—although it might seem like mission impossible—God could do it. I told the pastor this book was just about finished. I said, "I am sending it to the editors tomorrow, on Valentine's Day." I'd given the rough draft to my pastor's wife based on a prompting by the Holy Spirit, but that is a whole other story—for my next book, of course. I know Pastor was able to see how I was feeling. When I left the parking lot, the license plate on the car in front of me read "HAPI." God, you are so awesome. How do you do that?

One Sunday after returning to the North for the summer, I was worshipping at the church I now refer to as "part of my family." That day I had decided to wear my special jade cross necklace to church. I haven't worn it for years because I was always afraid of losing it. That day was so special. One reason was because I was able to hear a visiting pastor's wonderful preaching. He said that he thought God does have favorites and that my new church was one of God's favorite churches. I agreed. He mentioned he thought maybe we were cousins. It reminded me of how at one time I referred to my new church as my sister church. His message encouraged me so much because he talked about how we need to praise and worship God while we are waiting for what I call our miracle or answer to prayer. He also said, "It is better than you think." He was meaning God has already worked everything out and the results are better than we can imagine. I so agreed with that statement too. Ironically, this pastor's home church is in Las Vegas. That coincidence made me giggle. I thought about my desire to go to Las Vegas to give out this book. Maybe one day this book will make its way to his church and through it I will speak about how God has called His children to help solve the abortion issue by loving and serving moms in crisis first and foremost.

As I listened to the pastor's sermon, I was talking to God at the same time, and I felt so loved and special. At the end of the service one of the pastors from my home church announced, "We are going to give this gift basket to someone today by picking a seat. I will choose a section, row and seat number." As soon as he said that I started to giggle. I just sensed in my spirit that I was going to be the person sitting in that winner's seat. When the pastor said, "Section B, row 4, and seat 5 to the left" I felt my eyes fill with wonder and I started giggling even more. Finally, I stood up and with a wave of my hand I signaled that I was the winner. It was the second time I was singled out at that church. Another time, I had gone up for prayer and was covered with the prayer shawl after one of the pastor's said "It is finished. Your miracle is coming. You should be so happy. You should be running around this church." That day I thought about my crush, my family and this book. I knew it was all tied together and God had worked it all out. The pastor's words encouraged me and gave me hope that my miracles are coming true. I believed God was sending me a message that He was going to do so much for me. So this day out of over 1,500 people God chose me! It was confirmation that "yes" I was in the church God called me to and that my God will provide for me. I felt so favored and special that I started to cry. Through coincidences God was communicating with me. I received His message that He hears me talking to Him all the time. I sensed in my spirit that He loves that I trust Him to do a mighty work in my life and through my life. He most certainly has His eye on me. I want you to believe with all your heart that He has His eye on you too. He will do everything to build your faith and bring miracles to you. Keep the faith!

I've been blessed to discover many books that have encouraged me during my waiting time. SQuire Rushnell's second book, *When God Winks on Love*, is one of them. I found his ending to sum up my thoughts about what I've always called God sightings, so I think I'll ask SQuire if I can quote him. Here is what he has to say:

The small voice within:

You must continue to listen to the small still voice within—your intuition—and make the important choices in your life on your own, bolstered by an awareness that you are surrounded by the invisible safety net of the Almighty, confirmed by godwinks, that you are never alone.

Godwinks as Signposts

Signposts don't choose where you go.

You do.

But once you make your determination, the signposts are there to support your decision.

That's the role of godwinks in your life. They are signposts *affirming* that you are heading in the right direction: reassuring that you're getting closer to your goal; reminding you to stay within boundaries; and bolstering the choices *you* have made. (Squire Rushnell, *When God Winks on Love*)

Months ago, I had written this poem along with the footnote. When all this came together and fit perfectly at the end of this story there are no words to describe how truly amazed I was.

Soul Mates

Call it coincidence, a God sighting, or a "godwink."★
They all mean the same I do think.
It just means we are on the brink
Of seeing God in just a blink.
He is all around. You can see.
He's just connecting you and me.
As we work or play together,
He does show up just whenever
Two souls connect and become one,
Are about to get something done.
Sometimes God shows up for romance.
He wants two together to just dance.
He knows exactly what to do.
He does His best to get through to you.
So as you look for your soul mate,
Don't think you have to go on a date
For with God it is already done,
And when he's around it's pure fun.

You yourself can barely contain
Together you wish to remain.
It is just extremely bizarre.
It's almost like you caught a star.
You can hardly believe it's true
What God would really do for you.
When you're alone, you long to meet.
When that day comes, it will be sweet.
Will it be summer, winter, fall?
Spring's the best time for love for all.
When hearts are tender, made for love,
Holy Spirit on the wings of a dove,
You'll know in an instant you were meant to be.
It opens you up to truly see.
This feeling has power all its own.
Seems you aren't going to be alone.
You doubt it could happen this way.
Sometimes the thought you tucked away.
You deny you had that moment,
Or you wonder just where it went.
You think of all you both did say.
You wish those thoughts would go away.
They just dance around in your head,
You think, "This is the one I'll one day wed."
You wonder, are you just crazy?
And some days the thoughts are hazy.
Memories at times so very clear,
At other times they disappear.
Then you ask God, "What does this mean?"
That's when He shows up on the scene.
At times He finds a way to let you know
He is the one running the show.
Then all you can do is giggle.
At times you just start to wiggle.

You're hoping you'll see him again,
Waiting for the waiting to end.
God knows what first needs to be done.
He says enjoy your time together don't run.
For I am always here with you.
I'm in control. Enjoy the view.
That's when the Spirit does come through.
The rest is up to him to do.
So as we go about our day,
Rest in God's love, worship and pray.
One day with him you'll finally be,
And that is when the world will see.

*The term *godwink* taken from the book *When God Winks at You* by SQuire Rushnell.

Afterword

s I already mentioned, I recently moved my primary residency from South Carolina to Florida. From the very first night—even though I slept on an air mattress because my furniture hadn't arrived yet—I felt like I was home. I believed God wanted me in Florida for a particular reason and season, but sensing He was telling me and confirming it over and over has been awesome. Yes, I am a friend of God's, and sometimes He shares things with me. For sure, the spectacular sunsets I see outside my window have brought me a little closer to experiencing Him.

I asked God to lead me to a home church here. He answered that prayer request pronto and brought me to a local church that is working to make this area of Florida a place where the lost are able to know Jesus loves them and understands their pain. My church has big dreams to impact the area and see people begin to heal and change when they enter into a relationship with God. Although the church is a half hour drive away, I had no trouble finding it and arrived on time. That alone was a miracle. The minute I entered into worship, I knew it truly was "love at first sight." That Sunday, my pastor talked about the Feast of First Fruits. There was no doubt after God spoke to me; I knew what

I was to give for my first fruits. As of this point, I had lived in Florida for only three weeks, but I knew God had brought me there. After putting my gift on my credit card because I forgot my checkbook, I called my credit card company that night to make sure it would go through. God connected me to a fellow Christian that worked at the credit card company, and we talked for quite a while. It was after midnight when I called so he wasn't too busy to talk to me. He said he was going to go back to his church and promote my first book. Wow! That confirmed it for me. I was truly stepping out on a maybe with my book sales. That is the whole idea behind it. You give because you are expecting to get what God has for you already. For me, this went right along with the belief that God is involved and He is leading me on this journey that I am living and writing about. My Bible verse is "'For I know the plans I have for you,' declares the Lord, "plans to prosper you and not to harm you, plans to give you hope and a future'"(Jeremiah 29:11). I am expecting my books to sell so that the money will go to the ministry I believe God called me to support. Now let me tell you this is a faith walk and not a cakewalk. This isn't always easy to do and it is not for the weak of heart. It takes lots of spiritual muscle, but don't worry if you don't have enough God will build more. Metaphorically speaking, I am working out and physically I am too. But I don't want to get stress out and overdo it either. I have to find my balance and that is why sometimes I may look a little odd. I am easily excitable. That day I was torn between giving that gift to my church or to the ministry that provides free ultrasounds to women. God showed me the right answer pertaining to my situation was to give to my local church and have faith that He would financially bless and grow that ministry. I took the leap of faith. God promised me this ministry would benefit much more this way. I am counting on it. I also learned that even though we give our tithe through our local church the one true church is under the leadership of Jesus. It is His bride.

The night Bishop T.D. Jakes preached at my home church in Florida literally hundreds of people went forward to accept Jesus as Savior. I felt like I was seeing the beginning of revival. When I returned home that night as I laid in bed looking out my window at the city below I sensed God allowed me to see a glimpse of my prayers being answered. You see praying for revival is one of the callings God has put on my heart. I intercede for all those that don't know Jesus yet. I pray in the Spirit so I know my prayers line up with God's will. I also pray for all my pastors because they need our prayers most of all. I am so blessed to be a prayer warrior, and I encourage all of you to do that too. It is a wonderful calling to pray for others. Often times God rewards us by allowing us the opportunity to see the power that the name of Jesus commands. When we pray and call on the name of Jesus it is an awesome and wonderful honor to know our voice travels to the throne room where He intercedes on our behalf.

I have so much joy in my life. I can't resist sharing the latest coincidence with you. My neighbors directly across from me are this older married couple from, of all places, Germany. The husband just celebrated his eightieth birthday, and he still has a twinkle in those brown eyes that reminds me so much of you know who's eyes. They are the sweetest couple. They are teaching me some phases in German. My two favorites so far are "I see it in your eyes" and "Tell me the truth." I am over one thousand miles away from my crush, but some things haven't changed or have they? Now I am not going to say anything more than this because anything more I write will show you I am somewhat in a state of confusion right now. So let's just leave it at that. God brought me to Florida for a rest. I was to rest in Him, knowing it is all finished. He has prepared the way. I think He will bless me in numerous ways. I already sense He is going to connect me and use me in a way that will give glory and honor to Him. He knows that is my heart's desire.

I asked God to help me finish the book so it would be my very best. That was when He gave me the perfect title for one of the chapters I'd added after I gave Adam the manuscript. I titled it, "Stepping Out on a Maybe." I borrowed that line from one of my pastor's sermons because it summed up this entire experience. I am purposely not mentioning any of my pastors by name because this is about trusting God not promoting my local church. I am walking in faith, not by sight. Because God holds my hand and walks one step ahead of me, I am not afraid. There are no maybes about that!

I was going to title this book *Love at First Sight Really: Ruth and Boaz Twenty-First Century Style*, but God changed that too. He corrected the title. It makes sense, because my relationship with Ruth, Rebekah, Sarah, and Esther are of equal importance. Like Esther, I hope my brave act will save God's chosen babies from extinction. God, thank you for all the words and insight you have given me, down to the exact title of this book. I truly would not have been able to write this without you.

Please help women make the best choice for themselves and their unborn children by praying for all women who are in crisis because of unexpected pregnancies. Be open to what else God prompts you to do, so that women everywhere will make a choice that will give glory to God.

I'd like to borrow a line from the children's book *The Lorax* by Dr. Seuss. "Unless someone like you cares a whole awful lot, nothing is going to get better. It's not."

Love At No Sight

J find comfort considering the idea that when I was at the beach and met a guy I refer to as Angel, God was just using him to whet your appetite for my next book. The fact that he lives in a high rise too and we can see each other's balconies reminded me about the short film *Paperman*. The fact that he is also a writer and that he wrote some poems to me has me more than a little confused. The fact that in the very last poem I wrote to Adam I wrote a line stating I might meet a guy at the beach now seems like a foretelling. The fact that Angel is *seventeen* years younger than I am is hysterically funny! Oh God you most certainly do have a sense of humor. Only you could arrange all of these coincidences with such detail. Right now all I can do is pray, "God please help me!" I have to leave it at that.

When I try to write about this and figure it out, I feel like I haven't learned a thing in the last three plus years. I almost added Angel into the second book. Fortunately, I saw what a mess I was in at the moment even entertaining that thought. I have to look at this from all angles and, perhaps, contemplate the possibility that someone was using Angel to try to get me off course. I have to trust the idea that regardless of everything that has been happening to me lately God has already worked out every last detail. I am certain I will see His results before I finish the next book. I started that book a while back, but it is taking on a deeper meaning now. I see how my books have many layers to them because that is how I am made. I am somewhat like an onion. That would be how I would describe myself. I hope as I expose those layers about myself, it makes you cry. I hope you cry mostly those happy tears from laughing and also tears of joy when you read about how much God loves us. I have been crying a great deal lately myself and although many are happy tears some have been tears of sadness too. I have to look at this as God's way of doing some more healing work in me.

I have to learn to discern a few more things, too. I need to stay open with others and see how important that is for my recovery. Even if the other person doesn't want to acknowledge me, I have to do this work to keep myself healthy. As of this point in my single life I have learned one thing---there is a lot more to men than meets the eye. And men say women are confusing! Yes, we come from two different planets. Will Mars and Venus ever be able to live in harmony? I believe it is possible so I am doing my homework. I will use this waiting time as an opportunity to figure out how to relate to men. Some days I honestly have to wonder if I really do want a husband. Then, when I see the softer side of some men my answer is still *yes*.

So this is meant to be the bridge to my next book. The working title is "Love At No Sight." I am certain of that part of the title. I'm still debating about the subtitle. I am considering "My Jeans Are Too Tight" verses "Hold On For the Ride of My Life." Just in case you thought I might be having a baby, no way. I am going to be turning sixty-five in a few weeks. God knows the last thing I want is a baby. I want a spiritually, mentally and emotionally mature man. If he isn't as physically mature as I am that's okay. I know I will be living a long and satisfying life so we will have plenty of days together!

Bibliography

Beth Moore, *Here Now...There and Then: A Lecture on Series on Revelation*, (Houston: Living Proof Ministries, 2009), Introduction.

Eldredge, John and Stasi, *Captivating, Unveiling the Mystery of a Woman's Soul*, (Nashville; Thomas Nelson, 2005), 36.

Eldredge, John and Stasi, *Captivating*, 131.

Kurt Schwitters, *Lucky Hans and Other Merz Fairy Tales*, trans. Jack Zipes (Princeton: Princeton University Press, 2009), 29-30.

Kurt Schwitters, *Lucky Hans*, 41-47.

Kurt Schwitters, *Lucky Hans* 61-62.

Squire Rushnell, *When God Winks On Love: Let the Power of Coincidence Lead You to Love* (New York: Atria, 2004), 36.